New Year's
to
Kwanzaa

New Year's
to
Kwanzaa

Original Stories of Celebration

Kendall Haven

fulcrum resources
Golden, Colorado

This book is dedicated to Suzanne,
who created the idea and whose boundless enthusiasm
convinced me to write it,
and to the love of my life, Roni Berg,
who guided and shaped each story and held them
true to their purpose and intent.

Library of Congress Cataloging-in-Publication Data

Haven, Kendall F.
    New Year's to Kwanzaa: original stories of celebration / Kendall Haven.
      p.   cm.
    ISBN 1-55591-962-6 (pbk.)
      1. Holidays—Cross-cultural studies. 2. Ethnic groups—Social life and customs.
    I. Title.
    GT3930.H37   1999
    394.26'089—dc21   98-47873
                                                CIP

Book cover and interior design by Bill Spahr

Printed in the United States of America
0 9 8 7 6 5 4 3 2

Fulcrum Publishing
350 Indiana Street, Suite 350
Golden, Colorado 80401-5093
(800) 992-2908 • (303) 277-1623
www.fulcrum-resources.com

Contents

March

April

May

Contents

June

July

August

September

October

November

December

Acknowledgments

I owe a deep debt of thanks to many people for making the creation of this book possible. In particular, I owe special thanks to Dr. Rex Ellis for reviewing the Afro-American stories; to Geets Vincent and Rabbi Slater for their help with the Jewish stories; to the consulate staffs at the Colombian, Nigerian, and Ghanaian consulates in Washington, D.C.; to Ken Cline for his information about the Stickdance; to Kin Chuan for his help with the Chinese stories; to Keahi Allen, Director of the King Kamehameha Festival in Hawaii; to Hector Alverez for his review of the Mexican stories; and to Robert Price for his book on John Chapman, the only reliable source I found on this extraordinary American. Finally, I extend a heartfelt thanks to Roni Berg, whose wisdom and insight brought clarity, completeness, and a sense of storytelling to my accounts of each of these festivals.

Lastly, my thanks go out to you, the reader, for caring to read these stories. I hope they light a flame of curiosity and excitement in you for your own celebrations and for those of the other peoples who share your world. Search for similarities between celebrations, for common forms and concepts, common themes and motifs. We are all human. We all celebrate in the same ways and for many of the same reasons. We all use celebrations to express joy, pride, thanks, support, awe, and sorrow. Let our common celebrations help us understand and appreciate our fellow humans.

Introduction

I asked three different groups of upper-elementary students to tell me what a celebration is. Mostly I received hesitant shrugs. In all three groups someone said, "It's like a party." In all three someone added, "Like a wedding." Other tentative answers included "You mean like a birthday?"; "My mom celebrated her divorce."; "My grandma celebrated when she won a lot of money at Las Vegas."; "We celebrated when my Uncle Jackie got out of jail."

I said that those were all personal or family celebrations, and asked them to name any bigger, planned celebrations they participated in. Weddings were what they mentioned most. I began to list the major American celebrations: Presidents' Day, Easter, Passover, Memorial Day, Thanksgiving Day, etc. In each of the groups someone interrupted, "Those aren't celebrations. Those are school holidays."

Maybe we have such trouble articulating, verbalizing, and defining our celebrations because they are so tightly woven into the fabric of our lives that we can't separate them out and view them objectively.

We humans celebrate everything! We hold over ten thousand scheduled celebrations each year. That's almost thirty every day, worldwide. And that number ignores personal, family, and neighborhood celebrations mentioned by the kids I talked to.

Celebrating seems to confirm our humanity. We celebrate the origins of our countries, communities, and groups. We celebrate our independence. We celebrate our culture and the things we believe are important. We celebrate our history and the events that have shaped our common heritage. We celebrate past heroes and heroines. We celebrate stories—especially myths and legends. We celebrate religious occurrences and events. We celebrate planting; we celebrate harvest. We celebrate virtually every phase of the growing season. We celebrate time itself.

If you can name it, there's a group somewhere that celebrates it!

The dictionary defines *celebrate* as "to perform publicly (especially religious services or weddings), to honor or observe an occasion or event, to praise or sing the glories of, and to seize an occasion for being festive." But such a definition pales in comparison to the gusto, energy, and unbridled enthusiasm we pour into our celebrations.

Our celebrations help define who we are and what we value and believe. They define how we expect to act and interact. What and how we celebrate is a blueprint to us as humans, and to our cultures.

The question that fascinated me as I began research for this book was *why* we bother to celebrate. What drives us to set aside the time and energy required to organize, plan, prepare, and observe a celebration—especially in our harried, microsecond-counting, backbreaking, rat-race pace? Why don't we say, "I think I'll skip the celebration this year and simply relax and read a book"?

Certainly, some do exactly that. But most of us don't. Why? I believe it is because we *need* to celebrate. Participating in our own celebrations makes us feel connected both to our present community and to our history. It gives us a much-needed sense of belonging. It makes us feel human.

In this sense, it is the *doing* of any celebration that is most important, not a deep understanding of the celebration's purpose and significance. So, for many—perhaps, most—of us, we move through our celebrations by rote. We memorize the ritual. We hold tightly to the activity, the fun, the excitement. And we are willing to let the purpose, the origin, and the meaning of the celebration grow hazy and obscure.

That's a shame, because celebrations burst into rich and exciting color when we take the time to understand both what we do and why we do it. Knowing the origins and evolution of a celebration, its growth and reshaping over the years, gives heightened meaning and joy to the act of the modern-day version of the celebration.

This book is a collection of thirty-one stories of different celebrations from around the world. In picking the few I would write about from the vast number of potential celebrations, I tried to balance the following considerations: (1) spread the stories evenly across the months of the year with two or three celebrations for each month; (2) include representative celebrations from each of the world's major religions and for each of the general types of celebrations (cultural, historic events, independence, origins, myth and legend, historic figures, agricultural, and time); (3) include celebrations from each of the major population groups that have flowed into the United States; (4) include some well-known and relatively unknown celebrations; and (5) pick celebrations for which I could create good stories. The selection process thus became a multidimensional matrix balancing act.

My goal in writing each story was also multifaceted. Each story is designed to create a sense of what it feels like to participate in the celebration; to describe the modern celebration, its history and development, and the people and places where the celebration is observed; and, lastly, to entertain.

Each celebration's entry is divided into four sections. Before the story, a section titled "At a Glance," provides historical background and development information for the celebration. Following the story, sections titled "Follow-up Questions to Explore" and "Suggested Activities" list several questions and activities that flow from the story and are worthy of your time and energy to ponder and research. For some I have included factual answers. For others, the answers lie in your beliefs and opinions, and in those of your classmates.

Much of the information used to construct these stories has been based on personal interviews with those who have participated in the celebrations. You'll find many references in your library for some of these celebrations. For an equally large group you probably won't find any at all.

Well documented or not, each of the celebrations described in this book is an important celebration for some group of us in the United States. Each celebration is worthy of our understanding and study. What better way to understand humans throughout the world than to study and understand what and how they celebrate? What better way to understand their celebrations than to vicariously participate in them, to sense, through words, the sounds, smells, sights, taste, and feel of a few extraordinary celebrations?

January

New Year's

A Worldwide Celebration
About the Annual Cycle of Time

At a Glance

NEW YEAR'S IS THE OLDEST and most universal celebration in the world. Every country, every culture celebrates New Year's. Over the past five thousand years and in the hundreds of different cultures throughout human history, New Year's has been celebrated on at least forty different dates that span all four seasons and almost every month.

Marking and celebrating New Year's is how we track the flow of time, the cycles of our planet, and the ebb and flow of life itself. Over the years humans have burdened New Year's with countless beliefs, traditions, superstitions, ceremonies, and activities. They come and they go. They are popular for a while and then fade into disuse.

New Year's stories happen everywhere. This particular one happened in a small city in Guatemala.

New Year's

"Mother! I'm home!"

Twenty-year-old Tito Arguella stood in the doorway of his mother's trim stucco house in the coastal city of Puerto Barrios, Guatemala, and flopped his bag onto the tile floor. The afternoon behind him was warm, not hot, and pleasantly dry. But that's what you'd expect from late December. Why should December 31, 1991, be any different?

Tito called again, "Mother! I'm home!" From a back bedroom he heard the loud commotion of someone jumping up, startled, and then, in their haste, knocking over several things that clattered to the floor.

"Tito?"

His mother, forty-four-year-old Dolores Arguella, rushed into the hall still buttoning her dress and rubbing sleep from her eyes. "Tito!" She had lived alone in this house since Tito left for the university three years ago. She stopped five feet from him. Her fists slammed onto her hips. Her smile dissolved as a deep scowl crossed her face. "You're late."

"I said I'd make it home for New Year's. And I have."

Her finger wagged at him. "You also called and said you'd get here two days ago. I've been worried sick!"

Tito blushed. "Sorry, Mama. I had to go back to the university for a day for one of my projects. Then the bus was five hours late into Guatemala City and messed up my connection."

"You could have called."

"Do you know how expensive long-distance phone calls are in Guatemala?" He began to grin. "And I'm a poor and starving student."

Now she swept forward to hold her son in her arms. "Welcome home. You look wonderful!"

"So do you, Mama. Except you look really tired."

"It's New Year's," she explained.

"Mama. New Year's isn't until *tonight*. How could you be tired already?"

"You think it's easy to get properly prepared for New Year's?" Dolores demanded, her fists sliding up to her hips again.

"What's to prepare?" asked Tito. "You get a couple of noisemakers; we go to Mass like every year; we come home and wait for the church bells to peal midnight; we make a racket; and we go to bed."

"Ha! A lot you know," she scoffed. "I guess they don't teach you everything at college. I've been studying—a lot. And this year I'm prepared!"

Tito sighed, "Only my mother would *study* for New Year's as if it were a test." Again he sighed. "All right, Mother. What are you 'prepared' for?"

"New Year's is important," she answered. "What you do on New Year's Eve and Day determines your fortune and luck for the entire year to come. New Year's is the victory of renewed life over death, of light over dark. And we have to do it *right* if it's going to work." Dolores brushed past her son and stepped into the bright afternoon.

"Where are you going?"

"To bless Janus," she called back over her shoulder. "Come on!"

"Who's Janice? A friend of yours?"

She stopped where the cement walk to her house met the sidewalk. "*Janus*, the Roman god. January is named for him. In Latin, Janus means 'the gate.' So we are going to bless Janus by blessing the gate." She crossed her arms with a satisfied nod.

"You don't *have* a gate, Mother."

"If I *did* this is where it would be. So offer a blessing."

"We're going to bless a gate that isn't there because two thousand years ago Romans—in Italy which is six thousand miles from here—prayed to a god named Janus?"

"Exactly," she answered. "Now pray!" On the way inside Dolores clipped ivy from a trellis where the plant climbed up one wall.

"What's that for?" asked Tito.

"Ancient Druid priests hung sprigs of mistletoe over doorways to ensure the blessings of a bountiful harvest."

"But that's ivy."

"So? I don't *have* any mistletoe," she snapped. "I figured it's probably the thought that counts, anyway. Get some tape." Tito hung strands of ivy over the front door as his mother called, "Can you drag that bag of ashes into the kitchen?"

"Sure." He hoisted the heavy bag onto one shoulder, then paused. "What are you going to do with a bag of ashes?"

"On the Isle of Man …"

"On the Isle of *where?*" Tito interrupted.

"The Isle of Man—wherever that is," she said. "The women sprinkle ashes on the kitchen floor on New Year's Eve. Then in the morning they look to see if there are any footprints in the ashes. Prints facing *toward* a door mean bad luck and loss. Prints facing *away* mean good fortune in the coming year."

"The real question is who cleans up the mess," muttered Tito.

"Just sprinkle." With the kitchen covered in a fine layer of ash, Dolores shooed her son into the living room. "You have an hour before dinner. Write your New Year's resolutions."

Tito laughed. "I don't make New Year's resolutions."

"Of course you do! New Year's resolutions are like notes to the gods, telling them what you plan to accomplish. If they like your resolutions, they'll be pleased and help." Her voice turned dark and foreboding. "If you ignore them and don't write, they'll be *very* angry."

"Who dreamed up *that* idea?" laughed Tito.

"The Greeks. And you better do it. I don't want angry Greek gods in *this* house."

Tito held up his hands in surrender. "All right. I resolve to …"

"Don't say it. Write it. I've written over two hundred so far."

Afternoon faded into evening; twilight faded into twinkling stars. Dolores and Tito strolled the darkened streets on their way home from New Year's Eve Mass.

"Is it ten o'clock yet?" Dolores asked.

Tito glanced at his watch. "Three minutes of."

"Run!" commanded Dolores. "We have to turn on the TV."

"It's two hours to midnight," called Tito racing after her.

Sprinting into the house Dolores said, "If it's ten here, it's midnight in New York. I have to watch the ball drop at Times Square. I want to watch New Year's march across the land." As the chilled New York crowd cheered after their countdown to 1992, Dolores said, "Now pray."

4

"To which god this time?"

"It's a she, the Babylonian goddess of good crops."

"What's her name?" asked Tito.

"I don't remember. But pray anyway. The Babylonians did every year on New Year's and they survived for three thousand years." Dolores rose, smiled, and sucked in a deep, satisfied breath. "It's going very well, so far. Next is the Wassail Bowl ..."

"The *what?*" stammered Tito.

"It's Old English. The word comes from *waes hail,* which means 'be of good health.' On New Year's they drank a special punch and wished each other good health. Get the punch cups."

Tito started for the kitchen. "All right."

"Tito!" his mother screamed. "Walk out of the kitchen backward. I don't want any footprints facing the wrong way!"

Tito returned to find his mother stirring a pale brown bubbling punch.

"What's in it?"

"It's supposed to be spiced ale. But I didn't have any beer, so I used ginger ale. I didn't know which spices the English use, so I dumped in some cinnamon, one of my favorites." Tito took a cautious sip. His lips puckered. "That's terrible!"

She glared at him. "Say it."

"Say what, Mother?"

"*Say it.*"

He raised his cup. "Wassail. Be of good health—if this punch doesn't kill you first."

Dolores turned toward the hallway. "Quick now. We have to drown the old year before eleven. I want to watch New Year's in Chicago."

"You're going to drown someone?" asked Tito.

"Not someone. *Something,* the old year. It's a German custom. They build an effigy of the old year and drag it through town on New Year's Eve. Then they throw it in a river and watch the old year drown." Tito followed her into the bathroom. "We don't have a river, so I decided to use the sink. That meant I had to make a small effigy of the old year."

"That's just three twigs tied together," Tito laughed.

"So? An effigy is an effigy. Now carry it through the house ... but don't walk through the kitchen!" Tito returned and plopped the twigs into the full bathroom sink. "It's not drowning, Mother. The twigs float."

"Put a rock on top to hold it down," she said.

New Year's fell across Chicago. They watched partiers dance as confetti rained down. They heard a knock at the front door. "Aye yei!" Dolores wailed. "He's too early."

"Are you having a party?" asked Tito, following his mother into the hall.

"Mr. Ramirez," Dolores said at the door. "You're early. Wait outside. I'll bring you something to drink." She closed the door on the man outside and shook her head in disgust.

"Mr. Ramirez is one of the richest men in town," said Tito. "You can't leave him standing outside. Invite him in."

"I can't," wailed Dolores. "He's early. It's called 'first foot,' a Scottish tradition. If the first person to cross your threshold in a new year is wealthy and noble, it brings good luck. I asked him to stop by *after* midnight."

"Midnight is still fifteen minutes away. You can't leave him out there that long."

"I *have* to," she replied. "If he comes in early the good luck doesn't work." She thought for a moment, tapping her foot. "I know. Get the noisemakers!" Arms filled with pots and metal spoons, bells, horns, whistles, and firecrackers, Tito and Dolores stepped out the front door. Mr. Ramirez stood, crossly drumming his fingers against the wall.

"May I come in, now?"

Dolores tried to smile. "Inside? … No! It will be more fun to listen to the New Year's noise out *here*." She shoved two pots and a long string of miniature firecrackers into his hands. "Noise drives out the old year and makes room for the new one. It dates back to ancient India and Babylon."

Mr. Ramirez shoved his pots into Tito's arms and reached into a coat pocket. "When I make New Year's noise, I use this." He pulled out a chromed six-shooter. "Shooting guns at New Year's is an American southwestern tradition."

"Actually it dates from old Siam," corrected Dolores. "They believed that firing guns was the only way to frighten off demons born and grown during the old year."

"Really?" scowled Mr. Ramirez.

Tito shrugged apologetically. "My mother's been studying."

At three minutes to midnight, Dolores said, "Everyone inside. We have to open all the doors and windows … oops! Not you, Mr. Ramirez. You work from the *outside*."

6

"What's this supposed to do?" Tito asked.

"Opening the house lets the last of the old year flow out with the breeze, and lets the new year flow in to warm itself by the fire. It's an eastern European tradition."

"But there isn't any breeze, Mother."

"I'll turn on an electric fan."

"And you don't have a fireplace or a fire."

"I'll light a candle! Just get the windows open before midnight!"

Dolores called, "Now into the living room to watch the Times Square ball drop again … oh, Mr. Ramirez, you watch through the window." Eyes glued to the TV, Dolores Arguella watched the big ball drop for the second time that night. "Five … four … three … two … one … Happy New Year!" Dolores kissed her son, the American custom for good luck, and called, "Now you can come in, Mr. Ramirez … Mr. Ramirez?"

"He's gone," said Tito.

Dolores stomped her foot. "Drat! There goes our good fortune. Why'd he have to show up so early?" She struggled to shake off her disappointment. "Sing 'Auld Lang Syne' with me, Tito."

"But I don't understand any of the words. It's a dumb song."

"So?! *No one* understands the words. It's a Scottish tradition. You sing it for good luck."

Tito sank wearily onto the couch after singing. "Now can I go to bed?"

"No. Take this stick and follow me outside. It's a Russian tradition. We beat each corner of our house with a stick to drive out old demons before the new year can begin in peace and happiness."

"I thought Mr. Ramirez's gun drove them off."

"Don't argue. Just beat the house." Inside, Dolores picked up her Bible. "Keep your eyes closed while you open the Bible and point to one line. That line will tell your fortune for the next year. It's an English custom called 'Bible dipping.'"

"I'm going to bed, Mother."

"Not yet," she protested. "I have to give you a gold coin to hold tomorrow—a Spanish tradition, and some lemons."

"Lemons?"

"An Irish tradition for good luck." She followed him down the hall. "We have to be up at sunrise to inspect the color of the morning sky—an African New Year's tradition." Tito groaned and closed his door.

"And I have fourteen kinds of lucky food for us to eat tomorrow from eighteen different countries. Then there's the mummer's parade ..." Tito stuck his head into the hall. "I've made a New Year's resolution. Next year I'm going someplace *else* for New Year's!"

Follow-up Questions to Explore

1. What do you and your family do to celebrate New Year's? *Why* do you, and they, do it?

Answer

Compare your answers with those of other students.

2. Do you think it is all right to use the ceremonies of a celebration to seek good luck for yourself? Are there celebrations where you do it?

Answer

The most common is the wish made while blowing out birthday candles. We also have a simple ceremony where we make a wish each time we see a falling star. This book includes stories about at least five celebrations where participants wish for good luck. Are there things you don't think it's appropriate to wish for during a celebration?

Suggested Activities

1. In this story, people make wishes for good luck and good fortune on New Year's Eve. Research other ways and times when different cultures make wishes. Make two lists of these wish times: one on sticky notes that you place on a map by country, and one on a calendar by date or time of year. Decide how you want to list those wish times that are not specifically tied to a fixed date (e.g., when you see a falling star, or on the first star you see each night).

2. Write each of the New Year's traditions mentioned in this story on a sticky note. Place these on a world map by the appropriate country. Research other New Year's traditions and list those on your map. See how many you can find in the library and on the Internet.

Tet (Tet Nguyen Dan)

A Vietnamese Lunar New Year's Celebration

At a Glance

TET NGUYEN DAN (COMMONLY CALLED TET) is the Vietnamese New Year's celebration and literally means "first day." Tet was never as well known in the United States as Chinese New Year, the other major lunar-based New Year's celebration. There have been many Chinese in this country since the mid-1800s, but few Vietnamese. Chinese New Year is more of a public spectacle with Lion Dancers, Dragon Parades, and countless firecrackers.

Then, during the Vietnam War, the North Vietnamese attacked in great force during the Tet celebration on January 31, 1968. The bloody fighting became known as the TET Offensive, a well-known event to every U.S. serviceman and woman.

Now there is a large Vietnamese population in the United States, and it is time to recognize the "other" lunar new year, an intriguing mix of tradition, religious symbolism, and family celebration and ceremony.

⎯◌ Tet ◌⎯

Raymond Johnson lived alone on the sixth floor of a high-rise, turn-of-the-century apartment building in Oakland, California's Lake Merit district. From the building's one elevator he had to walk fifty feet down a wide but poorly lit hall to reach his apartment door.

On the rainy afternoon of January 28, 1980, Raymond hoisted a bag of groceries onto his hip and started down that hall. He wore jeans, work boots, and an army fatigue jacket. A burly man, Raymond worked as a school custodian for the Oakland Unified School District. His size and the permanent scowl on his face kept any of the kids at his junior high school from testing him and kept most strangers away.

Halfway down the hall a door on the opposite side from Raymond's apartment opened. The graying head of a short Vietnamese woman poked into the hall. Her broad, flat nose and face were covered with the deep lines of a lifetime of care and hard work. "Mister? You come?"

Raymond raised his eyebrows and pointed to himself with a finger of his free hand. "Me?"

"Mister? You come?"

Raymond glanced over his shoulder to make sure there wasn't someone else she could be talking to. There wasn't. "It's not 'mister.' It's Raymond Johnson. And come where?"

From deep inside the apartment behind the half-closed door the voice of a man with a thicker accent could be heard. "Wife? Do not invite him!" The woman's head popped back inside, but she left the door ajar. "I already did."

Now the man's voice spoke rapidly in Vietnamese. "Foolish woman! This is Tet. You know how important it is that only *good* things occur during Tet."

"What I know, husband, is that it's important for us to *make* good things occur during Tet."

Again Raymond heard the man's voice. His Vietnamese was rusty, still he recognized a few words. "He is a bitter American who hates us. If he comes to our home during Tet bad things will happen and our whole year will be ruined!"

The woman's head popped back into the hall, an apologetic smile on her face. "You come? It will be good for you to come."

"Come to *what?*" asked Raymond, curious and angered at the same time.

"Tonight. Eight o'clock. New Year's."

"New Year's? That was a month ago, lady."

"Tet. *Our* New Year's. You come?"

For the next five hours Raymond Johnson paced the floor of his apartment trying to remember why he said "yes," trying to think of ways to gracefully get out of going. He hadn't heard the word "Tet" for eleven years and had spent all that time trying to forget it. At 8:15 P.M., having run out of ideas for excuses, and wearing clean jeans, dress shoes, and his one and only tie, Raymond Johnson nervously knocked on the door of apartment 604. The same elderly woman opened the door, a beaming smile on her face. "Mr. Raymond. You come in."

"No. It's Mr. Johnson … that is, just call me Raymond."

Stuffed into the living room of the small two-bedroom apartment were twenty-four adults and children—all Vietnamese, all gathered for the traditional Tet celebration.

The woman bowed. "I am My Chau Phuoc." Her right hand swept toward the crowd in the living room and kitchen. "These are my husband's relatives who have graced us with a visit for this important night. I am—we are *all* glad you come."

Raymond frowned on top of his permanent scowl trying to remember: "*Phuoc.* … Doesn't that mean 'happiness'?"

My Chau beamed as she spoke rapidly in Vietnamese, and then turned back to Raymond as many of the adults behind her smiled and nodded. "I tell them it is very good that you know our language."

"I had to learn a little," he blushed. "But I don't remember much."

The last of the special Tet dishes was being arranged on the dining room table. My Chau nodded excitedly and pointed toward the table. "You eat?" The table was filled with platters of boiled chicken, sticky rice balls with meat and beans, and candied fruits and sweets, and with bowls of vermicelli soup and the five fruits that bring good luck. A shiver raced up Raymond's spine. His lips curled. He muttered, "Smells just like the rot we ate in the jungle. …"

"There! See?" shouted a chubby Vietnamese man with thinning salt-and-pepper hair. "I told you it would be no good."

My Chau dropped her head and gestured toward the man. "This is my husband, Le Thanh Phuoc." Raymond dipped his head in a slight bow as he remembered doing when he had met Vietnamese dignitaries during his tour in Vietnam. Le Thanh glared back as he sipped his drink.

"Try this one," said My Chau, gesturing to a platter of sticky rice balls. "It is *banh chung*."

"*Banh chung* …," repeated Raymond, struggling to remember if he had ever heard the name before. "*Banh chung*. …"

"It is a favorite food of the Tet celebration," My Chau explained. "Sticky rice, yellow beans, pig fat, and spices wrapped in bamboo leaves and boiled for half a day. We must have special food for a special celebration."

"Pig fat?" repeated Raymond lifting one of the cakes to his mouth. Then he added under his breath, "Good thing I haven't converted to Islam yet. Muslims can't eat pig … Mmmm! Delicious," he said around a mouthful and repeated the name, now trying to remember it for the next time he ate out in a restaurant. "*Banh chung*. …" Turning away from the table Raymond saw two things: first, every adult in the room stared at him, studying his every move and reaction, and, second, in the middle of the living room stood a bamboo pole.

"The *Cay Neu*," said My Chau. Raymond stepped close to the tall bamboo pole that scraped the living room ceiling. Several cactus branches had been fastened to it. A small lantern hung from the top, as did a square of woven bamboo. Red strips of paper with written inscriptions fluttered from the pole, so did gold and silver ones. Silver bells, tiny silver fishes, rooster feathers, wind chimes, and small baskets of areca and betel nuts also decorated the pole. The total effect was startlingly beautiful.

"It's like a skinny Christmas tree," said Raymond staring closely at the glittering decorations.

"But this bamboo pole and every item on it has a very specific meaning," said a younger, trim woman with long black hair, deep-set sad eyes, and a warm smile. She extended her hand. "I am Lia Huang Dan, cousin of Le Thanh. You have been invited to share the *Ong Tao* ceremony. We believe that every family has a household

12

spirit—*Ong Tao*—sometimes called our 'kitchen god.' On this last night of the old year, this spirit travels to the Jade Emperor to report on the affairs of the family. It is important that the spirit travels safely, that it leave here in a good mood, and that it makes a favorable report.

"During the week before Tet we must try extra hard to be polite, generous, and cheerful and to avoid anger and meanness. We must only allow good things to happen during Tet. In this way the spirit will carry a favorable report to the Jade Emperor. This party and its special food is supposed to send the spirit off in a good mood. This pole is designed to safeguard the spirit's trip."

"How does it do that?" Raymond asked.

"A bamboo pole is said to be the way a spirit travels to the Jade Emperor. The bamboo square blocks evil spirits from following our *Ong Tao*. The nuts are said to be a spirit's favorite food. The paper strips are messages to be carried to the emperor— the red ones are wishes, the gold and silver are notes of thanks. The fishes and rooster feathers scare off evil spirits and keep the *Ong Tao* from getting lonely."

Raymond chuckled. "I thought they were just decorations."

"Everything that is part of a ceremony should have meaning. Don't you think?" Raymond glanced down at his feet. At the base of the bamboo pole a large bow and arrow had been painted in white powder. "That smells like lime powder. I use lime to mark the lines on athletic fields at school."

Lia Huang softly laughed. "Yes. Lime. There are stories of evil spirits that are too mean and too clever to be stopped by the *Cay Neu*. The lime bow and arrow scare *them* away."

Raymond shook his head. "You're serious about helping your kitchen god make a safe trip."

"It is important. Our luck for next year depends on it."

Le Thanh Phuoc stood in front of a corner shelf where he and My Chau had built a simple family shrine with pictures, candles, and a branch with peach blossoms. He stared, brooding at the shrine as Raymond approached. "In Saigon I was a bank president. I had a large room for our family shrine and properly honored our ancestors. Here I am only a baker's assistant and can only afford one shelf."

My Chau said, "This is Tet, my husband. A time to be happy."

Raymond slowly shook his head through a sad laugh. "'Scuse me, but all my memories of Tet are the worst memories I got."

Le Thanh said, "Ahh, you were in the army for the '68 Tet Offensive?"

Raymond nodded. "The Mekong River Delta. I lost my three best friends when the North Vietnamese attacked. It was the worst fighting of the whole war."

Le Thanh smiled, a thin, sad smile. "They were our enemy, too. I lost *half* my family, *most* of my friends, *and* my country in the war."

With a hopeful smile, My Chau said, "Maybe you both should set aside your sorrow and loss and let *this* Tet be new beginning for a new year." The adults gathered their chairs in a circle around the *Cay Neu* for the *Ong Tao* ceremony to properly send off their kitchen god. Children sat on the floor. Le Thanh led them in prayers of thanks to their ancestors, and then to their relatives. They each said prayers of thanks for their past good fortune, and then prayers of blessings for friends and guests.

Raymond tried to be polite and cheerful and concentrate, but missed most of the words during this one hour of rapid-fire Vietnamese. Greetings and gifts were exchanged. Red envelopes were ceremoniously handed from giver to recipient with a formal bow. A few contained small amounts of money. Most contained hand-printed greetings. Raymond realized that for these people it was really true—the thought *did* count more than the gift. Each recipient seemed equally thrilled no matter what was inside.

When four envelopes were handed to him, Raymond began to squirm. He hadn't known to bring presents, hadn't expected to get any. Now he was on the spot and didn't know what to do. People were smiling at him as he held his red envelopes, too embarrassed to open them.

Clutching the four gift envelopes, Raymond rushed out of the apartment and down to his own. In three minutes he returned holding a white letter-sized envelope that he had colored red with a Magic Marker. Inside he had stuffed five Vietnamese coins.

Awkwardly he bowed and handed the envelope to Le Thanh. "They aren't worth anything anymore. I was saving them just as a souvenir. But maybe you lost more than I did in the war. Maybe you had to leave so fast you didn't get to bring *any* souvenirs with you."

Raymond turned to My Chau. "Thank you for tonight. I enjoyed seeing that there was a *good* side of Tet. Maybe tonight will be my new beginning. A new year."

My Chau laughed hard and patted her husband's arm. "I knew it would be a good thing if he came. And now I think it's going to be a very good year."

14

Follow-up Questions to Explore

This story is about people from a foreign land who have brought their old country celebrations with them.

1. Do you think it is all right for people to do this, or should they adopt the celebrations of their new country?

2. Can you think of any common American celebrations that started that way?

Answer

Compare your answers with those of other students. Examples of celebrations that have been brought to this country by immigrants include: Cinco de Mayo, Valentine's Day, Groundhog Day, Saint Patrick's Day, and virtually all religious celebrations, among others.

During Tet, each family's kitchen god travels back to make a report to the Jade Emperor. The family holds a send-off celebration to coax the kitchen god into making a favorable report.

1. Do you have any celebrations with similar reporting on behavior? Certainly Santa Claus collects reports on who's been naughty and nice.

2. Is this any different than the Jade Emperor collecting those reports?

3. This story turned out well because the celebration of Tet seemed to bring out the best in several characters. Do you think celebrations and ceremonies tend to bring out the best in people? Why?

Answer

Compare your answers with those of other students.

Suggested Activities

1. There are many ways and dates on which humans have celebrated New Year's. Research New Year's celebrations throughout history and make a list of all the dates used by each culture for New Year's celebrations. Why have different cultures celebrated New Year's on different dates?

2. This story makes reference to the Vietnam War. Interview Vietnam War veterans living in your community to find out their experiences during the war, and their memories of the Vietnamese people, culture, and celebrations.

3. Research other Vietnamese traditions and celebrations and share your findings with your class.

Chinese New Year

A Chinese Lunar
New Year's Celebration

At a Glance

SAY "CHINESE NEW YEAR" and most people will say back, "firecrackers." Most Americans think that the Chinese use long strings of firecrackers for the same reason we honk horns, bang on pots, and blow noisemakers at midnight on New Year's: just to whoop it up and welcome in the new year. But that's not true. Firecrackers, lanterns, and virtually every other item and act that make up the complex celebration of Chinese New Year has a very specific function and purpose.

Chinese New Year is one of the oldest continuously celebrated rituals on earth. Yet most of their real New Year's ceremony happens in the home and with the family, not out on public streets. It is also far more than just a New Year's celebration. In effect, it is a birthday party for every person in China. Regardless of a child's actual date of birth, he is considered to be one year old on New Year's.

Finally, Chinese New Year is also a spring festival. The emphasis on flowers and flower blossoms is an acknowledgment that the worst of winter is over and spring is on the way.

Chinese New Year

Wu Kin Li was coming home.

For seven years he had been away in America earning money that he regularly sent home to his parents. And now, on January 23, 1991, he was coming home to visit for New Year's as the Year of the Rooster dawned over the world.

"Clean everything!" cried Wu Ming-Way.

"We always do for New Year's," said Hung-Chen, her husband, writing good luck sayings on red paper scrolls in the living room of their downtown Yulin apartment. Yulin, in southern China, was too big to be a town or village, but too small to be a city. Like thousands of other small cities across China, it was unremarkable and ordinary, but was home to over fifty thousand Chinese.

"Clean better!" cried Ming-Way. "My son is coming home!"

But Shu Chang and Yi-Liang, Ming-Way and Hung-Chen's other two children, were already busy mopping and painting. Yi-Liang had arranged vases of plum blossoms, pussy willows, and water lilies in each corner of the living room. Hung-Chen and Shu Chang hung paper lanterns around the patio and garden. Ming-Way busily worked in the kitchen on the traditional New Year's dinner dishes. Shu Chang had purchased a potted tangerine tree for the living room (like our Christmas tree). And now Hung-Chen tacked his red paper sayings above each window and door.

Ming-Way nodded. "The five lucky signs of happiness (cleanliness, red papers, fresh flowers, lanterns, and traditional foods) are in place for New Year's. Everyone put on your new shoes. Kin Li will be here soon."

Hung-Chen worked for the government and so had a comfortable first floor apartment in an eight-story building. Their apartment had cement floors and concrete block walls, a large living room wired with electricity and a TV, and a kitchen with bricked-in wood-burning wok and grill. The apartment was modern, comfortable, and typical of a smaller Chinese city.

Ming-Way was excited because Kin Li, her firstborn son, had migrated to America and sent back more money than any of her friends' sons who had left China. Twelve-year-old Yi-Liang was excited because a brother she hardly remembered would walk through the door in a few hours.

But twenty-year-old Shu Chang was most excited of all. All his growing-up years, Shu Chang had felt like a welcomed appendage to his older brother, like a third arm. Shu Chang had never lived a day without his older brother for guidance, companionship, and support. Then Kin Li left for America, leaving a giant hole in Shu Chang's life that no one else could fill. Each year Shu Chang felt the emptiness of that hole most on New Year's when the Lion Dancers roamed the streets.

Kin Li and Shu Chang had been Lion Dance partners. Kin Li worked the head, ferociously leaping and shaking, mouth snapping open and closed, head rising and lowering to thrill the crowd. Shu Chang worked the body and tail, shaking and thrashing, prancing and twisting. Everyone said they had been magnificent. Shu Chang missed his brother most watching other Lion Dancers from the curb.

Shu Chang had retrieved their lion from its storage shed, mended the several small tears in the fabric body, and oiled the metal joints in the mighty head. He had already found three drummers and a cymbal player to agree to march with them and provide the music for their roving dance. This New Year's would be like the old times—only better. This would be a New Year's to remember for always.

A violent shiver raced down Kin Li's back as he stepped off the bus that had driven him over the last leg of his journey. Yulin looked *exactly* the same as it had on the day he stepped onto that bus seven years ago. The damp cold that wormed right through your clothes was the same. The gray sky, the bamboo scaffolds on buildings under construction or repair, the sounds, the smells, the drab buildings that looked as if they were about to collapse jammed next to each other on narrow, curving streets, the thick mob of bicycles everywhere. Nothing had changed— except Kin Li. Suddenly it felt very important to Kin Li that everyone see that, even if nothing and no one in Yulin had changed, *he had*.

Kin Li was greeted with loving cries of delight at the family's front door. He swaggered in, showing off his new three-piece suit and brilliant yellow tie.

Ming-Way clasped her hands to her face, then to his arms, then back to her face as tears of joy trickled down her cheeks. Yi-Liang bounced up and down, squealing. Shu Chang (who was now taller than Kin Li, to both of their surprise) locked his brother in a tight hug.

"Easy, little brother. You'll wrinkle my new suit."

"You haven't changed a bit!" cried Shu Chang as he dashed into his bedroom, saying he had a present for his brother. Kin Li breathed in the familiar smells of the house and food. He noted the five lucky signs, carefully set out as they had been for countless centuries of new years before.

And he needed these people to see that he *had* changed. He was different. He was an American now.

Shu Chang returned, thrusting a small box into Kin Li's hands. "What's this? … Gloves? … I have gloves." ·

"These are your Lion Dance gloves, Kin Li. We can Lion Dance together tonight."

Kin Li scoffed, "I'm too old for Lion Dancing."

Shu Chang pleaded, "I mended and oiled our lion."

"I'm not interested."

"But we were the *best* … please."

Kin Li shoved back the gloves. "Maybe another time."

Shu Chang stomped out the front door feeling alone for the first time in his life.

Hung-Chen scowled at his oldest son. "There is no other time. This is New Year's. Your brother is crushed."

Kin Li shrugged. "He'll get over it. Did I tell you I'm an important real estate agent in San Francisco now? Here's my card."

Hung-Chen frowned as his wrinkled hands held the business card. "What's this?!"

"You like it?"

Hung-Chen's frown spread into a scowl. "Who is McKinley Wood?"

"It's me, Dad. McKinley was a president and it sounds like Kin Li. And Wu doesn't sound American, so I changed it to Wood. 'McKinley Wood' makes me an American."

"But you're *not* American. You are still my son. You are still Chinese. Shu Chang is still your brother. These things will not change."

Hung-Chen's parents, brother, and his family arrived before any more could be said. They all gathered in the living room for the New Year's ritual. Hung-Chen took down the paper image of *T'sao Wang,* the god of the kitchen, from its bamboo shrine in the kitchen. Each year on New Year's Eve the kitchen god traveled to heaven to report on the family's behavior. Yi-Liang had decorated a paper chariot for *T'sao Wang* to ride in and gave this to her father.

Hung-Chen placed these images on the living room family shrine, a corner shelf. He said prayers of thanks to the gods and then to their ancestors. Each member of the family placed sweets before the image to make him happy before his journey. Hung-Chen's father smeared honey on *T'sao Wang*'s lips to encourage him to report only sweet things about the family.

Kin Li sat nervously in one corner, head down, afraid to look at *T'sao Wang,* for fear of what he might report about how badly Kin Li treated his brother. Shu Chang sat quietly across the room and would not look at his brother. Hung-Chen carried the paper images out to their small courtyard. The family followed, Kin Li and Shu Chang last in the line.

Hung-Chen said, "We have performed the proper rituals to send *T'sao Wang* safely off to heaven. Tonight we will light lanterns to safeguard his trip and set off firecrackers to frighten evil spirits away. Now it is time to send *T'sao Wang* on his journey."

Ming-Way brought a lighted straw from the kitchen. Hung-Chen's parents said more prayers. Hung-Chen set the paper images on fire, for only in smoke and fire can a god ascend to heaven.

As the paper turned to ashes, Yi-Liang lit the first string of firecrackers. The older people jumped. Everyone laughed. Then they hurried back inside to eat the food they had been smelling for the last hour as it cooked.

The table was set up and quickly filled with food. Along with soup, rice, and vegetables that were the mainstay of every meal, three traditional New Year's dishes were served: *lohan chai,* or "vegetables of the saints," to remind everyone of good and proper behavior; *yu sang,* a dish of raw skinned fish mixed with onions, peanuts, lemon, and ginger, to remind everyone of the gifts from the earth and the ancestors; and "thousand layer cake" to wish everyone a long life of good fortune.

The food was cleared and New Year's greetings were exchanged. First each person offered gifts and thanks to honor the family ancestors.

Next, Hung-Chen's parents sat in straight-backed chairs and, one by one, all other family members knelt before them to offer greetings and small gifts for good luck. When Kin Li knelt before his grandfather, the old man asked, "You have been good to your family while in America. Are you also being good to them while you are here?" Kin Li dropped his head and did not answer.

After the grandparents, Hung-Chen and Ming-Way sat in the chairs and received greetings and gifts. Then *lay shee,* or good luck money in red envelopes, was given first to the children and then to the adults.

By now it was dark. Hung-Chen lit the candles inside each paper lantern to create a soft glow across the courtyard. Drums sounded in the distance. Lion Dances were starting. Hung-Chen said, "Come, we will all go out and watch." Kin Li excused himself, saying he was tired from his travels and wanted to sleep.

Without a word or glance at his brother, Shu Chang marched out into the night. Hung-Chen sighed and followed, slowly shaking his head.

A lion for the Lion Dance is a giant, brightly colored cloth-and-paper head over a metal frame that looks more like a dragon with great rolling eyes than a lion. One dancer stands erect inside this head prancing, turning, raising, and lowering the head until it looks like a real monstrous cross between lion and dragon. A second dancer follows behind, bent over in the flowing cloth body of the great beast. The prancing lion is accompanied by marching drummers who pound their drums hard enough to rattle the rib cage of each watcher. Long strings of miniature firecrackers explode like machine-gun fire at the dancer's feet, sending thin clouds of smoke rising around the great lion bodies.

Something seemed wrong with the third lion to pass by on the main street near the Wu apartment. The body seemed to trail lifelessly along the ground behind the wildly shaking head. Three drummers marched with the lion, pounding so hard that windows shook. Firecrackers exploded on all sides. The cymbals clanged. Ming-Way reached up to cover her ears. The lion's great eyes rolled. Steam snorted from its nostrils. The mouth snapped open and closed. The lion's mane thrashed and shook. But the body did nothing. Everyone stared in wonder. What was wrong with the second dancer?

The lion stopped before the Wu family. The head was lifted high, revealing a sheepishly smiling Kin Li underneath, panting hard. "I had forgotten what hard work this is." He bowed to Shu Chang. "I apologize brother. It would be an honor to dance with you tonight."

"But I'm not wearing the right clothes or shoes," protested Shu Chang.

"Get in," softly commanded Hung-Chen.

As Shu Chang scampered under the cloth body and grabbed his handholds, Kin Li said, "And father, you are right. I will always be proud to be Wu Kin Li."

The drums beat like thunder. The cymbals crashed like jagged lightning. Firecrackers blasted like pelting hail. The lion leapt with a mighty roar down the street as people cheered.

Ming-Way beamed beside her husband and nodded toward her dancing sons disappearing around a corner in the street. "Finally, Kin Li has come home."

Follow-up Questions to Explore

1. Why does Chinese New Year jump from date to date from year to year?

Answer

Chinese New Year is one of the many celebrations based on a lunar, rather than the twelve-month solar calendar we use. Because the moon does not complete an even number of orbits around the earth in the 365 days it takes the earth to complete one orbit around the sun, the start of the lunar calendar shifts back and forth. Tet, as well as many Christian and Jewish celebrations, is based on a lunar calendar and so shifts from year to year. Islamic celebrations are based on yet another calendar. They also shift from year to year, but in a different way than lunar calendar–based events.

2. Why are strings of small firecrackers such a big part of Chinese New Year?

Answer

It is believed that their noise scares evil spirits away.

Suggested Activities

1. Research the twelve animals that represent different years in the Chinese calendar. What is the meaning of each animal? When and why did the Chinese begin to use this system for identifying different years? Which Chinese year were you born in? What is that supposed to tell you about yourself and your future? Make separate lists of the behaviors and attitudes the Chinese zodiac predicts for you that you agree with, and the ones you don't agree with.

FEBRUARY

Carnaval

A Brazilian
Pre-Lent Catholic Celebration

At a Glance

EVERY COUNTRY IN THE WORLD with a large Catholic population has a wild party just before the beginning of Lent, the forty days of somber fasting and reflection that precede Easter. In Germany this party is called *Fashing*. In New Orleans it is *Mardi Gras*. Most of the world calls this celebration *Carnaval*. The name comes from the Latin words *carne vale,* which literally mean "a farewell to flesh."

Most think this title symbolically means a farewell to the pleasures of the flesh, to frivolity, to hedonistic indulgences, and to rich foods, in anticipation of the forty days of sacrifice and self-denial that are Lent.

Certainly this interpretation is true. But there is an older meaning to the words *carne vale,* stemming from a five-thousand-year-old pre-Christian spring ceremony in which priests actually flogged (whipped) members of the tribe to purify them before the new year started with the onset of spring. Flesh was literally torn from people's backs by the priests' whips—farewell to flesh.

The early Christian Church in Rome incorporated elements of this, and many other pre-Christian celebrations, into the celebrations marked on the Christian church calendar. Thus, elements of *carne vale* were folded into the Christian celebration marking the beginning of Lent, and Carnaval was born.

Nowhere on earth is Carnaval celebrated with such wild abandon as in Rio de Janeiro, Brazil. There, Carnaval is the biggest, most spectacular celebration of the whole year.

Carnaval

Frantically Madeline Debolt folded, unfolded, and then refolded the Rio de Janeiro street map across her lap, across the dashboard of their tiny Brazilian rental car, and then across the windshield.

"Move that map!" bellowed her husband, Thorton Debolt. "I can't see where I'm driving!"

"You shouldn't drive *any*where until I figure out where we are," she protested.

"How can we be lost already?"

Mrs. Debolt answered, "Rio is *impossible* to follow on a map. It's a maze of bays, lakes, peninsulas, and twisting streets."

"And crowds," added their eight-year-old son, Henry, peering out the small backseat window as he shoved his glasses back up his nose and wiped his mouse brown hair out of his face. "This is worse than New York."

A great party crowd milled along every sidewalk. Most were dressed in costumes—but not ordinary Halloween costumes. These were elaborate, outlandish costumes sparkling in glitter and sequins. Everyone seemed charged with an air of expectant excitement. The feeling might have been driven by the pounding samba beat of distant drums, or by the clock ticking steadily through the afternoon of this next-to-last day of Carnaval. Either way, the crowd seemed ready to explode in wild, spontaneous celebration at the slightest encouragement.

Henry said, "Why does everyone dress so weird in Brazil?"

"It's Carnaval time," laughed Mr. Thorton Debolt. "Those are Carnaval costumes. Carnaval is why we're here."

"They're having a carnival?" asked Henry.

"Not a carnival. *Carnaval!* The greatest, wildest pre-Lent bash in the world!"

"Look out!" screamed Madeline, bracing against the dash.

Thorton braked and swerved to miss six costumed partiers who wandered into the street in front of him. Tires squealed and he blasted his horn. Madeline crashed forward, shredding her street map. Her tall glass of sparkling water sprayed across the map and windshield. "The map's soaked! We'll never get back."

The revelers merely laughed, waved, and continued to saunter across the street. Two were dressed as devils, the other four like circus clowns.

Thorton honked in frustration as he sat hunched over the wheel. His head scraped the car roof. His left elbow stuck out the window because there was nowhere else for it to fit. "Why do Brazilian cars have to be so small?"

Three costumed people plopped down into the curb lane of this busy four-lane street to hold a tea party. Car horns honked and drivers yelled for blocks behind them. One of the partiers was dressed as the German Kaiser Wilhelm with a propeller beanie on his spiked helmet, one as the Mad Hatter, and one woman was dressed in golden glitter and wore a nine-foot-high foam rubber headpiece depicting a map of the Amazon River.

"It's as if they were *trying* to be wild and dangerous," sighed Madeline.

"That's Carnaval," answered Thorton, "a time to cast off your inhibitions, a time to walk on the wild side."

"Why?" asked Henry. "It's kinda scary to see so many people acting crazy."

"Brazil is a Catholic country. For the forty days of Lent they have to sacrifice, to deny themselves physical pleasures. Carnaval is a time to get wildness all out of their system just before Lent starts." Thorton added, "We've been to Mardi Gras in New Orleans. This is the same thing, only Carnaval is bigger and *much* wilder."

Henry grumbled, "It's freaky to see every adult in the whole city gone insane. They weren't acting so crazy on the beach at our hotel."

"Ahh, the beach at Ipanema," sighed Thorton. "I've wanted to see that beach for all my life. It's supposed to be the most beautiful beach in the world."

"Let's go back there," suggested Henry. "It's more fun than *this.*"

"First," answered his father," I don't think I could turn the car around in this crowd …"

"Second," interrupted Mrs. Debolt, "I don't know where we are. We may *never* find our way back to the hotel."

"And third," continued Mr. Debolt, "we flew five thousand miles to see Carnaval. The most spectacular part of Carnaval is the samba school parades. We've got tickets for bleacher seats on the main parade route this afternoon, and *that's* where we're going."

"I just wish it wasn't so hot," said Henry, wiping a trickle of sweat off the back of his neck. "How can it be this hot in February?"

"Rio is below the equator," answered his mother. "Down here February is the middle of summer. Besides, Rio is so near the equator, it's hot all the time."

Thorton stomped on the brakes and swerved around a second group of costumed partiers who danced across the street. Three were dressed as bright blue winged cows with golden full-moon faces. The other two looked like overstuffed cats with lampshades for heads. The crowd grew thicker and more frantic with every block the Debolts crept along the boulevard.

"Aveneda Presidente Vargus!" screamed Madeline pointing at a street sign. "That's the street we're looking for. Turn here!"

"Turn through this crowd?" stammered Thorton.

"Just turn! Our seats are near the intersection with Aveneda Rio Branco six blocks down this street."

The crowd pressed in tight against the Debolts' car so that Thorton had to inch along at a walking pace. Each person seemed to try to be wilder and more outrageous than the next—both in costume and in action—as if this were a graded craziness parade and each person was fighting for a first-place trophy.

Mr. Debolt slowly shook his head. "It's hard to believe this is a religious holiday."

"*This* isn't," answered Madeline. "The religious holiday, Lent, begins with Ash Wednesday, day after tomorrow. There's nothing religious about Carnaval."

They parked and walked the last three blocks. "These parades are bigger, wilder, and more musical than anything you've ever seen," said Mr. Debolt. "Just listen to that music!"

Even though the parade route was still three blocks away, the throbbing beat of great samba drums shook the street and vibrated Henry's tennis-shoed feet.

Henry hung back by the car. "This place looks scary-wild."

His parents took tight hold of his hands. "This is going to be the greatest show on earth!" shouted his father to be heard.

"Hold our hands tight," yelled his mother. "I can't imagine what we'd do if we got separated in this sea of people."

Firecrackers exploded down all side streets like at Chinese New Year. Costumes of glittering sequins shined in all directions. It looked to Henry like they were backstage at some gigantic circus just before a wild finale.

Hand-in-hand they wormed their way through the crowd to the parade-route street just as the first of the samba schools passed by. Confetti rained down blizzard thick. The countless thousands in the sea of faces that made up the watching crowd yelled and sang with the samba music.

"Our seats are this way," screamed his father over the deafening racket. "Hold hands and stay together!"

On the street before them over two hundred costumed members of a samba school danced by. Their theme was the rainforest. Some were dressed as jaguars, some as turtles, alligators, monkeys, toucans, and herons, many as tall trees. Each costume was flowing blotches of blue, green, and gold covered with forests of glitter. Each school member sprouted shimmering wings so that all two hundred seemed to float on invisible clouds as they samba-pranced down the street.

A band with a dozen trumpets and horns and rows of flutes led the dancers. But what captivated Henry were the drums. Fifty drummers pounded a frantic samba beat at the head of the parade. The drums rattled through Henry's chest. They rumbled through his stomach. They seemed to fill the whole world. The pounding base drums felt like shock waves slamming into him. The high-pitched soprano drums beat on him like machine-gun fire.

Henry's body vibrated with the sound. It vibrated *to* the sound. Henry couldn't speak. He could barely breathe. His head throbbed with the pulsing samba beat. Henry felt that the pounding of the drums could flatten him as easily as a hurricane.

A second samba school approached with even more drummers. Henry's knees wobbled. The drums were too powerful. These dancers used the theme, "the fire within." They looked like red and yellow swirls of colored fire rolling, pulsing down the street.

Henry glanced up to say something to his father. And realized the man holding his hand was not his father.

Henry held the hand of a total stranger!

"Your not my son!" bellowed the man.

"You're not my father!"

"Oh, dear! Our hands must have gotten switched while we watched the samba parade. My Karl must be with your parents!"

Henry felt a wave of fear wash over him. He would have screamed. He certainly would have cried. But the samba drums shifted rhythm, their beat now faster, more frantic, more overpowering. The tears were swept from his mind by the all-powerful pounding of the drums.

The man bent down to be heard. "I'm Aldo Finster from Germany. Looks like we're stuck with each other till we find your parents and my Karl."

The trumpets blared, the fire dancers swirled like raging wildfire, the crowd roared.

"Isn't it glorious? Fantastic?" yelled Aldo.

"No. It's scary."

Aldo laughed. "That's Carnaval! A whole country trying to go wild, to let every inhibition go. It's planned national insanity! In America you have Mardi Gras. In Germany we have Fashing. But they are nothing like … *this!*"

Henry yelled, "How will we find my parents?"

"In this madness? We won't." Aldo had to yell it three times right into Henry's ear before he could hear it over the great din of drums and voices. "But they must be along the parade route somewhere near here. We'll let them find us."

"How?" mouthed Henry.

A wild sparkle danced across Aldo's eyes. "We dance down the street with this samba school. Within a couple of blocks they're bound to spot us."

Henry's face recoiled in horror. "*Me?* Dance with *them?* I can't dance!"

"It's the only way to find your parents and my son, Henry."

"But … but we don't have costumes." Surely this was the craziest idea of all.

"This is Carnaval," laughed Aldo. "A time to *be* crazy! There are no 'can'ts' and no 'don'ts' at Carnaval. At Carnaval there is only 'do'!"

The pounding drums throbbed in Henry's mind. He couldn't remember what the world sounded like without their deafening beat. Swirling dancers looked like glowing balls of dancing fire. Henry's head and heart hung back, but his feet leapt into the street when Aldo pulled him forward. The driving samba beat took over. Henry jumped like a sizzling flame. He twirled like smoke. He spun and pranced like a whirlwind with the other samba fireballs. He strutted, he roared, his feet pounded on the street to match the brutal pounding the drums gave his body.

Henry glowed as he danced just behind the samba band, the brightest, hottest fireball of all. Aldo danced beside him. The crowd roared in approval.

Then Henry heard another sound.

"MY HENRY! MY BABY!"

His mother rushed into the street and snatched up her son.

"My Karl!" cried Aldo Finster, rushing to where his son huddled next to the Debolts.

Driving back to their Ipanema hotel Henry's mother said, "Mr. Finster and his son were so nice. I can't wait for them to visit us for Mardi Gras next year." Her face darkened with concern. She leaned over the seat and took Henry's hand. "It must have been awful, terrifying to realize you lost us in that madness, Henry."

Henry nodded and pushed his glasses back up his nose and swept his mouse brown hair out of his face. "Yeah, it was pretty scary," he said. Then a bright sparkle danced across his eyes. "But … em … I wouldn't mind going back again tomorrow."

Follow-up Questions to Explore

1. Carnaval arose because Catholics wanted to be wild for a few days before Lent and "get it out of their systems" before the forty days of somber sacrifice that are Lent. Do you think it's all right to have a celebration that's all about intentionally acting wild? Are there other celebrations like this? Do you participate in any? Do you think it's all right to have one celebration that's about doing all the things you're not supposed to do during the next celebration?

Answer

Fasching in Germany and Mardi Gras in New Orleans are the same kind of pre-Lent celebration that Carnaval is. Holi, in India, calls for the same level of public wildness. To a lesser extent, so do April Fool's Day in Europe and North America and Homowo in Nigeria.

Suggested Activities

1. Carnaval takes place in Rio de Janeiro, Brazil. Get a map of Rio and mark the places mentioned in this story. When is Carnaval held each year? What is the weather like in Rio then? Research Carnaval and mark all the places where Carnaval parades and concerts are held. How many people come to Carnaval each year? How many people participate in Carnaval activities? How would you get to Rio? How long would it take to get there? What time zone is Rio in?

2. Rio de Janeiro is in Brazil. What places and sights in Brazil outside of Rio would you want to see during your trip? Two of those sights would probably be the Amazon River and the Brazilian rainforest. Research the Amazon River and the Brazilian rainforest. Why are they important? Describe the ecologies of these areas. What unique animal and plant species live there?

Valentine's Day

A Western Celebration of Romance and Love

At a Glance

WHEN WE THINK OF VALENTINE'S DAY we think of buying a pack of valentine cards, of deciding who in your class you want—and don't want—to give one to, of cute little cupid and his arrows, and maybe of a class party. Valentine's Day didn't used to be so harmless, or so easy. For several centuries in England, Valentine's Day was about picking and being picked as sweethearts—for the whole year! Worse, in many cultures you didn't get much say about who you were paired with. In some places you were assigned a valentine sweetheart by random draw. In some, your valentine was the first person you saw that morning.

But what does Saint Valentine have to do with lovers and cupid and this day? The answer is, not much. At least not much that is known for sure. What is known is that Valentine was bishop of the church in Terni, Italy, who was killed for his faith by Emperor Claudius on February 14, A.D. 273. That happened to be the same date as a popular Roman festival for spring fertility and lovers, Lupercalia.

In the seventh century, the Catholic Church created a day to honor Saint Valentine, and placed it on the anniversary of his death. Since the pagan festival, Lupercalia, was by then outlawed, many of the customs and beliefs of the old festival grew to be associated with the new Christian celebration for Saint Valentine.

Stories abound of how Saint Valentine helped young lovers, and championed their cause. But none can be substantiated. Over the centuries, new customs and meanings have been added to this celebration of love. One of the most important for how we now celebrate Valentine's Day is the sending of cards to sweethearts. Some think that tradition was invented by an American greeting card company. But it started much earlier. In fact, sending Valentine's cards can be traced to the year 1415 and the French Duke of Orleans.

Valentine's Day

"A blanket, a dry blanket! Is there not one single dry blanket in all of London?"

"I'm sure there is, gov'ner," laughed the jailer, huddled around his flickering torch for warmth. "Jus' ain't any in *this* place."

The date was February 7, 1415. But it was hard to keep track of days under the endless gray sky and dreary rain of winter in London. The prisoner collapsed back onto his moldy cot. "Don't call me 'governor.' I am a duke."

The jailer labored up from his chair and shuffled to the small grate in the prisoner's door. When young and spry he had been a sergeant in the army. Now old and plagued by arthritis he could do little but watch prisoners in the dreaded Tower of London who were so securely locked and chained they needed little watching. The Tower was the most famous and hated prison in all England.

As his teeth loosened and fell over the years, his laugh drifted toward a cackle. His stubbly beard and scraggly hair looked little better than his prisoner's. "Don't *look* much like a duke ta' me, gov'ner."

Again he cackled as he shuffled back to his seat and guard post. The guard paused and shrugged. "'Course, three years in this tower'd make anyone look like a moldy lump o' rags."

Summers in the Tower of London were bad, but survivable. Some days the sun shone. Occasionally its warmth penetrated the thick walls. But winter in the stone tower felt worse than death. The bitter, soggy cold of London never gave a moment's peace. There was no place to hide from it's ever-present torment.

For the thousandth time that winter Charles, the Duke of Orleans, shook his fist at the walls and sky and screamed in rage at his terrible fate. So nobly he had led his army in gold-plated armor and velvet trim. So dashing he had looked, mounted before his cheering soldiers. So bravely he had fought. So easily he had been captured as the battle lines shifted.

After three years in chains in the Tower he stopped scratching lines in his cell wall to mark the passing of days. Time had lost its meaning. All that mattered to him, all he thought of now, was the love of his life, his dear wife, left far behind in happy France.

But the French army hadn't been able to forge the victories it would take to win the duke's freedom. His family couldn't pay the hefty ransom to buy his way out.

Wind lashed a spray of rain through the wall slit that served as Charles's window, causing him to scream in frustration.

"Don't complain so, gov'ner," chided the old guard. "Gave ya' a corner room with a view. Best suite in the whole bloomin' hotel." Then he cackled again at his own humor.

The view of freedom was a torment, especially to a man who only wanted to view the smile of his sweet wife. The slit only let in the rain and fog.

"If only I could get word to my wife that I was still alive. If only I could tell her how much I love her …"

An idea slowly spun into focus deep in his mind.

"Jailer! What month is this?"

The guard cackled, "As if months mattered to someone who's going to rot in this dungeon."

"What month?!" demanded Charles, now pacing his cell.

"Oh, February, I guess, gov'ner."

"And the date," continued Charles, now hanging on the bars of the small grate in his iron cell door. "What is the date?"

"Who cares about dates in a place like this?" shrugged the guard.

"The date!" bellowed the Duke of Orleans.

"No need to get testy, gov'ner. I believe it's the eighth. No, the seventh."

Over and over the duke muttered as he paced, "The seventh of February … the seventh of February … one week to Lupercalia …"

"Luper-what?" asked the guard now curiously peering through the grate. "What's got you so agitated, gov'ner?"

"Saint Valentine's Day—the Festival of Lupercalia—the day of lovers is in one week away on the fourteenth. That is the perfect time to tell my wife how I love her."

"Beggin' yer pardon, gov'ner. But since yer locked in here, and she's in France, how are you going to accomplish that?" The jailer frowned and rubbed his rough beard. "You're not planning an escape are you?'"

"Paper and pens," commanded the duke. "I need paper and pens."

The jailer shook his head. "Sorry, gov'ner. Not allowed."

"It's *duke*, not governor. And I'm begging you, man. All I'm asking for is paper and pens."

Again the jailer shook his head in the dim, flickering hallway light of the torches. "You're a clever one, your dukeship. You might figure how to use a pen as a weapon to overpower some poor guard—like me, fer instance."

"I need to *write*," Charles insisted.

"You might figure how to use the paper to help your escape. I don't think I ought ta do it."

"I will not escape," said Charles. "But I must write *today* for my letter to arrive on time."

The suspicious jailer folded his arms. "And what might be so special about today for a prisoner who's sat in that cell for over three years?"

Charles, the Duke of Orleans, reached pleadingly toward the bars, his blue eyes blazing through three years of matted, unwashed hair, grime, and beard. "Have you heard of Saint Valentine's Day, man?"

"Yes. But don't expect anything from me."

"On that day, February 14, the Romans held one of their most important festivals, Lupercalia, in honor of Lupercia, goddess of spring and fertility, and of

Cupid, the son of Venus, goddess of love and beauty. It was a day for lovers to meet and for marriages to be bonded."

"But what's that got to do with Saint Valentine?" interrupted the jailer.

"Valentine was an early Christian bishop who was martyred on the eve of Lupercalia in the year 273," explained the duke. "By the sixth century, Saint Valentine's Day, a day to remember the faith and devotion of the martyr, and Lupercalia were merged."

Now the duke poured out his story rapid-fire. "But there is more, far more. I often heard this story even as a child. During his service as Bishop of Terni, Valentine defied a command by Emperor Claudius forbidding potential soldiers to marry. Married soldiers, you see, wanted to stay home, not march out on long campaigns to fight. Valentine invited young lovers to come to him in secret to be married with the blessings of the church. I was told he secretly married hundreds of couples before he was caught, and killed—on Lupercalia, the day of lovers."

"'Scuse me fer askin', gov'ner—er, I mean dukeship," interrupted the jailer. "but what does this have to do with you?"

"February 14th is the day for lovers. I cannot be with my love this year …"

"Or next year, or the next ..."

"BUT," continued Charles to silence the interruption, "I can send my love to her—if I had paper and pen to write and draw."

"You'd draw a bloomin' picture fer a *woman?*" gasped the jailer.

"I would gladly draw a thousand to express my love for my wife," answered the duke.

The jailer whistled low and shook his head. "That's *something*." Then he nodded. "That kind of love should be rewarded. I'll see what I can do."

The jailer shuffled down the hallway—then stopped. "I suppose this means you'd want me ta sneak the letter out of the Tower of London fer ya, too?"

Charles nodded. "I have no other way to get my Valentine's letter there."

Before nightfall the duke had completed a detailed drawing of winged Cupid aiming an arrow at the likeness of the duke's wife, all surrounded by a ring of hearts.

With the drawing went a two-page letter ending with the wish that his wife would again be his on Valentine's Day.

The jailer tucked the folded Valentine's letter into his rough tunic. "I'll get it posted with a courier to France. But don't expect I'll start giving ya extra rations. This is still a prison, ya know."

That unnamed jailer shuffled out of the Tower of London and straight into history as he mailed the world's very first Valentine's card.

Follow-up Questions to Explore

1. Valentine's Day is named for a Catholic saint. Do you think it is odd that Valentine's Day has nothing to do with the man for whom it is named? Can you think of other celebrations that have drifted away from their origins?

Answer

St. Patrick's Day is becoming such an event in the United States. U.S. Labor Day and Memorial Day are also drifting away from their original intent.

2. Why do *you* send Valentines? Are you hoping to find a sweetheart for the year? Do you believe sending a Valentine will help?

Answer

Compare your answers to those of your classmates.

Suggested Activities

1. Research Valentine's traditions over the past century in this country to see if they have changed. Interview your parents, grandparents, and other relatives to learn what they did for Valentine's Day when they were your age. Read books on Valentine's Day customs in the late nineteenth and early twentieth centuries.

2. Write down what you *want* to happen, and what you think most likely *will* happen when you send a Valentine. How does your answer compare to your classmates' answers, to your parents' and grandparents' answers?

MARCH

Ibu Afo

A Nigerian
New Year's Celebration

At a Glance

EVERYBODY CELEBRATES NEW YEAR'S. Most of the world celebrates New Year's Eve on the night of December 31, based on the solar Gregorian calendar. Some countries (China and Vietnam, for example) base their calendar on the cycles of the moon. Their New Year's falls in January or February. Many agricultural countries used to celebrate New Year's at the beginning of the planting season. For these cultures, New Year's coincides with the spring equinox, the date when the sun crosses the equator into the Northern Hemisphere. A few societies still celebrate New Year's on this date.

But these are not the only times of the year when New Year's celebrations are held. The Druids of Ireland and Scotland, for example, used to celebrate New Year's around the fall equinox. No matter which date is picked, virtually every culture has designated one fixed date (based on either a solar or lunar calendar) for their New Year's celebration. The date never varies. It is the same every year.

But not every culture.

The Igbo tribe in Nigeria, Africa, is one of the few cultures with a floating New Year's. In America, the *Farmer's Almanac* tries to make weather forecasts a year in advance and, from these forecasts, prints advice on the best times for planting. We tend to look at these forecasts as just guesses, and wait to see computer and satellite data before we make any major decisions.

The Igbo Council of Elders makes the same kind of long-range forecasts. The result of their forecast is a decision for the date and time of New Year's. That decision then defines the start of the spring planting season for the Igbo people's main crops—yams, cassava melons, and rice.

Not only is the Igbo system for picking New Year's unique, their New Year's celebration itself is unique. The Igbo New Year's celebration Ibu Afo, mixes the universal joy of a new year's dawning with something like the fear of meeting the boogieman to create a moment of danger and fright—even terror—for Igbo children.

Ibu Afo

Ebantu Ugonna clapped her hands to gain her children's attention. "Aliengi? Tennensu! Nap time."

Born in 1983, now seven-year-old Aliengi frowned at the idea of a nap. She was generally as bright as sunshine, as bubbly as a cool spring, a happy girl who seemed to always find a reason to laugh and a way to turn any time into playtime. Her skin was velvety smooth and a lighter brown than either her younger brother, Tennensu's, or her parents'. Her braided hair was clipped at the top of her head with a barrette to let any breath of breeze that might stir in the steamy heat of southern Nigeria blow across the back of her neck. Frowning seemed hard for Aliengi, as if she had to concentrate on making her mouth curl down.

Though only three, Tennensu was already the mirror of his father's dark face—not only dark in color, but in that his face was set in a permanent scowl. Many Igbo males wore this scowl (eyebrows furrowed, lower lip extended), which could not be broken by smile or laugh. They were not angry at all, but looked that way to an outsider who didn't know how common that facial structure was.

"Aliengi! Tennensu! I said it's nap time."

"But I'm too old for naps," protested Aliengi. Tennensu, knowing he could stall as long as his sister kept up her argument, continued to play in the corner of their living room.

"Not on Ibu Afo you aren't," said their mother. "If you're going to stay up and see the new year safely in, you had better nap this afternoon!"

"Why is today New Year's?" asked Aliengi.

"Because the Council of Elders says it is Ibu Afo."

"But how do they *know*, Mommy?" pressed Aliengi, her eyes now sparkling and her white teeth flashing through her wide smile.

"Every year for all time the Council of Nze Elders has decreed which day and which hour is the start of the new year. It lets us know when to begin planting."

"We don't plant," interrupted Aliengi.

"No, but many of our friends do," answered Ebantu. "Most of the people with accounts at your father's bank grow yams, cassavas, or rice." Her eyes narrowed. "Are you just stalling to get out of a nap?"

"Do we *own* the bank, Mommy?" asked Aliengi, ignoring her mother's suspicious glare.

"Your father is the bank manager. Now get into the bedroom for a nap!"

"But it's too hot to sleep."

"No more stalling! Go! ... And you, too, Tennensu." Seeing his sister sigh in defeat and head for the back room of their cinder-block house, Tennensu rose, a contented scowl on his face, and waddled after her.

In truth, Aliengi was right. The steamy afternoon heat pressed down like a giant hand, squeezing the energy out of everyone, making every movement uncomfortable and difficult. But it often felt this way in the wet, fertile lands of southern Nigeria. Farther north, Nigeria was scrub brush and deserts. Here, in the town of Ithitenansu, it was tall palm trees; lush, thick vines; wide shade trees; and humid heat that crept into every nook and made the earth feel like a sauna.

Cities and rural villages were worlds apart in Nigeria. Ithitenansu was in between. Cities had paved streets, tall metal and glass buildings, electric power, office and factory workers, and Western clothes. Villages were mud huts with thatched roofs, dirt roads, small farm plots, goats everywhere, and flowing traditional robes. Ithitenansu was a town—a little of both, city and village mixed together. There were no tall buildings or noisy traffic jams. But there *were* neat streets of cinder-block and wood houses where the "citified" Igbo people lived. That included the Ugonna family.

Just as Aliengi flopped onto her mattress, the front door opened to their father, Nnabuenyi Ugonna. Nnabuenyi was tall and slender and moved with the grace of a dancer. His face wore the classic Igbo scowl, but he smiled and laughed almost as much as his daughter.

"Great news!" he cried, his face radiating excitement.

Recognizing an opportunity to skip her nap, Aliengi bounded out of bed and ran to her father. "Hi, Daddy!"

"*What* news?" asked Ebantu.

'The Oba, himself, will walk through Ithitenansu for Ibu Afo!"

"The Oba? Here?" gasped Mrs. Ugonna. "Oh, my! That *is* exciting."

"I want to see him!" squealed Aliengi. "He's the richest man in the whole world!"

"I want to see, too," said Tennensu.

"You don't even know who the Oba is," scoffed Aliengi.

"I do so!"

"I'll tell you," laughed their mother, squatting on the cement floor next to her son. "The Oba, or Emir, is the tribal chief. And Aliengi is right. He is a man of great power and wealth—though not the richest in the world. He wears beautifully embroidered flowing gowns, and his slippers are decorated with gold and silver. His crown is heavy with jewels. Twenty drummers walk before him to announce his coming. A servant walks behind him holding a wide colored umbrella over him that is stitched with gold thread and bears the golden crest of the Oba."

"Several hundred years ago Emir Mousa went on a pilgrimage to Mecca," added Nnabuenyi. "It took a thousand camels to carry his gold."

"Not a thousand, Daddy," laughed Aliengi.

"That is what they say," he answered. "And the Oba has asked *me* to walk with him to discuss the state of local business."

"You get to actually walk with the Oba, Daddy?" gasped Aliengi.

"This will be a *very special* Ibu Afo," agreed Ebantu.

But Aliengi's face curled into her second frown of the day. "What time will the Oba walk by our house?"

"I can't say," answered her father. "I'm not even sure he'll walk down this particular street."

"What time is Ibu Afo?" demanded Aliengi.

"The Council said the new year begins at eleven tonight."

Fear replaced Aliengi's frown. "What if the Oba comes at Ibu Afo?"

"He *is* coming tonight," said her mother.

"No! I mean, what if he comes *exactly* at Ibu Afo?!"

"Ahh. I see your problem," smiled Nnabuenyi. "Then you'd want to be outside to see him, and inside to be safe, all at the same time."

"Why?" asked Tennensu.

Mr. Ugonna answered, "Because as the old year departs, like a wicked old goblin, it will snatch up any children it catches outside and carry them away with it. We must all make lots of noise to drive the old year away and make the land safe for a new year to enter. Children must run inside, lock the door, and pound extra hard to stay safe."

"Oh, that. I remember that," said Tennensu.

"You do not," chided his sister. "Last year you slept through everything."

"I do, too!"

"Back to bed," insisted their mother. "Tonight will be a very special night, indeed!"

By 8:30 that evening word raced down the street like crackling wildfire that the Oba was in Ithitenansu. Aliengi wormed her way through the milling crowd to the middle of the street so as not to miss him when he came.

By 10:00, Aliengi heard the Oba's drums pounding his greeting in the distance. The sound rose above the growing rumble of the excited crowd waiting for New Year's. "He's coming this way, Mommy!"

"I hope he hurries," Ebantu said. "It's getting close to Ibu Afo time."

By 10:30 most children had tiptoed back inside, or at least had edged nervously to doorways. None wanted to look cowardly, but neither did they want the cruel, horrid old year to snatch them away as it did all foolish children who lingered outside too long and disobeyed the advice of their parents.

Adults and teenagers outside had begun the early pot banging, horn honking, yelling, and cymbal crashing of Ibu Afo. By the hour of Ibu Afo, their noise would rise to a deafening crescendo, loud enough to drive the old year out of town.

"The drums are louder, Mommy. I know he's close!"

"How can you tell?" Ebantu screamed over the growing noise, so as to be heard. "I can't tell the Oba's drums from the other New Year's noise."

"I know he'll come," Aliengi repeated. "He *has* to!"

At 10:50 Aliengi was the only child still outside. Ibu Afo noise had risen to a great din, washing away every other sensation. Like a mighty gale, the noise seemed to drive Aliengi back toward her door.

"Where is he, Mommy? I can't see!" Using gestures to point to the time and the door, Ebantu urged her daughter to go inside.

"I can't hear his drums in all this noise, Mommy."

"I can't hear anything!"

At 10:55, Ibu Afo noise had risen to a fevered pitch. Like giant waves, the noise throbbed and pulsed across town and through Aliengi's body. The street under her feet vibrated with the racket.

All the other children were inside, doors bolted, screaming at the top of their lungs, pounding on the door to drive away the danger of the old year.

"Where is the Oba?"

"Get inside, Aliengi!"

"Not yet, Mommy! I know he's coming."

Aliengi's heart pounded with dread. Would the old year sweep down the street and snatch her off forever in its evil tentacles?

10:57 … 10:58. The noise became deafening. Buildings shook. Windows rattled.

"Aliengi! Go!"

"He's coming, Mommy! I see his umbrella down the block!"

"Run, Aliengi! Run!"

At 10:59, like a sinister, shimmering shock wave speeding through the air, Aliengi saw the old year rushing toward her. Electric bolts seemed to stretch out ahead of the wave like rivulets of energy, like blue-clawed tentacles, grasping, clutching, groping for foolish children still lingering outside.

With a silent scream of terror, Aliengi leapt inside. She slammed the door, her trembling hands fumbling with the bolt. Heart hammering like a hummingbird's, knees trembling, Aliengi beat on the door. The whole world filled with dreadful noise. Rushing air and grabbing tentacles scraped at the walls and windows around her.

Eyes squeezed shut, Aliengi cried and pounded.

Then Aliengi heard a new sound, lighter and happier. She heard cheering, clapping, and laughing. "Come out! Open the doors!" called the adults. "It's a new year! Come out!"

Aliengi stopped her crying and rubbed the tears from her eyes. Her still-shaking hands inched open the door. Cautiously she poked her face through the crack.

"And this is my daughter, Aliengi," said her father. "Come out and meet the Oba."

Open-mouthed, eyes bulging in wonder, Aliengi stepped outside and was face-to-face with the gold-and-jewel crown and brilliant robes of the Oba. A gold-encrusted hand reached down to touch her chin. "Ahh. This one is a bright ray of sunshine—and such a brave girl, too!"

As if from a thousand miles away, Aliengi heard the call for the New Year's feasting to begin. But none of it mattered to her. She had seen the horrid old year screeching after her and had escaped. She had met the Oba and he had smiled and touched her chin—all in the same minute!

Aliengi knew there could never be another Ibu Afo as special as this.

Follow-up Questions to Explore

1. Do you think it is all right to scare children as a part of a celebration with stories like the one about the old year in this story? Why do you think such stories evolved?

2. Do you make noise around midnight on New Year's Eve? Why do *you* do it? Why do you think New Year's noisemaking started?

Answer

Compare your answers to those of your classmates.

Suggested Activities

1. Make a list of the events, celebrations, traditions, and ceremonies during which we try to scare children. Make a list of what scares you.

2. Plan a time to tell scary stories you create about the changing of the years from old to new. What makes a story sound scary, the story itself, or the way the story is told? Which stories that you have heard were the scariest? Why?

Stickdance

An Athabascan Indian
Memorial Celebration

At a Glance

EVERY SOCIETY HAS CREATED RITUALS AND CEREMONIES to deal with the trauma of death. As a group, these ceremonies have three purposes: (1) to ease and facilitate the journey of the departed individual into the next life or to the dwelling place for their afterlife (Heaven, Nirvana, the Elysian fields, etc.); (2) to ease the grief of the departed's family and friends and provide a mechanism for the larger community to express their sympathy and show their emotional support; and (3) to provide physical support for the departed's family through their difficult transition as they adjust to life without that family member.

Every culture has these ceremonies, these celebrations. Some are more public, some more private. But none brings final closure for family and friends in a better and more supportive way than the Stickdance of the Athabascan Indians of Alaska.

Stickdance

My father died exactly three years ago in 1989. He had flown the 350 miles from our home in Nulato to Fairbanks to testify at a government hearing on fishing rights along the Yukon River. The Yukon is the lifeblood of our people. From November to May it is our frozen highway to the rest of the world. In the summer it provides our water and much of our food for the year. My father felt honored to represent the 450 people of Nulato on such an important issue. We Athabascans are a small tribe, but have lived in Alaska longer than the Eskimos. As far as I know, for all that time we have lived along the Yukon River.

On the return trip, Father's small plane had mechanical trouble and crashed.

I was ten and my world crashed with that plane. There was a funeral. But I don't remember it. I was numb with shock and sorrow. So were my mother and two brothers. My father's best friend, Daniel Cline, made all the funeral arrangements. None of us could have. Afterward I remember feeling empty and feeling that I had never had a chance to say good-bye to my father.

Since then my family has been very busy, adjusting to life without Father, and getting ready. By the darkest days of this past winter, Mother said we were prepared. So this year my father is being honored at a Stickdance.

My name is Crystal Shuaba. My older brothers, Billy and Wadi, have been busy replacing our father, fishing and hunting. So Mother and I have had to do most of the work to prepare for the Stickdance. And, believe me, getting ready for a Stickdance is long, hard work. But the work has been a blessing. It has kept Mother busy and made her see how much my father meant to Nulato, and how much the community has given to support our family.

See, the Stickdance is a chance to say a final farewell to my father, and a chance for us to say "thank you" to the community for their friendship and support. And *that's* where the preparations come in. We will give a present to every person who comes to the Stickdance. That's hundreds of presents to buy or make. For most families—including ours—it is mostly *make.* It takes years to stockpile the furs, cloth, wood, time, and money to make enough presents.

The last Stickdance was two years ago. That one was held in Kaltag, thirty-five miles downriver from Nulato. Sometimes there are three or even four years between Stickdances. It just depends on whether the families have prepared. I was eleven for the Kaltag Stickdance. My father had only been dead one year, and that was the first time I really connected the celebration with death. I remember watching the families of the departed thinking that someday soon that would be me.

A Stickdance lasts for a week. For the first four nights there are gatherings in the community center. Some nights these gatherings are full potlatches with moose, salmon, beaver, and rabbit meat. (A *potlatch* is like a formal, structured potluck dinner.) Some nights there is only cake and coffee. But always there is singing and dancing. Not ceremonial songs. Just fun songs and fun dancing. People eat, sing, dance, talk, and remember. The hall becomes more crowded each night as more people arrive in Nulato.

Friday night the formal ceremony begins. This year it is Friday, March 12, 1992. A huge crowd—many hundreds of people—have gathered. My father is one of six being honored at the Stickdance tonight. The sun set around 4 P.M. The temperature had already dipped below zero degrees Fahrenheit.

As women dance in a big circle, five men, including Daniel Cline, whom we have asked to get dressed for my father, carry the fifteen-foot-tall trunk of a young spruce tree into the hall. This pole (it is the "stick" for which the whole ceremony is named) has been stripped of branches and wrapped in ribbons. The men stand this pole in the center of the big hall in the community center.

People begin to sing and dance. The families and close friends of the dead hang gifts of fox, wolf, and beaver fur and cloth on the pole. Throughout the night more and more gifts will be added to decorate the pole like a Christmas tree.

Tonight we will sing the thirteen sacred songs. Because they may only be sung during a Stickdance, few know all the words. The old ones lead. The rest of us try to follow and pick up some of the words we don't know. Someday we will be the old ones and will have to lead the singing.

We dance around the pole. Really, what we do is closer to a shuffling march in long lines around the pole, over and over as the songs are chanted. People drop out of the dancing to eat and rest, then join back in. Soon I can't tell how long I have been dancing, or how many laps around the stick I have made. I can't remember when I started. It feels like I have danced around this pole with the memory of my father forever.

Almost in a trance, I circle the stick, dancing, shuffling, hearing the chanted songs from the elders. The words wash over me, through me. I see my father, smiling, waving, carrying a basket of salmon for me to clean. I see him laughing while we eat in our small house in Nulato. I see him waving good-bye, saying that life is a wondrous mystery for us to enjoy. The music and words carry me around the pole, over and over in countless laps as I relive my life with my father.

The singing and dancing go on all night. When the sun is up Saturday morning, climbing above the southern mountains on its short arch across the sky, the elders agree that it is time for the pole, the stick, to be carried outside. The furs and cloth are removed. They will be some of the gifts given out tonight.

Men carry the stick past each house in Nulato. People watch through windows and wave. Some step outside to watch the stick carried by. After the men have passed every house, they carry the stick to the river, break it into pieces, and throw them far out on the ice. In May, the Yukon will melt and carry these pieces out to sea.

Friday night of a Stickdance is very spiritual and private, each person dancing with their own thoughts. Saturday night is a great public celebration, a formal potlatch at the community center. The room is packed with hundreds of people, many I have never seen before, but who knew one of the others being honored.

Near the end of the meal a sheet is tacked up hiding part of the stage. One by one the people who have been asked to dress for one of the dead step behind the screen. We can partly see their shadowed forms as they are dressed in clothes of, or clothes which remind us of, the person they are dressed for.

When they step out from behind the sheet, they have become the dead person. My heart jumps to see my father stand before me again, even though I know it is really Daniel Cline who wears his clothes. A beautiful feeling washes over me. Timidly I wave and whisper, "I love you."

Speeches are made about each of the honored dead. Then those who are dressed for the dead leave the hall. Outside, by the river, they perform a ceremony to shake the spirits from their clothing. I cannot see this ceremony, nor will I until I am chosen to be dressed for some departed friend or relative.

Now it is time for gifts. Every person in the great hall receives a present from the family of each of the honored dead. The gifts are our way to thank the community for their friendship to my father while he lived, and for their support, help, and friendship to us since he died. It takes hours to distribute all the gifts Mother and I have worked on for three whole years. Long past midnight, it is done and we go home to sleep.

Sunday morning, those dressed for the dead visit each house in town to shake hands and say a final farewell. Our house is almost last. Mother weeps as she opens the door and faces Daniel Cline dressed in her husband's clothes.

"I know," says Daniel, dressed as my father. "We will all miss him. But it is time to move on like the flowing river."

Mother smiles and squeezes Daniel's hands.

Billy and Wadi have decided they don't want to cry again as they did at the funeral three long years ago. They both scowl to hold back their waves of sadness and formally shake hands with the man being our father.

"You do him honor in how well you take his place," says Daniel.

It is my turn. I, too, had planned to shake hands as I did at the last Stickdance when I was eleven. But then I had hardly known the people being honored. Now it is my father. Tears begin to flow. I rush forward and hug the man being my father.

"I will always miss you," I sob.

"I will always be with you in spirit," Daniel answers.

As he says these words I know they are true. I feel stronger. My father has died, but now I can go on. Inside, my heart glows with warmth and love. It bursts out as a smile. Life will go on. I wave as the door closes. The Stickdance is over.

Follow-up Questions to Explore

1. What ceremonies and events does your culture use to say farewell to those who have died? Are there any that happen as long after a death as the Stickdance?

2. During the Stickdance the family of the deceased gives a gift to each person who attends. Is that a unique concept for giving gifts? At which celebrations do you give or receive gifts? How does your culture decide

who gives the gifts and who receives? Can you find cultures and celebrations where it is different than yours?

Answer

Compare your answers to those of your classmates.

Suggested Activities

1. This story is about the Athabascan people of central Alaska. Research the Athabascans. What are their customs and history? Where do they live? How long have they lived there? Where did they come from? How do they make their living? Now research the other Native tribes living in Alaska. In what ways are the Athabascans similar to other groups? In what ways are they unique?

Holi

An Indian Spring, Religious Myth, and Public Wild-Time Celebration

At a Glance

HOLI IS UNIQUE AMONG THE CELEBRATIONS OF THE WORLD. Partly it is an agricultural festival celebrating the winter harvest in northern India. Certainly there is nothing unique about an agricultural and harvest festival. Partly it is a spring festival, marking the passage of seasons and of the year. Nothing unique there, either.

Partly, Holi is a religious celebration, honoring the triumph of good over evil, and the victories of the Lord Krishna. Nothing unique yet. But the combination of religious, seasonal, and agricultural celebrations rolled into one event is unusual.

Then there is the playful side of Holi. Holi is a time of planned and sanctioned madness, a time of public wildness. Again, this is not unique. Carnaval, Mardi Gras, and Fashing are also celebrations of public wildness. But no one does it like Holi!

On the day of Holi, colored powder may be sprayed, colored water may be squirted or thrown in water balloons onto anyone—anytime! And no one gets angry. No one grows resentful. It is Holi!

What makes Holi unique? Two things. First, there is no other celebration in the world that wraps all four of these types of celebrations into one event. Second, there is no other celebration where people are allowed to act in the wild way they act on Holi.

Holi

"I saved some *real* firewood for you this year." Mr. Sahir stood at the door of his whitewashed one-story house in the town of Pharenda, northern India. A late afternoon sun blazed fire red down the street, making his deep-set green eyes glow more fierce and suspicious in the doorway. A light breeze flowed through his thin cotton shirt and pants to cool his skin this warm February.

Mr. Sahir motioned at a pile of kindling and wood he had stacked inside the door, then blocked the doorway with one arm before either boy could step inside to scoop up armfuls of the precious stuff. "I'm giving you *lots* of wood this year. So no Holi tricks. No squirting."

Both ragamuffin boys in front of him blinked innocently. "No, Mr. Sahir. We won't get you on Holi this year." With dirty faces, loose-fitting white pants and white linen shirts, and broad smiles, both boys stepped forward to wrestle the wood outside.

Pharenda is a small city nestled against the Churia Mountains. Kavi and Rajak were two of hundreds of children scrounging wood for the great Holi fires. As they dragged their load down the winding dirt street toward a great town clearing at the river, Kavi and Rajak stopped next to a cluster of bushes.

"Do you have the bamboo blowpipes?" asked Kavi.

"And the yellow and red powders," answered Rajak, pointing at their secret stash hidden beneath the bush.

"I've got the water balloons."

"We're ready for Holi!" And both boys laughed. "Watch out, Mr. Sahir!"

The sun hung like an orange ball on the hills through the haze to the west. "Hurry," said Kavi. "The moon's going to rise. We've got to get our wood to the bonfire."

A full moon was due to rise this evening of March 25. That meant tomorrow was Holi. Tonight was the night before, a night of magic followed by a day of wild fun.

Kavi and Rajak dragged their blanket-load of wood to the great clearing next to the Rapti River. A monstrous pile of wood, paper, discarded furniture and crates, torn straw and baskets—all gathered by children of Pharenda for the Holi bonfire— filled much of the open dirt clearing.

A great crowd buzzed around the mound. Friends and neighbors laughed together. Music played from a hundred instruments carried to the river clearing.

Kavi and Rajak added their load of wood to the great mound just as the sun disappeared in a fiery blaze in the west and a golden full moon rose in the east over the low hills of the jungle. The sweet smells of growing grass and of fragrant tree blossoms spilled across the clearing. The night blew warm and friendly. The heat and mugginess of the monsoons were still a month away.

With rounds of applause, burning torches were brought forward and soon the great Holi bonfire blazed hot and bright. People laughed and cheered. Sticks of sugarcane were passed to the children.

Young children romped and wrestled around the blazing Holi bonfire. Adults sang. Clusters of young women with large almond-shaped eyes began folk dances around the fire.

Kavi and Rajak sat with their families watching the pulsing glow of the flames and the dense smoke billow into the spring night to turn the rising moon a deep red. Music floated up with the rising heat from a dozen impromptu groups around the fire.

One of the town elders—a tall, powerful man with thick beard and flowing, waist-length black hair wrapped inside a turban—climbed onto a platform and called out, "I will tell you the story of this bonfire."

The crowd cheered. The bearded elder, wearing a flowing robe, began. "We have a bonfire tonight because long ago the female demon, Holika, came down each spring to devour the children of the village. The villagers tried to hide their children, but the demon smelled them out, and gobbled them down one by one, until she was full.

"One year the villagers banded together with burning torches, surrounded Holika, and burned her in a great bonfire. She never returned to that village. So now we burn great bonfires each spring before Holi to remind Holika not to return."

The crowd cheered as the elder bowed.

An older man with a straggling white beard cried, "Not true! Holika was evil, but she ate no children. She was the sister of an evil, demon king. The king's son, Prahlad, was a wise child sage. The evil king was jealous of his son and, with his sister, schemed to kill the boy. But each attempt failed because the goodness of Prahlad was protected by the great god, Krishna.

"Finally, Holika, whose magic power protected her from fire, had a great bonfire built and lured Prahlad to sit in its middle with her, knowing he would burn to death. But just the opposite happened. Holika burned and Prahlad lived! Holi is a celebration of the triumph of Krishna's good over evil and of renewed life with each new spring."

Again the crowd cheered, and music erupted from drums, horns, and stringed instruments around the great fire. People sang, danced, and laughed. The glowing full moon poured down its light. It was a night of radiant magic.

Rajak asked his father, "Which story was the truth?"

"Maybe both. Maybe neither," he answered. "They are myths. What is important to remember is that the Holi fire represents the triumph of good over evil."

One by one families drifted off to home and sleep as the bonfire faded to glowing red embers.

As the sun climbed hot and clear over Pharenda the next morning, families drifted back to the bonfire clearing. Each person dipped a finger into the warm ashes and marked their forehead to wish for luck in the coming year.

Then the fun of Holi began!

Kavi and Rajak dashed away from the bonfire clearing, the first red rays of morning lighting their faces, and stopped next to the bush with their stash of Holi weapons.

"Soon we'll make *everyone* see red," laughed Kavi, snatching up a two-foot-long bamboo blowpipe and bags of red and yellow powder.

"Especially Mr. Sahir!" said Rajak, filling three balloons with yellow water.

But Mr. Sahir was already hurrying through the maze of narrow streets toward his shop. "I must get safely inside while it's still early."

"There he goes," cried Kavi. "He's ahead of us."

"Through this alley. We'll cut him off," answered Rajak, already sprinting through a narrow gate opening.

The boys heard, "Balloons away!" and glanced up as two water balloons plummeted on them from above.

One exploded in the alley right in front of Kavi spraying red water across his pants and bare feet. The other, a perfect shot, crashed into Rajak's upturned face, soaking him with saffron-stained yellow water.

"Holi!" cried the laughing children from above.

"Fire back!" cried Rajak.

"No. First we have to get Mr. Sahir," answered Kavi.

Mr. Sahir rounded the corner and stepped toward his linen shop. Kavi whispered, "Blowpipes," and both boys poured generous amounts of colored powder into one end of their pipes.

With a soft "Now!" the boys sprang into the street and blew out their yellow clouds at Mr. Sahir.

"Holi!"

A saffron yellow cloud enveloped Mr. Sahir. He ducked. He turned. He screamed. But he could not escape the dust of Holi.

"But you promised!" bellowed Mr. Sahir, wiping saffron powder from his eyes and teeth.

"Balloons!" cried Rajak. *Splat!* A red water balloon exploded across Mr. Sahir's shoulder.

"Promises never count on Holi!" And both boys dashed down the street, laughing—and straight into a great cloud of colored powder blown by three girls. "Holi!!"

No one wore good clothes on Holi.

By noon Kavi and Rajak were out of powder and balloons, and were painted head to toe in bright red and yellow. So were most other children in Pharenda. So were many adults.

The boys parted, each toward his own home and the family feasts that would mark the end of Holi.

The food was plentiful and succulent. But it was the cries of "Holi!" and the perfectly timed attacks with powder and water balloons that would linger longest in the boys' memory.

Follow-up Questions to Explore

1. Do you think people get mad being sprayed and splattered on Holi? Would you? Why or why not?

Answer

In India no one seems to mind being splattered on Holi because that is what they expect to have happen. It is usually your expectations, rather than an event itself, that makes you angry.

2. Why do you think people spray yellow and red powder onto each other during Holi?

Answer

Holi began as a spring festival. Yellow and red were colors associated with spring blooms and spring fertility. The colored powders were not originally sprayed on people, but rather on the ground where the spring celebration was held. It is most probable that the first powder to hit people did so by accident. But they were accidents that called for revenge. Over time, revenge escalated into the daylong free-for-all India enjoys today.

Suggested Activities

1. Research the games we play that involve getting dirty, wet, or messy. Make a list of all you can find. How many have you played? Which ones did you enjoy most? Why?

2. Myths are an important part of Holi. Invent a myth to explain the importance of one of your celebrations. Read your myth to the rest of the class. What are the characteristics of a good myth? What makes them seem plausible or believable?

APRIL

April Fool's Day

A Western Celebration of Foolery and Pranks

At a Glance

APRIL FOOL'S DAY, THE FIRST DAY OF APRIL, is celebrated worldwide. There are no parades, no festivals, no speeches, no organized ceremonies. Still, April 1 is looked forward to, planned for, and enjoyed everywhere. April Fool's Day is the only worldwide celebration that does not include any formal ceremony, festival, or acknowledgment by religious, governmental, or community organizations. It is a day for foolery, for personal spontaneity, for pranks, for jokes. It is a day for people and play. And no where is April Fool's more enthusiastically celebrated than in Western Europe and North America. This story unfolded in Quebec, Canada, in 1986. But it could have happened (and might well have) in any of fifteen other countries.

April Fool's Day

Nine-year-old Eugenia Cuvier called up the curved stairway to her ten-year-old brother, "Arna! Breakfast!" Then she giggled and rubbed her hands together. Her dark eyes sparkled. Even her black, braided pigtails seemed to snicker with mischievous glee.

"Coming," called Arna, still tucking in his shirt as, blond hair bouncing across his forehead, he bounded down the stairs of the family's two-story row house in an older neighborhood on the west side of Montreal.

Eugenia slid into her seat next to the children's grandmother, trying to cover another giggle.

"Sugar for your oatmeal?" asked Gram Methena.

"No thanks," blurted Eugenia.

"I'll have some," said Arna settling into his seat.

Eugenia watched out of the corner of one eye as Arna scooped two heaping spoonfuls of sugar onto his cereal. He shoveled a large bite into his mouth, chewed twice, and wrinkled his face in disgust "Bleah! This tastes terrible!"

"Want more sugar?" laughed Eugenia.

Arna's eyes widened in understanding. "It's salt! You put salt in the sugar bowl."

"April Fool's!" she laughed.

"I'll get you!" Arna reached across the table but was stopped by Gram Methena.

"Not during my breakfast, you won't." She turned to the smug Eugenia. "Don't gloat, young lady. The day is still young, and they say that the last one fooled is the biggest fool of all."

Their mother, Mrs. Cuvier, joined them and breakfast finished in a strained truce between brother and sister.

As Arna and Eugenia stacked their dishes in the sink, Gram Methena pointed toward a corner counter. "I made some chocolate-covered fudge balls. If you call an April Fool's truce and behave today, you may both have some later."

Both children nodded enthusiastically in promise.

As they headed for the door and school, Arna turned for the front closet. "I'll get your jacket, Eugenia."

Seconds later both children leapt down the front stairs zipping jackets against the swirling wind and cold, book bags dangling from one shoulder. Piles of snow lingered across the small front yards. The first buds and grass were still weeks away. The air felt more like snow than spring.

Paul Moreau, a classmate of Arna's, joined them on their walk to school. "Hi, Arna, Eugenia." Then, *whack!*, he kicked Eugenia hard in the rear.

"Ow! What was that for?!"

Paul shrugged, "Just doing what the sign says."

"What sign?" demanded Eugenia. But she didn't need to hear the answer. She knew. Arna had already doubled over laughing. "April Fool's!" he called. Then he sprinted off down the street.

Eugenia stripped off her jacket to see a large "Kick me!" sign taped onto the back. "I'll get you!" she called after her brother.

Eugenia steamed all through morning studies planning revenge. Mr. St. Clair, her teacher, towered over the class. "I will not tolerate any April foolishness during the school day. Pranks here will land you in the principal's office." He paused studying his students. "Who knows the origin of April Fool's?"

A friend of Eugenia's, Catherine Monet, raised her hand. "My father said it started as a pre-Christian celebration in France to scare off evil spirits at springtime."

Mr. St. Clair nodded and rubbed his bushy eyebrows. "I have heard the same theory."

Catherine sat taller in her chair and nodded smugly to her classmates.

"But it is incorrect," he continued. "The celebration of April Fool's started because of the Gregorian calendar. Write that name down. Gregorian. It's the calendar we now use. England and the North American colonies did not adopt the Gregorian calendar until the 1750s. But King Charles IX in France adopted the Gregorian calendar in 1564.

"New Year's had previously been celebrated on the spring equinox, March 23. The Gregorian calendar moved New Year's to January 1. Many, however, continued the traditional New Year's celebration that lasted for a week from the spring equinox on March 23, to April 1. Those people were ridiculed and teased. Tricks were played on them. Invitations to nonexistent New Year's parties were delivered. Over the years that trickery grew into what we celebrate as April Fool's."

Now he glowered at the children. "April Fool's may appear on your next test; however, it will not appear in my classroom. Understood?"

But Eugenia couldn't quit while Arna had the last laugh. At recess she pocketed a bottle of glue and raced to the school's cement play yard. In two minutes she was ready and hid beside a stone stairway just as Arna's class was released. Arna sprang out the door, down the steps, and stopped dead in his tracks. "A quarter!" he cried. "It's mine. I saw it first!"

He dropped to his knees and reached to scoop up the shiny coin. Classmates stopped to watch. Arna's hand swept out, closed over the coin, and started back for his pocket. Then it stopped. It didn't have the quarter. He reached out a second time. Again his hand came up empty. Now he clawed with both hands to pry up the coin. Try as he might he could not lift it from the cement.

Other kids laughed, "Arna's too weak to lift a quarter!"

"No," pleaded Arna, still clawing at the quarter. "It's stuck. It's glued down."

The ring of kids laughed all the harder.

"April Fool's!" cried Eugenia leaping from behind the stairs.

Everyone laughed. Arna screamed, "I'll get you!"

Ten minutes later, Arna swaggered to where Eugenia played with three friends. There were still five minutes left in the morning recess.

"Mr. St. Clair wants to see you *now*," Arna sneered.

"Me?" gulped Eugenia. "Why?"

"Somehow he found out about your April Fool's prank."

"You told!" hissed Eugenia. "I'll get you!"

Arna grinned, "But first you have to see Mr. St. Clair."

Alone and trembling, Eugenia reentered her classroom and marched across the polished wood floor to Mr. St. Clair's desk.

His bushy eyebrows wrinkled into a frown. "What do you want?"

"You wanted to see me," answered Eugenia, her voice barely a whisper.

"About what?" demanded her teacher.

"About my April Foo—" Then her mouth slammed shut. Her eyes widened. "Arna!" she hissed.

"Your *what?*" continued Mr. St. Clair.

"Ahhhh ... nothing, sir," smiled Eugenia backing toward the door.

"It must be about something, young lady. Sit in your desk until either you remember or until recess is over."

Blushing bright red, Eugenia sunk into her desk. Her mouth silently formed the words, "I'll get you, Arna."

Arna was first home from school, still gloating over his prank.

"Don't act so proud," cautioned Gram Methena. "The day is far from over and remember, the last one fooled is the biggest fool of all."

The front bell rang. Arna open the door.

Then he screamed. The top edges of a paper lunch bag burned—smoldered— on the front steps.

Arna lifted one foot and stomped onto the bag to put out the fire. Sparks showered up around his leg as his foot sank into a thick mound of manure hidden inside the bag. Manure squished up around his shoe and over his pants and sock. The stench of smoldering manure stung his nose.

"Yuck!"

"April Fool's!" laughed Eugenia stepping from behind a bush.

Gram Methena shook her head and shut the front door to keep the smell out. Arna sprang off the porch shaking his foot to shed the worst clumps of manure and tore after his laughing sister. "I'll get you!"

At 5:30 that afternoon Gram Methena sternly summoned both children into the kitchen. A scowl etched her face. "My chocolate-covered fudge balls are gone. Which of you took them?"

"Not me" answered Arna. "Honest."

"I'd never take something of yours, Gram," stammered Eugenia.

Foot angrily tapping the linoleum floor, Gram Methena crossed her arms. "Someone here is concealing the truth. Besides me, you are the only two who have been in this house this afternoon. Now who took them?!"

Both children stared in numb shock and slowly shook their heads.

"Since no one will confess to being the thief, both of you up to your rooms and get to your homework. I will get to the bottom of this later."

Twenty minutes later, just before their parents were due home, the children were summoned downstairs. Gram Methena sat in a high-backed chair. Burly police sergeant Yves Tyers stood in his uniform in the middle of the room, hands resting on his gun belt.

"Hi, Uncle Yves," said Arna.

The sergeant stared, grim-faced.

"Who took the fudge balls?" demanded Gram.

Arna shifted uneasily. "Gram? … Uncle Yves? …"

Eugenia stared in silent terror at the policeman.

With a wave of her hand Gram turned her back on her grandchildren. "Take them away, officer."

Tears streaming down her face, Eugenia stammered, "But Gram …"

"Not a word," growled Sergeant Tyers and gestured toward the door with his head.

But Gram Methena reached under her chair and pulled out a ribboned box. She giggled, "I just remembered, *I* took them. They're right here!"

She opened the box to reveal the plate of chocolate-covered fudge balls. "April Fool's!" she and Sergeant Tyers laughed, as the children's mouths dropped open.

"A trick? Oh, Gram, I was so scared," gasped Eugenia.

"This was all a prank?" squealed Arna.

"Now you know what a *real* April Fool feels like." And Gram extended the box. "Have one."

Arna reached in, lifted the largest fudge ball and stuffed it into his mouth. His face wrinkled up in disgust. Around the white wad in his mouth he cried, "Ids nod fudge. Ids cotton!"

"April Fool's again!" sang Gram Methena. "And remember. The last one fooled is the biggest fool of all!"

As she tucked her grandchildren into bed that night, each one whispered, "Next year Gram, we'll get *you!*"

Follow-up Questions to Explore

1. Do you do April Fool's pranks? What kinds of tricks do you think are not acceptable to do? Discuss instances of pranks that got out of hand, when someone got hurt, or when someone's feelings were hurt.

2. Do you think a day of playing tricks and pranks is enough to consider April Fool's a real celebration? What has to happen in order to make the event a celebration? Is it the number of people who participate? Is it the things those people do? Is it the purpose for which they do them?

Answer

Compare your answers to those of your classmates.

Suggested Activities

1. Research April Fool's pranks that have been used in the past. As a class, make a list of all the pranks you can find, separating the ones you consider acceptable from the ones you consider unacceptable.

2. Design an elaborate April Fool's joke you can pull as a class. How will you make it fun, and still protect your victim from being hurt?

Easter

A Christian Celebration
of Jesus' Resurrection

At a Glance

ASTER CELEBRATES TWO OF THE THREE most important events in the Christian calendar: the death and resurrection of Jesus. (Christmas celebrates his birth, the third event.) Interestingly, neither the celebration's name nor most of the images we associate with Easter come from Christianity or Christian history.

The name *Easter* is derived from the name of a Germanic goddess, Oestara. Germanic and Anglo-Saxon tribes held spring festivals to Oestara. In some regions Oestara appeared as a hare, or rabbit. In some she rode a giant hare. Eggs and rabbits are both symbols of fertility, renewed life, and spring. Thus, most of the symbols we associate with Easter have nothing to do with the Christian celebration, but were added to it as Christianity spread into other cultures and as other celebrations merged into Easter.

Not all Christians even agree on when Easter should occur. Russian and Greek Orthodox sects set their church dates by a different calendar from that used by the rest of Christendom. The Orthodox sects split from the Roman Catholic Church in 1054 over a dispute concerning the role and power of the pope. The Greek Orthodox reverted to a pre-sixth-century calendar.

This story focuses on the activities of Greek Orthodox Easter. Their Easter is the same basic ceremony all Christians celebrate, but features slightly different customs and traditions.

Easter

Saturday afternoon, April 8, 1981, an air of expectancy hung over the small city of Amtiklia, Greece, much like the feel of an oncoming thunderstorm before it hits.

"Hurry, Mito! Hurry, Aura! There's still much to do!" called thirty-five-year-old Calantha Panopoulos to her two children. Her voice echoed through their trim whitewashed stucco house with red tile roof and brilliant green trim around doors and windows.

"Coming, Mother!" replied seven-year-old Mito with short, curly black hair, and six-year-old Aura, whose long brown hair flowed behind her as she hurried to her mother's call. Far from feeling resentful at their mother's driving demands, the children were eager to get the work done, get the house ready. Tonight was Easter!

The same uncontrollable giggle of anticipation rolled from Mito's and Aura's lips that besets many children during the final days before Christmas.

"Aura, you're on flowers. I want bouquets of spring flowers in every room."

Aura giggled without even being aware of it. "Yes, Mother."

"Mito, you help me with the lamb and potatoes."

"Hooray," cried Mito. "No more fasting!"

The Panopoulos family belonged to the Greek Orthodox Church, as did most of the families in Amtiklia. For the forty days of Lent they had followed the church's strict fasting guidelines. At first Mito had been terrified he wouldn't get to eat at all for over a month. He was greatly relieved to find out they would only be *limited* in what and when they ate, but then equally upset to find out they couldn't eat his two favorite treats—honeyed sweets and lamb. But now Lent was over and a lamb feast was on.

"Afterward you may both help me dye the eggs."

"Yea!" cheered the children. Aura bounced and clapped as she cheered.

"Aura," warned Mrs. Panopoulos, "be careful as you bring in the flowers. It's very windy today."

"Yes, Mother." And Aura was off like a whirlwind, her flowing hair struggling to catch up.

Amtiklia was nestled against the north face of the Oeta Mountains, just below Mt. Parnassós, eighty miles northwest of Athens, ten miles south of the Thermopylae plain and pass, made famous by a Spartan battle almost 2,500 years ago. Amtiklia was pleasant in the summer when soft breezes stirred around the mountains. But it could be chillingly cold on winter and spring afternoons when icy winds roared down from Mt. Parnassós.

The children's grandfather, Papa Nestor, stood scowling in the kitchen doorway. Exceptionally tall and lanky for a Greek, his bushy white mustache hid any trace of an upper lip. "Flowers and hard-boiled eggs! Bah! These aren't part of *Pascha.*"

Calantha answered, "Dad, even the priests say eggs and flowers are an acceptable part of Easter …"

"And don't call it Easter!" interrupted Papa Nestor. "That name isn't Christian. It's the name of some Anglo-Saxon god. Call it Pascha. That's its true name."

"We have this discussion every year, Papa," laughed Calantha. "I say: Easter, Pascha, who cares what you call it? What's important is the feeling of joy and hope the day brings. And *you're* the only one around here who's a grumpy sourpuss with no Easter feeling."

She kissed him lightly on the cheek and patted his backside to scoot him all the way into the kitchen. "Now help Mito and me with dinner."

By 2:00 that afternoon Aura and Mito clustered around the kitchen table with a dozen hard-boiled eggs and bowls of colored dye.

"I want red ones," declared Mito, dunking two eggs into the red bowl. "Red eggs do better in the breaking battles!"

"Pascha should be a time for soul searching and deep religious thought," said Nestor. "But these non-Christian add-ons have him thinking only about battles and games."

"It's not a battle," corrected Calantha. "It's a ceremony. Breaking your egg against another person's egg lets the blessings of the new year escape."

"It's a battle!" insisted Mito. "And I'm going to win!"

Aura pulled on her mother's sleeve. "Help me tie leaves onto my eggs before I dye them, Mommy. I want a pretty leaf pattern on mine."

Mito and Aura proudly surveyed their work as the full dozen dyed eggs stood drying in their holders. Aura asked, "Why did some countries have Easter last week?"

"Most Christians and countries switched to a different calendar a long time ago," explained Papa Nestor. "We didn't. We kept the old calendar. Different calendar means Pascha falls on different dates."

"But which is the *real* Easter?" she continued.

"The real Easter is the one you celebrate in your heart," said their mother. "Now scoot upstairs to fix your ikons."

The front door opened and their father, Cyrus Panopoulos, stepped in. "Happy Easter! The flowers look wonderful."

Aura beamed. "I did it all by myself, Daddy."

Papa Nestor grumbled, "Pascha, not Easter."

Cyrus was a short man with bright, black eyes and thick hands from his years of working at his leather and shoe repair shop. Today he had closed the shop early for Easter.

"Will you help me make my ikon, Daddy?" called Aura, dashing up the narrow stairs.

"In a minute, precious," he called after her.

Ikons are small, personal altars usually built above a person's bed. Typical of most, Aura's featured a framed picture of Jesus mounted over a small shelf where she had a candle, a cross, and several personal trinkets she put there because they were special.

"Very nice," said Cyrus, surveying Aura's work from her door. Papa Nestor added, "Now *that* is something worthwhile to do on Pascha."

"Now to sleep," concluded her father. "We have a long night ahead of us."

"I'm way too excited to sleep," Aura answered, still giggling uncontrollably.

"Rest then."

"I can't."

"Lie quietly."

With a disgusted "hurrumph!" Aura crossed her arms and flopped onto her bed. Two minutes later she was sound asleep.

"Hurry, Mito! Hurry, Aura!" shouted their mother. "It's ten forty-five P.M. Aren't you dressed yet?! We'll be late for church."

"Coming Mother," Mito and Aura answered, both struggling with their new shoes.

"And get a wrap, Aura," she added as the children tumbled to the foot of the stairs.

"No, Mother. I don't want to hide my beautiful new dress."

"But it's cold and windy tonight. You need one."

"No!"

"Yes! And hurry."

The family walked the narrow streets of this hilly part of Amtiklia, listening to the wind, the crickets, and the nearby honking cars. Other families, also bundled against the bitter wind, walked toward the traditional midnight church service.

"Everyone have everything?" asked Mr. Panopoulos. Everyone nodded for each item he recited. "Offering envelope? … Colored eggs for the ceremony? …"

Mito held up his three bright red eggs. "Ready for battle!"

"It's not a battle," insisted his mother.

"Not fair," protested Aura. "I only have two eggs."

"So? You're only six."

"Quiet!" barked Papa Nestor. "It's Pascha."

"Candles?" continued Mr. Panopoulos.

Everyone nodded. Then Aura froze, mouth dropped open, hands covering her face. "I forgot my candle."

"Oh, no," groaned Mito.

"You'll have to go back for it," sighed Calantha.

Papa Nestor agreed, "Eggs are pointless. But you *do* need a candle to receive the light of the new year."

"Hurry, sweetie," said Mr. Panopoulos. "I'll go with you." Turning to his wife he added, "We'll catch up before you reach the church."

Aura already raced back up the street. "My candle. I need my candle!"

Aura still panted as they slid into a pew at church. Her long hair was tousled into a hundred tangles from her run through the wind.

Black drapes covered the stained-glass windows of the church. Tall candles stood unlit along the isle and across the altar. The lights were dimmed. The choir sang hymns softly from the front of the church.

As the minutes passed from 11:00 to 11:30 the lights slowly faded. The choir sang in increasingly hushed tones. By 11:50 the church was completely black except for one oil lamp that always burned beneath the ikon of Christ above the altar. The choir sang in a muted whisper. No other sound could be heard save the wind moaning against the windows.

Mito almost fell asleep in the dark stillness. Then the booming church bell bonged the first stroke of midnight. A single priest in splendid white robes stepped from behind the altar carrying a lighted candle. Holding the glowing taper high he called, "Come ye and take light from the eternal light." Almost instantly the black drapes were pulled down, lit candles blazed across the church. The choir boomed out a triumphant hymn in their loudest voices. The midnight Easter service began.

The rumbling boom of dynamite rattled through Amtiklia. Papa Nestor growled, "They shouldn't be allowed to do that."

"Throwing dynamite from mountaintops at Easter midnight is an old tradition," said Calantha.

"It's dangerous and should be stopped."

As the service ended each person lit their candle with the new year's light, some from altar candles, some from the candle of another person. "Christ is risen," they repeated with each new lighting.

In the courtyard neighbors chatted, the choir sang over the continued rumbling of distant dynamite, each person struggled to protect their candle flame, and Mito's egg battles began.

Mito's strategy was to bonk the pointed end of his egg into the weaker side of someone else's, hoping theirs would break before his. They were both supposed to say, "Christ is risen," as they broke the eggs and offer best wishes for the coming year. Mito often forgot that part.

"Red eggs attack!" cried Mito as he smashed the green egg held by an older boy.

Mito found Aura and held out his red egg, offering to let her hit it with her leaf-pattern one. As her hand started forward, Mito blew out her candle. Aura screamed, "Not fair," and, *smash!* Mito crushed her egg with his red one. "Red eggs attack!"

"Not fair!" Aura called after him, then turned to her mother to relight her candle.

The family started the happy walk home through the early hours of Easter morning. Streams of lit candles marched down the darkened streets. Experienced handlers knew to cup one hand around the flame to protect it from the swirling wind. Aura walked beside her mother, staring at the tiny flame she surrounded with the fingers of her free hand as if it were more precious than gold, more delicate than a spider's web.

Busses glowing with lit candles drove noisily down the cobbled street. Three boys riding donkeys ambled past protecting their candles. Several couples crept by on bicycles, afraid to ride any faster for fear of blowing out their lights.

Nearing the house Aura tripped over a loose paving stone and tumbled to the street. *Splat!* She crashed into mud. Her new white dress was splattered dripping brown. Her ankle had twisted and began to swell. Still Aura smiled. "My candle didn't go out, Daddy!"

Her father carried her the rest of the way home and up to her room. Inside she proudly pushed her candle into the holder on her ikon shelf and flopped happily into bed, washed by the candle's soft glow.

She had protected and carried the sacred flame all the way to her very own alter where it would burn bright in her heart for another year. All was well with the world. It was Easter!

Follow-up Questions to Explore

1. Why are there differences between the Easter celebrations of different Christian religions? Is that all right, or should everyone celebrate Easter exactly the same way?

Answer

The general concept, purpose, theme, and basic mode of celebrating Easter are the same for all Christian sects. It's the details of the pageantry that differ to meet the differing needs of different groups and different areas.

2. What do you do for Easter that has nothing to do with the religious aspects of the celebration? Where did these events come from?

Answer

The many nonreligious aspects of Easter commonly include new Easter bonnets, new clothes, Easter parades, colored Easter eggs, the Easter bunny or rabbit, and Easter baskets. Virtually all of these elements came straight from pre-Christian spring festivals in several European countries. Many think they have survived, and now dominate our image of Easter, simply because they are fun for children.

Suggested Activities

1. In part, Easter is a spring festival. Research spring festivals around the world. Make a list of the activities and symbols used in spring festivals. Design and hold your own spring festival.

2. Easter is primarily a religious celebration. The six most widely followed religions in the world, in chronological order of their emergence, are: Hinduism, Judaism, Confucianism, Buddhism, Christianity, and Islam. Pick three major celebrations of each religion. List the purpose and activities surrounding each celebration. Can you find common themes and ways of expressing religious wonder and joy? Are there similarities in the ways these different religions conduct their celebrations?

3. Research Easter baskets. Where did they start? From what can they be made? What things can go into an Easter basket? What is the origin of each item? Design an Easter basket to contain each of the items you researched that you might want. Can you use these items to tell the story of the renewal of life with each new spring?

Passover

A Jewish Remembrance and Freedom Celebration

At a Glance

A CENTRAL JEWISH HOLIDAY, considered by some to be their most important, Passover is really a celebration of freedom, and of the pain-filled road to reach it. Passover (the Hebrew name is *Pesach*) is a weeklong celebration of the Jewish people's escape out of bondage (slavery) in Egypt, across the Red Sea, and into freedom in what is now Israel.

The primary ritual of this celebration is the *Seder* (which means "order"). The Seder comes at the beginning of Passover week. It is a household or family ceremony over a ritualized dinner following a script contained in a book, the *Haggadah* (or "narration"). The Seder is a time to remember both the bitter oppression of bondage and the salvation and deliverance by God of the Jewish people into freedom.

As is true with the finest Chinese plays, every item, every action, every word in the Jewish Seder has symbolic and historic significance and meaning. It is through these symbols that the full meaning of the Seder is revealed.

Passover

"Mom, can I go to Joel's house for dinner?" Ten-year-old Steven Jensen stood inside the back door on the sunny afternoon of April 17, 1992, and yelled the question at his mother, working in her home office, just off the kitchen.

"Tonight?"

"Of course, tonight. Joel said it's a big dinner and he could bring a friend."

She rolled her chair across the office floor and poked her head out the door, "A 'big' dinner? Are you sure it's all right with Joel's mother?"

Steven heaved his shoulders and sighed. "Yeeeees, Mother. At school Joel said his mother said he could invite a friend for Seder. I said, 'You're eating cedar?' He said, 'No, Seder was the name of the whole ritual they did at dinner.' He said that sometimes it lasts for hours. I said, 'Wow. Dinner at our house only lasts fifteen minutes.'"

"Oh, thanks," said his mother.

"So I asked what they were having. Joel said it was the Seder. I almost didn't want to go 'cause I thought I tried Seder once and it tasted fishy, so I was going to say I was a vegetarian and couldn't come. But he said Seder was the ritual, what they *did,* and that there'd be lots of great food. So can I?"

His mother nodded. "You've been invited for a Passover Seder. Wonderful. I think it will be good for you to see. Yes, you may."

Joel Meyers sat like a worn-out lump on the kitchen floor when Steven arrived.

"I had to help clean the *whole* house yesterday! I'm still tired."

"Just for *dinner?*" Steven asked.

"No, dummy. For *Passover.*"

Steven grimaced. "Doesn't sound as much fun now that I know cleaning is part of it."

"Especially," Joel continued. "I had to get up every crumb of leavened bread. We can't have any leavened bread or food at all during Passover."

"What's wrong with Mr. Leven's bread?"

Joel punched Steven's shoulder. "Not a *him,* dummy. It's a kind of bread. Any bread that is soft and has air holes all through it is leavened. Anything made from grain is leavened when it's allowed to ferment or rise. In Hebrew it's called *hametz.*"

"*All* bread is like that," protested Steven.

"Not *matzah.*"

"What's matzah? Sounds like a Japanese movie monster. Matzah meets Godzilla."

Again Joel laughingly punched Steven's shoulder. "Matzah is a Hebrew word. Matzah is quickly baked, unleavened bread we eat during Passover."

"Why?"

"Because when the Jews fled Egypt they left in such a hurry they didn't have time to bake bread for the trip and threw unleavened loaves of dough into backpacks. Along the way the sun baked it into hard, flat loaves. We eat it to remember the story."

Joel led Steven into the dining room. "See? There are three pieces of matzah in that cloth sack. And remember, everything we say and do at the Seder is important. It tells about our history."

As other family members entered the dining room and were introduced to Steven, Steven studied the Seder table. Everyone had wine glasses. Every place had fancy china with no chips in it. The seat at the head of the table had big pillows. There were two tall candles, and a bag with the three matzah slices. In the middle of the table sat a platter with five skimpy food items on it.

Steven's heart sank. "Is *that* dinner—for all of us?"

Joel's mother laughed. "Aren't you familiar with the symbols on the Seder plate? These items help tell the Passover story. *Zeroa*, a roasted lamb bone to remind us that God passed over the houses of the Israelites in Egypt marked with lamb's blood. *Betzah*, a roasted egg, for the ancient temple sacrifices and as a symbol of spring. *Maror*, bitter horseradish, to remind us of how bitter slavery is. *Haroset,* the mixture of nuts, apples, spices, and wine that looks like brick mortar, to remind us of the work the Jews did as slaves. Finally, *karpas*, parsley, as a springtime symbol."

Greatly relieved, Steven slid into his chair next to Joel. A total of fifteen gathered at the long table. Joel's father handed Steven a round cap to wear. "We get to wear hats during dinner?"

Mr. Meyers answered, "It is a Jewish custom to cover our heads out of respect for God."

Steven nodded. "Cool. My parents make me take hats *off* at the table."

Everyone seemed happy, but still serious, as if they were very glad to be here, but felt the evening was important and that they had to get it right.

Joel's mother lit the candles. His father filled the wine glasses, including the small ones for the children.

"You get to drink wine? Cool!" whispered Steven.

"It's for the Seder," answered Joel. "Don't drink it."

Tall paperback books were passed out around the table.

"Is this the menu?" whispered Steven.

"No, dummy. It's the *Haggadah,* the script for the Seder."

Joel's father rose and gave a blessing, a prayer.

"It's a blessing for the wine," whispered Joel. "Lift up your glass like everyone else."

"Cool. Specialty prayers. We just say, 'God is great, God is good. Now we thank Him for this food,' and dig in."

Bowls were placed around the table. People poured water over their hands into these bowls.

"Did they forget to wash before dinner?"

"Shhhh!" hissed Joel. "No talking. This is part of the Seder."

"But your dad's talking."

"He's reading from the *Haggadah.* He's reading the script."

Next, a plate of parsley was passed around the table. Everyone took a sprig.

"No thanks. I'll skip the salad," said Steven, waving his hand.

"Not salad, dummy! Parsley symbolizes the fruits of the earth. You dip it in that salt water, which represents the tears of bondage, and eat it."

Steven shrugged. "How was I supposed to know? I can't understand a word your dad's saying."

"It's Hebrew, the language of the Jewish people. Some families say the Seder all in Hebrew, some all in English. We do some of both. It'll be mostly English later."

Joel's father rose and slid the middle matzah out of its cloth sack. Holding it he read more from the *Haggadah* and broke the crackerlike bread into two pieces.

He slid the smaller piece back in with the other two matzahs and wrapped the larger piece in a napkin and set on the edge of the table.

Joel giggled and jabbed Steven with an elbow. "That's the *afikomen*. It will be mysteriously hidden during Seder. After dinner we get to search for it. Finder gets presents!"

Every family member read carefully in their *Haggadah*, following every word of the Seder. Steven didn't understand much of the meaning, and found it more enjoyable to watch the people around the table.

Joel's father asked, "Would anyone like to ask any questions?"

Steven almost raised his hand. A glare from Joel made him realize this wasn't the time.

Joel's younger sister stood to read four questions from the *Haggadah*.

Steven whispered, "Why does she get to do it?"

"Because she's the youngest."

Joel's sister smoothed her dress and followed the words with her finger in the book. "On other nights we eat either hametz [leavened bread] or matzah. Why on this night do we eat only matzah? On other nights we eat all kinds of vegetables. Why on this night must we eat bitter herbs? Why on this night do we dip our vegetables [in salt water]? Why on this night do we eat reclining?"

She smiled at having not made a mistake. Everyone else told her what a good job she had done.

Mr. Meyers began to read a long story from the *Haggadah*. It was a story of slaves and pharaohs. God brought down ten plagues upon the Egyptians because they would not let the Jews go. On the night of the tenth plague, which was that the Angel of Death would swoop down and carry off the firstborn of each household, the Jewish families marked their doors with fresh lamb's blood so that the Angel of Death would pass them by.

In grief the next day, the pharaoh told Moses to take his people away. Moses told the Jews to flee for their lives before the pharaoh changed his mind. There was no time to bake bread for the journey. There was no time to gather possessions.

The Jews raced toward the Red Sea. But the Egyptian army pursued them. They would have been recaptured except that God parted the waters of the Red Sea and let the Jews escape.

"Cool story," whispered Steven.

As each of the ten plagues was listed, each person at the table dipped one little finger into their wine and dripped one drop onto the table.

"Don't spill!" hissed Steven.

"We're supposed to," whispered Joel.

"You get to spill on purpose? Cool! But why do you do it?"

Joel's older brother explained, "It is to show compassion for the suffering of the Egyptian people, our old enemies."

Now Joel's father turned to the platter of symbolic foods and read a passage that explained each. Steven felt very smart for being able to remember what each meant from Mrs. Meyers's earlier explanation.

Again bowls and water were brought out for hand washing.

"I did it already and my hands are still clean."

"Shhhh, dummy!" hissed Joel. "We do it again. It's part of the Seder."

Steven whispered back, "Are we ever going to eat?"

"Comin' right up," smiled Joel.

First they ate a bite of matzah, then the horseradish, then the bitter herb sandwich.

"Is that it?"

"Shhhh," smiled Joel.

At that moment, a grand dinner was served with heaping platters and steaming bowls of food Steven had never seen before. Every time Steven emptied his plate, platters were passed around again and it filled back up.

After everyone was stuffed, dessert arrived. After dessert, on a signal from Joel's father, the children sprang from the table.

"Come on," cried Joel. "We have to find the *afikomen*. It's been hidden somewhere in the house."

"I didn't see anyone leave to hide it."

"You never do," answered Joel. "But it's hidden."

In three minutes a cousin cried "I found it!"—holding high the napkin-wrapped matzah. Everyone clapped and all the children received small gifts.

Back at the table, another blessing was said over fresh glasses of wine. An extra glass, the biggest glass of all, was filled and set in the middle of the table. Joel's father said, "Joel, would you like to open the door for Elijah?"

"Who's Elijah?" whispered Steven as Joel pushed back his chair. "A friend who's late?"

"No. Elijah the prophet."

Steven shook his head. "Whoever he is, he's *way* too late for dinner."

Joel rolled his eyes and hurried to open the front door. A slight breeze blew through the open door, rustling the curtains. Joel's sister squealed, "I can feel him!"

As Joel returned to the table, a cousin pointed to the large wine glass in the middle of the table. "Someone drank from Elijah's glass!" All gasped. The wine was down a good half-inch.

"But … but no one touched that glass," stammered Steven.

"Elijah did. And he has offered us his blessings," replied Joel's father. Joel and his sister glowed with pleasure and excitement.

There was more laughter now, more merriment around the table. Everyone began to sing Passover songs. Joel's favorite was a beautiful one they sang before dinner called, "Dayenu."

Steven's favorite was one about some water that put out the fire that burned the dog that ate the cat that … It reminded Steven of the children's rhyme about the house that Jack built. Everyone sang it chorus after chorus and laughed. Joel said they called it "One Goat."

By this time it was late and Steven had to leave. He thanked Joel's parents for including him.

"Did you learn something of our people tonight?" asked Joel's father.

Steven thought for a moment before answering. "I didn't know Jews were ever slaves. With the pharaoh, and the ten plagues, and Moses, and escaping through the Red Sea, it's a great story! The only slaves I knew about were the black slaves in America."

"Many peoples have been enslaved. Each has an important story to remember and tell. The Passover Seder tells part of ours."

Back at home Steven's mother asked him how he enjoyed his first Seder.

"It was a great dinner, Mom, once we finally got to it. And they did lots of cool symbolic stuff. They get to wear hats at the table and even the kids get some wine. And it's a great story with lots of history." Steven paused and scratched his head. "But how does Joel get his homework done if dinner takes two hours every night?"

Follow-up Questions to Explore

1. The Passover food to be eaten, the words to be said, the actions to be taken are all symbolic. Are there symbolic acts and words you perform in your celebrations?

Answer

Here is a list of seven common American celebrations: St. Patrick's Day, Easter, Fourth of July, Halloween, Thanksgiving, Christmas, Kwanzaa. Can you find symbols and symbolic acts in each of these? Can you think of other celebrations that involve symbols?

2. The purpose of Passover is to remind the Jewish people of a time when they were enslaved in Egypt. Why do you think Jews want to remember the bad times of their history?

Answer

There are many reasons to remember all parts of personal, national, and cultural history. Some of then are: remembering past ills honors the ancestors who suffered through them; those past ills are the Jewish people's common history; from bad came salvation and arrival in the promised land; and actively remembering past ills helps to ensure those times are never repeated for new generations.

Suggested Activities

1. Find Israel, Egypt, and the Red Sea on a map. Trace the path of the Jewish people during and after their escape from slavery. Research this heroic escape. How did they escape from Egypt? Why did the Egyptian pharaoh agree to let them go? Where did they go after their escape? How did they survive?

2. Symbolic items and words are an important part of any ceremony. Pick a common American ceremony and research the symbols used in it. What do they represent? How are they brought into the ceremony? How are they used? What are they made of? Now create a new ceremony at school—the "End (or Beginning) of the Week" ceremony, or the "End of the Year" ceremony, for example. What symbols will you include in your new ceremony? How will you use them? As a class, agree on the whole ceremony and the parts each student will play in it.

MAY

May Day

A Western
Celebration of Spring

At a Glance

WE DON'T DO MUCH FOR MAY DAY in the United States anymore. We used to. There was a time when it was an important annual celebration, when towns and parishes looked forward to May Day through long, dreary winters, when they planned for it weeks and months in advance.

Before we dismiss May Day as an unimportant and minor celebration, we should remember three things. First, May Day is our only remaining celebration dedicated to the return of spring, of warm days, of flower-carpeted fields, and of the coming glories of summer.

Second, May Day is one of the oldest of all continuously celebrated human festivals. Early Romans held a spring festival in honor of Flora, goddess of flowers, with processions of floral garlands from April 28 through May 3 by our calendar. Before that, Greeks and Egyptians held spring celebrations around the same time. Even before that, Druids held a spring ritual called *Beltane* on this day to honor the return of the warm, life-giving sun to the northern parts of the earth. In medieval Europe long garlands of hawthorn branches (called "may") were woven on May Day as people talked of going "a-maying." Cultures across Asia, Europe, Africa, and North America have celebrated a spring festival around the first of May for over three centuries.

Third, May Day celebrates pure joy—the joy of living, the joy of frolicking in the warm sunshine, the joy of flowers and of life itself. Almost every other celebration centers on some other, more culturally, religiously, and/or historically based purpose. The heart of May Day, as it has been passed down to us, is rooted in a celebration of the pure joy of living.

May Day

"Slower and more gently, Erika. You'll gather more dew."

"But it's too dark to see," complained eleven-year-old Erika Dolk.

Her mother, Rakel, squatted with her in the misty grays of a predawn meadow. Rakel held Erika's hands in her own to guide her. "Sweep slowly and evenly across the grass this way."

Around them more than a hundred other women from Matfors also squatted under the first faint streaks of predawn light in meadows and fields, heavy with dew, to wash their faces in handfuls of the precious liquid. Dew washing marked the beginning of each year's May Day celebration. Some sang. Some talked and laughed. Some delicately washed in silence.

Behind them thick chimney smoke rolled into the predawn sky from houses all over the picturesque river town and hung like a thin cloud, caught in the evergreen treetops. High above, a grand spray of stars blazed like diamonds in the clear northern sky.

Four A.M. did not usually see many lights on in Matfors, Sweden, a small river town nestled along the banks of the Ljungan River, sixty-two and one-half degrees north of the equator, only four degrees below the Arctic Circle. But every year on the morning of May 1, lights blazed at 4:00 A.M. from many, if not most, of the steep-roofed wooden houses climbing up the hills away from the icy river. May 1, 1978, was no exception.

"This is the only part of May Day that isn't fun," grumbled Erika.

Her mother smiled as she rubbed soft dew water across her cheeks and eyes. "Washing with morning dew is good for your complexion and it's women's special way to welcome spring."

"But why can't we do it after lunch when it's nice out?"

Her mother laughed and shook her head. "The dew would not be fresh and pure then. No more grousing, Erika. It's May Day!"

But Erika Dolk had never gotten up easily and without complaint—especially when it was still dark and cold. Even on May Day, rising had been a struggle for Erika.

"Get up, Erika! We'll be late," Mrs. Dolk had hollered, shoving her feet into fur-lined boots.

Erika's groggy voice called back from her room, "It's too early to get up."

"Nonsense," said Mrs. Dolk, clicking on the lights in her daughter's room. "It's May Day."

"It's too cold to be May Day," protested Erika tucking her face and straight, shoulder-length blond hair deep under the covers.

"The day will warm with the sun. Now up and out!" snapped her mother. Then she added, "You'll never be chosen May Queen if you waste the morning in bed."

Erika's blue eyes had popped out of the covers. The May Queen! She had dreamed of being chosen May Queen since she was a mere child of eight watching with envy as Katrina Olsson wore the garland crown of daisies, as she was carried through the streets to lead the parade, and as she was admired by everyone in Matfors. Katrina had been eleven when she was chosen May Queen.

With a nervous lump churning in her stomach, Erika had dragged herself out of bed and into her clothes for the journey outside to wash with dew. In eight hours, at noon, the May Queen would be chosen!

Cheeks aglow, calling farewells to other girls and women, Erika and her mother whisked back inside as the sun first peaked over the slate gray waters of the Bay of Bothnia. Soothing warmth radiated from the living room wood-burning stove as they stomped their feet and brushed their coat sleeves to shed the thick layer of dew that clung to their clothes. Rakel rubbed her reddened cheeks. "What a lovely way to start a day of merriment."

"What a *cold* way to start," corrected Erika.

Erika's red-bearded father, Arne Dolk, puffed contentedly on a long-stemmed pipe, still wearing bathrobe and slippers. An eighteen-year-old boy, Misha Chapaen, eagerly paced the room before him. Clean-shaven Misha was visiting from Moscow, Russia, on an exchange program. Over the past few days he had been as excited about the upcoming May Day as Erika. "Now that the women are back, will the men gather for a worker's parade?"

Arne puffed and shook his head.

"We'll gather for speeches, then?"

"No," answered Arne. "The day's pretty full with the children's parade and Maypole dancing and picking a May Day Queen."

"*Children?*" Misha scowled in confusion. "In Russia, May Day is for workers."

"Here we celebrate the return of warm spring. After eight months of cold, I think that's worth celebrating."

After breakfast Erika bounded upstairs to change.

"Your good white frock," called her mother. "I ironed it yesterday."

Erika smoothed her frock in front of the mirror, wondering if this dress would sit on the throne of the May Queen in a few hours. Her mother wove bright daisies and violets into her hair. "Now you *look* like a May Queen."

By 10:30, a happy crowd streamed into the open square in front of Christ's Lutheran Church. Like iron filings racing toward a magnet, they seemed drawn by the frolicking parade that circled the square and nearby streets.

"The chimney sweeps and milkmaids have started," cried Erika, dragging her parents in a gallop toward the growing crowd. Misha followed, searching for signs of worker solidarity and placards expressing pride in working men and women. All he saw were streaming garlands of green and wreathes of flowers festooned across roof lines, windows, and doorways.

Many of the girls wore white dresses and frocks similar to Erika's. Most boys wore white shirts and light-colored pants. Several dozen young men, dressed as chimney sweeps and then covered with greenery so that even their faces could barely be seen, pranced like dancing clowns across the square. A group of young women, dressed as old-fashioned milkmaids, danced with them, playing tricks on the gathering audience, gathering laughter and applause in return. The dancers trailed flowing garlands of sweetbrier stuffed with flowers—cowslips, primroses, violets, oxlips, and flowering currant.

"Why is everyone so happy?" asked Misha.

"It's the feeling, Misha, floating thick as pudding in the air," laughed Arne, trying to find the right words. "It's the feeling that warmth and joy have once again conquered cold and gloom. Don't you *feel* like singing and dancing?"

Arne leapt into the parade behind the chimney sweeps, dancing with his pipe across the square. He scooped up the end of a long garland and flung it to his wife and daughter. The crowd cheered. Rakel and Erika laughed as they caught the garland and joined the throng of dancers. Misha frowned but tapped his foot with the music of drums and brass instruments now playing with the parade as it circled toward the Maypole.

The Matfors Maypole, a towering birch trunk over eighty feet tall, rose from the center of the square. Garlands of greenery entwined around it. Over fifty long ribbons trailed from the top, billowing in the breeze like stockings hung on a clothesline.

Children rushed forward to grab the ribbons, alternating girl, boy, around the pole. The band played and the Maypole dance began as the crowd cheered and danced on their own. Girls marched and skipped one way around the pole, boys the other, weaving in and out, creating a crisscross pattern with their bright ribbons around the pole.

The ribbons were tied at the bottom of the pole to keep the pattern from unraveling, and the mayor announced it was time to pick a May Queen. Only children got to vote. It was soon clear from the cheers and shouted names that two were the favorites this year: Hanna Gustoffson, daughter of the parish minister, and Erika.

Both girls were ushered forward to stand on the raised steps of Christ's Lutheran Church and face the sea of faces below. Hand-in-hand, Rakel and Arne held their breath.

A voice vote was taken. The children cheered louder for Erika. Erika won.

Rakel and Arne let out a deep sigh and raised their joined hands in a cheer of triumph.

Erika's knees wobbled and her stomach churned as the crowd applauded and the mayor placed the May Queen's daisy crown on her head. These were not common meadow daisies. These were special red and violet daisies grown just for the queen's crown. Erika glowed as if a beacon of golden light had been placed on her head. As if floating on the soft clouds of a wonderful dream, Erika stepped to the queen's thrown. She had won!

The puffy clouds of morning pushed aside. Sunbeams poured into the square as if a heavenly spotlight had been turned on to illuminate the new queen.

Queen Erika and her throne were lifted on thick broomsticks and carried out into the square. The May Day parade was off again! Bands played. People cheered. Fresh garlands were strung out, several over twenty feet long, and carried through the crowd.

It felt as if not a care or worry could be found on the streets of Matfors. The music and dancing swept them away for another day.

Many in the romping crowd carried baskets of flowers. Occasionally someone would hang their basket on a doorknob as they passed.

"Are the baskets left at homes of honored workers?" asked Misha.

"Those are May baskets," laughed Rakel. "They are left on the door of someone you secretly admire."

The parade wound into a grassy park. Queen Erika and her throne were placed in the middle of a great ring of watchers. Two thick-armed college students stepped forward and bowed. All eyes now turned to Queen Erika. Her hands trembled as she waved her queen's banner and proclaimed, "Let the battle begin!"

The two giants lunged at each other in a well-rehearsed mock wrestling match.

"Does one represent labor and the other management?" asked Misha.

"No, no. Nothing so serious," laughed Arne. "The one in gray is winter. The one in green is summer. Summer always wins the May Day battle. Of course, there was a time when the fight wasn't rehearsed and people believed this battle determined whether spring and summer would really arrive."

The battle ended with the enthusiastically expected triumph of summer. Winter was defeated again. Dancing erupted across the new grass of the park. A lavender parachute was unfurled and held on all sides by adults. One by one children piled into the middle to be thrown, squealing with delight, into the air. Flower petals were tossed in with the children to spray like confetti across the crowd.

Arne pushed Misha onto the parachute. He tumbled into the middle and was tossed into the air, arms and legs flailing to regain his balance. "Huzah! Huzah!" Over and over he was flung into the sky as Queen Erika and the crowd cheered.

As evening crept across the sky, great bonfires were lit. Families quieted and drew close to watch the glowing embers and remember the day. "Folks used to believe these fires drove evil spirits away. Now they're just a fun way to end May Day."

Misha nodded. "In Russia, May Day feels serious, important. But your May Day is more fun. I guess sometimes fun is important, too."

"Fun? *Fun!?*" gasped Erika. "May Day is more than just 'fun'! This May Day was perfect!"

Follow-up Questions to Explore

1. Why a May*pole* (instead of a May basket, or bush, or chair)?

Answer

Originally whole trees were brought into town squares instead of just the bare trunk—the Maypole. These trees were erected in front of early churches because it was believed that the trees, usually birches, could ward off evil spirits on May Day. (A similar belief led to the origins of our Christmas trees.) Over time, the May tree was reduced to just its trunk, or pole, and that alone was dragged into the village square.

2. What happens on May Day in Russia? Why is that different than what happens here?

Answer

After the Communist takeover in Russia in the early 1900s, May Day was converted to a day honoring not spring, but labor and military power. May Day was made a major state holiday. The day has been devoted to long military parades of polished troops and shiny rows of tanks and rocket launchers, and to political speeches honoring workers and promoting the Communist system. Since the collapse of communism in the former Soviet Union, May Day has become less important. There are still parades and speeches, but they are less formal, with corners of the spring festival roots of May Day creeping back in.

Suggested Activities

1. Plan a May Day celebration that honors community and school members. Create paper baskets and fill them with paper flowers you make. Deliver them anonymously to the people you choose to honor (school janitors, secretaries, librarians, etc.).

2. Build your own Maypole. Usually, long, wide ribbons are attached to the top of the pole. The class members stand in a wide circle around the pole, each holding the loose end of one ribbon. Alternate girl, boy, around the circle. Girls walk (or skip) clockwise, boys go counterclockwise, weaving in and out of each other with their ribbons to weave the ribbons onto the Maypole. Calculate how long each of your ribbons will have to be to circle the Maypole ten times as they spiral down, and just reach the ground at the end of the tenth revolution.

Cinco de Mayo

A Mexican
Historic Celebration

At a Glance

CINCO DE MAYO! THE FIFTH OF MAY. Some think Cinco de Mayo is a celebration of Mexican independence. Some think it celebrates Mexico's winning of a past war for independence—much as we look to Cornwallis's surrender at Yorktown as the moment of victory in our war of independence (although it was not).

But Cinco de Mayo celebrates neither of these events in Mexican history. It *does* celebrate a victory in battle, and that battle *was* fought during the war for Mexican independence. But the battle fought on May 5, 1862, in the small town of Puebla, Mexico, where a poorly trained and supplied band of two thousand Mexican militia commanded by General Ignacio Zaragoza defeated an invading army of six thousand French regulars, was fought five years before the successful end to the war.

The victory at Puebla marked, instead, the *first* victory by the newly formed Mexican army. It represented hope, a signal to the Mexican people that they had a chance to triumph, a symbol that they might finally throw out the European invaders who had first stormed into and conquered their country over three hundred years before.

As early as 1863 the fifth of May was called *la gloriosa fecha* (the glorious date), and celebrated throughout Mexico. Cinco de Mayo is now widely observed throughout Mexico and the United States, both as a memory of sweet victory and as a celebration of Mexican, or Chicano, culture.

In the United States, Cinco de Mayo is celebrated with mariachi music, feasting on Mexican dishes, parades, the flying of Mexican flags, and speeches honoring *La Raza* (the Mexican race) and Chicano culture. However, in many parts of Mexico, the date is celebrated through reenactment of the original battle. The town of Cerro Peñon, near the Mexico City airport, boasts one of the grandest, most elaborate such reenactments.

Cinco de Mayo

At 10:50 A.M. on May 5, 1994, Jose Huerta struggled toward the front door of his comfortable apartment. "Hurry! I'm going to be late!" His round, bronze face and black eyes that usually sparkled like friendly laughter were etched with worry and frustration. His thinning salt-and-pepper hair was matted down with sweat on this hot, muggy day.

His wife, Carla, answered around three safety pins clamped between her teeth. "Don't move. The seam in your pants will rip."

"This uniform must have shrunk since last year," huffed Jose.

"The uniform is fine. But you gained ten pounds sitting at your desk and nibbling all day," laughed Carla.

Jose Huerta shrugged. "I'm a banker. I'm supposed to sit at my desk."

"Today you're supposed to be the trim, dashing General Zaragoza. Today you are supposed to win a great battle for Mexico. So suck in your stomach." Carla snapped in the last two safety pins to reinforce a bulging seam. "There. Now go and lead your army in the parade."

As Jose reached the door she added, "Don't bend over or that seam will never last!"

Jose adjusted the wide-brimmed hat of the elegant *charro* suit he dusted off once a year to play General Zaragoza in the Cerro Peñon Cinco de Mayo pageant, and adjusted the elaborate gold braid and sparkling gold shoulder boards. He checked to make sure his rows of shiny medals were straight. He hooked his sword into a white, cross-shoulder sash, stomped his polished black boots to adjust the way they sat on his feet, and hurried toward the plaza. Overhead a steady line of airline jets screeched through the hazy sky like angry dragons as, landing gear down, they turned onto their final approach to the Mexico City airport.

The parade director nervously paced in front of a crowd of volunteer soldiers, each struggling to adjust the uniforms they wore once a year for the battle reenactment. "Where is General Zaragoza?" he demanded through his megaphone.

"Here! I'm here!" called Jose, rushing into his place at the front of the parade, sweat dribbling down his cheeks and off his chin.

"Looks like you gained a few pounds," laughed Manuel Ortega, a friend and grocer who was playing Marshal Lorencz, the French general.

"I did not!" insisted Jose. "This uniform shrank."

The crowd of men playing the part of 1862 soldiers all laughed. Jose blushed. The parade director hissed, "Those pants better not split during your sword fight this evening!"

The director checked his watch and blew a whistle blast. "Move the band up here. It's time!" Several women dashed into the ranks of soldiers to straighten their husbands' uniforms, and then scampered back to their spots along the sidewalk.

A great brass band leads the Cinco de Mayo parade each year as the procession starts down Catalina Street toward the plaza. A huge crowd lined both sides of the street cheering, laughing. The day holds the feel of a raucous party where jokes and pranks are as important as the battle reenactment.

Jose Huerta, as General Zaragoza, followed the band riding on a great palomino horse. Jose unfurled a banner of green, white, and red vertical stripes with the words "Viva Mexico." The crowd cheered. Behind him Marshal Lorencz waved a small banner that read "Viva France." The crowd laughed and booed.

Carla Huerta wormed her way to the front row of viewers waiting for the parade to reach the Cerro Peñon plaza before it turned down the wide main street of town to the park. Next to her stood a young man in jeans and cotton T-shirt. "Why are the marchers in old, nineteenth-century uniforms?" he asked.

Carla answered, "They are going to reenact the Battle of Puebla. The large rocks behind the plaza are our pretend fort for the Mexican army to defend. That fight is what Cinco de Mayo is all about."

"No solidarity marches? No speeches?" asked the young man.

Carla laughed. "This isn't a political holiday. It's a celebration."

"I come from San Francisco," said the young man. "I'm Arturo Chavez. And in California Cinco de Mayo is a chance to stand against the oppression of the Chicano people and to honor *La Raza,* our heritage, our birthright."

"Here we honor our victory and the hope and success it represents."

The crowd at the plaza cheered and waved flags as the parade marched past. Carla Huerta clapped and cheered as her husband rode by, looking very grand and very much like a great general.

Soldiers representing the French army were dressed in the red trousers, blue sack coats, and white leggings of the Zouaves expeditionary soldiers who fought for France in the mid-1800s. Many carried old muskets. Some carried loaves of French bread or jugs of red wine instead. The crowd roared and cheered.

Many of those representing the Mexican army wore peasant clothes instead of uniforms. "Did they run out of uniforms?" asked Arturo.

"General Zaragoza's army was a citizen army," said Carla. "Many came straight from the fields to fight and were not trained soldiers."

Arturo laughed. "Look! Women are marching as soldiers. Did you run out of men, too?"

"Those women represent the *soldaderas,* the women soldiers," Carla corrected. "Many cooked and cared for the men. They carry food and babies. But see the ones with rifles? Over fifty women actually fought in the Battle of Puebla."

The crowd fell in line behind the soldiers and final mariachi bands for the three-block walk to the Cerro Peñon park. There a great fiesta was prepared. Families ate and laughed under the shade of broad trees. Bands strolled through the crowd playing.

Arturo scowled. "There should be speeches calling for an end of gringo intervention in Chicano life. There should be cries of 'La Raza!'"

"Here we celebrate our victories," repeated Carla.

"In California we honor our struggles."

"La Raza?" asked Jose.

"La Raza," repeated Arturo. "The race. The mestizo nation. The bronze culture. The rightful owners of the American Southwest."

Roving bands of French and Mexican soldiers tried to steal food and drink from families dressed in uniforms of the other side. Some tried to sneak off with "enemy" rifles and ammunition. Everyone laughed at their antics and cheered at their successes.

The director called over his megaphone for both armies to report to starting places for the mock battle. Soldiers gulped final swigs of beer and punch.

The Mexican soldiers, led by Jose Huerta, climbed into the giant rocks behind the plaza. The French soldiers lined up across the plaza as the crowd booed.

At 3:30 P.M. the director blew his whistle and the first assault began. The crowd pressed close to watch as the French soldiers, rifles and French bread loaves gleaming through the smoggy haze, started up the slope toward the "fort." Children were lifted onto their parents' shoulders to be able to see. Many climbed onto benches and car tops for a better view.

By 4:15, right on schedule, the French had been pushed back to re-form near the fountain on the south side of the plaza. Refreshments were passed around. Those who were designated as casualties during this first attack got to happily join their families in the audience for the rest of the pageant. Bands played during this break in the action. Wives rushed into the ranks to repair tears and snags in the uniforms.

On signal from the director, grocer Manuel Ortega, acting as French marshal Lorencz, called for his troops to rally and assault the fort again. By 5:00 the French were pushed back a second time. Many of the weary volunteer soldiers asked to be declared casualties so they could sit out the final assault.

At 5:45 the final charge began as bands played, flags waved, the Mexican defenders hooted and jeered, and late-afternoon sweat rolled down the faces of the French attackers. By 6:30 the French fell back for the final time.

Great cheers erupted from the crowd as the Mexican army rushed from the fort and streamed toward the plaza on the attack. Now came the grand finale of the reenactment, a sword fight across the center of the plaza between General Zaragoza and Marshal Lorencz.

Sword drawn and gleaming, Jose Huerta sprang off his horse to challenge the French general. Manuel Ortega, already puffing from his repeated charges uphill to the fort, drew his sword for the face-to-face combat.

The crowd and bands hushed to watch the two leaders duel through well-rehearsed choreography across the square and up the steps of the plaza monument. Near the end Jose lunged, forcing Manuel down off the steps. *Rip!* The seam at the back of his trousers gave way. Jose blushed. Carla groaned. The crowd laughed. The director threw up his hands.

Manuel Ortega took advantage of this diversion to rush forward and score a mock stab with his sword. The crowd booed. Jose recovered and, holding the back of his pants together with one hand, won the fight right on schedule at 7:30, as he did every year.

The crowd applauded. The soldiers cheered.

As sunset darkened the eastern sky, a giant fireworks display erupted over Cerro Peñon, the final tribute to the bravery and courage of the fledgling Mexican army of a century ago. Hand-in-hand, families gathered in the plaza to watch and to "Ooooh!" and "Ahhhh!" with each multicolored burst.

Arms haughtily folded, Arturo turned to Jose and Carla. "This was a fun celebration. But in America we have to remember our culture and our fight for recognition."

"Here we live our culture," answered Carla. "We have to celebrate our past glories and victories."

Follow-up Questions to Explore

1. Do you think it's all right for one celebration to have two very separate and different purposes or themes? Is this true for any of your celebrations?

Answer

Compare your answers to those of other classmates. The United States' Thanksgiving is a combination celebration both honoring the harvest and giving thanks for past victories and salvation.

2. Do you celebrate anything that is celebrated differently in different parts of the country or world, or by different groups of people? What and why?

Answer

Several common U.S. celebrations are good examples. Christmas is certainly one celebration that has evolved differently in the United States than in Europe. Santa Claus and the dominant emphasis on gift giving exists only in America. In much of Europe, Saint Nicholas and presents arrive on December 6. Christmas is then primarily a religious celebration. Saint Patrick's Day is celebrated very differently in America than in Ireland. Can you think of others?

Suggested Activities

1. Cinco de Mayo celebrates a battle victory. Research other specific battles celebrated around the world. List each battle celebration and the victorious side on sticky notes and place them on a world map. Are there patterns to the list you have created, or are battle victories celebrated everywhere?

2. Hold a Mexican feast in your classroom. Research traditional feast dishes from different regions of Mexico. Research traditional activities, games, and dances for feasts. Plan an "all-Mexico" celebration, incorporating all of the unique regional activities and dishes you have discovered.

Girl's and Boy's Days

A Japanese
Cultural Celebration of Youth

At a Glance

MANY COUNTRIES AND CULTURES AROUND THE WORLD have set aside days to honor specific family members—Mother's Day, Father's Day, Grandparents' Day. Some countries celebrate a children's day to honor their youth and the qualities to be developed during childhood. Only one major country has separate ceremonial days to honor girls and boys. That country is Japan.

For fifteen centuries, March 3 has been called *Hinamatsuri*, or the Doll Festival, in Japan. It is a day to honor girls and the traditional role and virtues of girls. May 5 is called *Tangomatsuri*, the Boy's Festival (sometimes called the Festival of Flags), and honors the traditional skills and disciplines to be learned by boys.

As the societal roles and duties of males and females have merged in the second half of the twentieth century, so, too, are the separate Girl's and Boy's Days merging. Japan has created a national holiday on May 5 designated as Children's Day. But in many Japanese and Japanese-American homes the older, traditional ceremonies are still honored. Such is the case in the home of Kimoko and Mikato Sunita.

Girl's and Boy's Days

March 3 dawned wet and gray. Ten-year-old Kimoko Sunita was bitterly disappointed watching raindrops splatter against her window as she lay in bed. Why couldn't it be bright and clear? Peach and plum tree blossoms started budding over a week ago. Many of the branches were covered in glorious pink and white yesterday afternoon. The nightingale had been singing for three weeks to awake the spring.

But Akita, on the northern coast of the Japanese island of Honshu, is controlled by the cold waters of the Sea of Japan. The warmth of spring always comes late to Akita.

Kimoko's mother stepped into her room wearing a brightly patterned red ceremonial kimono and classical *obi* belt. "Get up, Kimoko. I've gotten out the boxes, but we have much work to do before anyone can view your doll display."

Still Kimoko pouted, "Mother, why does it have to rain on Doll Festival Day?"

Her mother said, "The dolls will stay warm and dry. They won't mind the rain. The tea and cakes will be scrumptious. They won't mind the rain. And with your new empress and musician dolls your display will be the prettiest on the street."

"In the whole city!" insisted Kimoko, her round face smiling at the mention of her two new dolls.

"But first we must get you dressed."

Her mother helped Kimoko into her red-and-yellow ceremonial kimono, helped with the white face powder and red lipstick, and brought out a great pink bow to place in the side of Kimoko's straight black hair. "Oh, it's lovely, Mother!"

Mrs. Sunita smiled. "Now you look even lovelier than your dolls."

Downstairs the furniture had been moved away from one wall of the living room. With cinder blocks and boards, five tiered display shelves had been assembled and covered in bright red silk cloth. Over twenty boxes were stacked on the floor.

"I want to start with my new empress doll, Mother." Kimoko lifted an eight-inch-high doll of the classical Japanese empress of the old feudal period from its box. Perfect in every detail, from ceremonial brocade gown to headdress, to fingernails, to painted porcelain face, the empress was placed on the right side of the top shelf.

Beside the empress went the majestic doll of the emperor.

"That doll was your great-great-great-grandmother's. It has been in our family for over two hundred years."

Kimoko placed a golden screen behind these two dolls and ornate lamps beside them. On the second shelf went dolls of three ladies-in-waiting to serve the royal couple. Each time a box was opened and a new doll emerged, Kimoko "Oooo-ed" and "Ahhh-ed" over the perfect figurines she had not seen since last year's Doll Festival.

"They are all so beautiful, mother!"

On the third shelf, five musicians were arranged to play for the emperor and empress.

"You're opening the boxes too slowly. I want to see them all right now!" cried Kimoko.

"I must dust each doll and make sure their clothes did not wrinkle in the boxes."

On the fourth shelf stood two ministers and three courtiers. Beside these Kimoko placed miniatures of lacquered cherry and orange trees.

On the bottom shelf Kimoko placed household items that the royal couple might need: a tiny dressing table and chest of drawers, mirrors, makeup, miniature plates and teacups, a sewing box, a bookcase filled with the tiniest books, even a carriage for the royal couple to ride in.

"Perfect!" exclaimed Kimoko, admiring her placements.

"Your doll display grows lovelier each year," agreed her mother.

An almost exact replica of this doll display was created that morning in over a million other homes. For this was Hinamatsuri, the day of the Doll Festival, and these doll displays of the Japanese feudal court were the central focus.

Mikato, Kimoko's eleven-year-old brother, drifted downstairs and haughtily strolled past his sister's display. With a loud "Hurmph!" he turned his back, spread his legs, and folded his arms across a long, imaginary samurai sword. "Dolls are silly and pointless."

But inside he wished he could look closely at the detail of those dolls. How could anyone make them so perfect?

That afternoon the visits began. First Kimoko and her mother visited three of her friends to "Oooo" and "Ahhh" over their displays and to share tea and colored cakes. Mikato was left alone to swagger and feign indifference to his sister's wondrous display.

Soon Kimoko returned and others came to visit her. As each girl and mother arrived they praised Kimoko's doll display, claiming it was the best in all Akita. Then Kimoko's mother brought out bowls of tea and tricolored (white, green, and pink), diamond-shaped rice cakes.

Kimoko served as the other girls settled to their knees on floor cushions in front of the display. First Kimoko offered tiny cups of tea to the emperor and empress. Then she placed tiny rice cake fragments on doll plates for them. Only after could she serve her friends. There was much giggling, praising, and sipping. Kimoko glowed at how perfectly her day had gone.

"How silly," scoffed Mikato. "They never wrestled, or ran, or played." But inside he wondered if the cakes tasted as good as they looked.

:ᗝ̣ ᗝ̇ ᗞ̣:

May 5 dawned clear and warm. A strong wind rolled across Akita from the southeast, sweet with the rich smell of growing barley and soft green grass.

Mikato lay on his futon under an open window savoring the glorious fragrance and day. "This is *my* day!"

Mikato was already up and dressed in a bright kimono when his father called for him to come downstairs.

"The sun is up, Mikato. It is time to announce to the world that I have two brave sons."

Swelling with pride, Mikato said, "I will fetch the kites, Father."

Deep in a closet Mikato opened a storage box and lifted out two cloth fish-shaped kites (looking much like brightly painted airport windsocks) that had been carefully folded and stored since last year's Tangomatsuri. One was small and bright red and yellow. That one was for Mikato's baby brother. The other was a black-and-red beauty over eighteen feet long. That monster was Mikato's kite.

In the garden of their trim house, which butted against the houses of neighbors on both sides, Mr. Sunita had erected a tall bamboo pole that rose like the mast of a sailing ship high above the red tile roofs to poke at the deep blue sky. Pulley ropes climbed one side of the pole.

Thick string, which had been sewn into the open mouth of each carp-shaped fish kite, gathered at a metal hook. Mikato tied this hook into the pulley rope. His long kite went above because he was older. His brother's went below.

Now Mikato and his father pulled on the rope to haul the carp kites high into the morning sky. The open mouths of each kite caught the wind, puffing out their long bodies. Mikato's heart soared at the sight of his kite fluttering in the wind as if the mighty fish were swimming hard upstream above the rooftops.

Almost every house in Akita also flew carp kites to honor the sons of the house. The skyline resembled an endless school of carp, their open mouths turned into the wind.

From her room Kimoko scoffed, "Flying fish in the air is silly. Besides, you can't play with them, or even look closely at them when they are way up that pole." But inside she wondered how exciting it would feel to hook her own kite onto the rope and pull it up to fly above the house.

In an alcove of the living room, Mr. Sunita set up a samurai display for his sons. Three fierce warrior dolls of ancient heroes were surrounded by swords, bows and arrows, miniature spears, and two ancient helmets.

"One of these was worn by my great-grandfather during the feudal wars. The other belonged to his grandfather."

Mikato's hand reverently reached out to touch the three-hundred-year-old leather as his father continued. "The displays prepared for you this day symbolize the qualities of manhood. The carp must be powerful to fight its way upstream and overcome difficulty. The armor represents bravery and strength."

Outside they heard a happy, yelling commotion. Mr. Sunita laughed, "Run outside and join your friends in mock battles, Mikato. Today, in your heart and mind you are a samurai."

As Mikato whooped and bolted out the door, Kimoko sneered, "My display was much prettier." But inside she wondered what the sword of a samurai would feel like in her hand.

Outside gangs of boys romped up and down the streets and parks of Akita all day imitating the feats and battles of samurai warriors of olden feudal days, challenging each other to contests of speed, agility, and strength. From the window, Kimoko wondered how many of those boys she could challenge and beat.

Covered in sweat and dirt, Mikato burst through the door just in time to devour ceremonial sweet rice cakes wrapped in oak leaves, and round dumplings made of sticky rice wrapped in bamboo leaves.

"I'd rather have *colored* rice cakes and tea," said Kimoko, turning up her nose, but still wondering if her brother's treats tasted as sweet as they smelled.

As the children drifted off to sleep that night, Kimoko and Mikato each whispered the same thought, "My day is better, but I wish I could do both."

Follow-up Questions to Explore

1. Do you think separate celebrations to honor girls and boys is a good idea, or do you think it would be wiser to have one celebration honoring all children?

2. Do you think the idea of a country promoting separate qualities for girls and boys is appropriate for today's world? What do you think are the plusses and minuses of such a system?

Answer

Compare your answers to those of your classmates.

Suggested Activities

1. As a class, create a celebration to honor all children, regardless of sex, age, or privilege. What themes would you use as the focus of your celebration? What qualities and attributes of youth would you want to honor and promote? What name would you give to this celebration? What activities and ceremonies would you include? Why? What will make this celebration special and meaningful for all children?

JUNE

King Kamehameha Day

A Hawaiian Celebration
of Their First and Greatest King

At a Glance

KAMEHAMEHA UNIFIED THE SEVEN HAWAIIAN ISLANDS into a single kingdom in 1795, at about the same time the thirteen American states were forming a new country along the Atlantic coast of North America. The Hawaiian unification came at the end of a decade of bloody civil war between chiefs ruling either separate islands or parts of islands.

As the victor of this civil war, Kamehameha became the first king of Hawaii. He was followed by six other kings (four his direct descendants) and one queen. The kingdom survived for less than one hundred years before the monarchy was overthrown and Hawaii became a territory of the United States.

Only one hero emerged from the time of the Hawaiian kingdom: Kamehameha. He was called the Napoleon of the Pacific, the George Washington of Hawaii. As a bigger-than-life hero, he embodied the spirit and greatness of the Hawaiian race. His every deed became legend. He is called Hawaii's greatest warrior and statesman.

Beginning in 1871, June 11 was designated King Kamehameha Day. Now the celebration is held on the weekend closest to June 11. Kamehameha is the only one of the eight Hawaiian monarchs to be honored with a day of remembrance and celebration.

King Kamehameha Day

The parking spaces and lots around the Honolulu Civic Center had long been filled. The grassy area of the center was jammed all the way back to the Judiciary Building on one side and out to the street in front of the Iolani Palace on the other. Faces lined every window of the governmental office buildings on both sides of the Civic Center. It was 4 P.M. Friday, June 7, 1996, a time when you'd think the Civic Center would be emptying as office workers rushed home to start their weekend.

But not on the opening day of the King Kamehameha celebration.

"What time is it now?" asked twelve-year-old Aleta Jackson.

Her mother, Shirley Jackson, glanced at her watch. "Five minutes after four."

"Can we move, Mom? The sun's in my eyes and I'm hot." Aleta was a plump black girl with a round face and her hair braided in neat cornrows. Her mother, Shirley, was lean and muscular, with a wide, bright smile that seemed to stretch from ear to ear, and a great fuzz-ball of hair she still wore in an Afro, made popular in the seventies and eighties.

"Move?" scoffed Shirley. "Look around this place. You see any open space to move to? We're lucky to have gotten a place to sit at all."

"But it's too hot," complained Aleta.

Although the temperature hovered in the mid-eighties, the afternoon trade winds hadn't kicked up today. The air felt oppressively close and muggy. The only clouds, a few soft puffs of cotton, gathered in the east, out past Diamond Head, the picturesque extinct volcano at the east end of Waikiki. There was no hope of relief from the unrelenting sun until it dropped toward the western ocean long after the opening ceremonies were over.

"What time is it now?"

"Aleta!" snapped her mother.

"Well, I'm bored."

Shirley said, "We didn't fly all the way out here from Chicago just to whine, or to play on the beach. We came to learn about Hawaiian culture by attending this festival. The Hawaiians are people of color, you know. And they had their own kingdom, right here on these islands."

Aleta shifted and stretched indifferently. "Did you bring a deck of cards?" When her mother glared at her, Aleta said, "Well I don't see any Hawaiian culture here. All I see is a jammed-in crowd, a hot sun, and a big brown statue."

"Bronze," corrected Shirley. "And it *is* big. But then Kamehameha was big— over seven feet tall."

"Did he play basketball?"

"They didn't have basketball two hundred yeas ago."

With nothing else to do, Aleta studied the statue. "He looks strong, powerful." Her mother nodded. "But his face looks sad. Why isn't he smiling if he was the king?"

Shirley said, "He was called 'the lonely one.' He saw most of his friends and many of his family killed by war or white-man diseases." She shrugged. "Being king is a hard job. Maybe that's why he's sad."

Aleta laughed. "Maybe he's sad 'cause he had to work every day instead of play on the beach."

The Royal Hawaiian Band began to play. With a loud squeal the microphone clicked on as the band finished its first piece. Two brief speeches were made from the grass mound next to the Kamehameha statue, part of one in the Hawaiian language.

"I love the sound of the Hawaiian language," whispered Shirley. "It flows like waves gently rolling up the beach. It only uses thirteen letters, and has no past or future tense."

Aleta said, "Maybe I'll pick Hawaiian when I have to study a foreign language next year."

Several women carried long *leis* to the statue.

"What's a lei?" asked Aleta.

"A flowered necklace. Just imagine how many flowers are strung into each of those big leis! I bet some of them weigh fifteen pounds."

Lei after lei, many thirteen feet long, were draped over the bronze statue's head, flowing down its front, until the statue was buried beneath the bright floral leis. Only Kamehameha's sad eyes and the top of his helmet rose about the sea of flowers. The cameras of banks of reporters clicked and whirred in the front rows.

Four grass-skirted women began a hula dance on the grass stage to music provided by the band.

Aleta whispered, "Hula looks kinda dumb. You'd get laughed at doing *that* back home."

"It's not just a dance," said her mother. "It's a story. The movements are a story told in actions and gestures set to music."

Aleta cocked her head, eyebrows arched. "That's a story?"

"Watch their hands," whispered her mother.

"What do they say?"

"They're telling about Kamehameha as king. He brought peace to the islands and made life safe. He restarted farming, which had been pretty well destroyed during the civil wars. He introduced reforestation and conservation—the idea of planting a new plant or tree for every one you harvest. He started schools and a medical college. He introduced new plants and animals to the islands—over a dozen new vegetables from the mainland: pineapples, sugarcane, horses, and dogs. He established trade with countries all over the world ..."

"You're just making that up," interrupted Aleta.

"No. I studied hula when I was a university student here in the seventies."

Aleta studied her mother to see if she was telling the truth.

The music changed from twanging electric keyboard to pounding Hawaiian drums. Three male dancers leapt in front of the statue, their feet stomping, punishing the grass with every step, their hands and arms flashing through sharper, larger gestures and images. "What are they saying now?"

"This is a story about Kamehameha the warrior," answered Shirley. "It's the story of Kamehameha's great victory at a sea battle during the civil wars." Shirley translated for her daughter as the dancers beat their way through the music.

It was in the spring of 1791. A hard southwest wind blew the waves into choppy whitecaps. A dark band of clouds hugging the western horizon threatened rain by nightfall. Scouts had reported that a great armada of outriggers and double-sided war canoes with the combined armies of Maui and Oahu were on the way. The reports told that Maui's Chief Kahekili had purchased cannon from fur traders and mounted them on his lead war canoes.

Outnumbered ten to one, weary from the civil war for control of the big island of Hawaii, Kamehameha's fleet of seventy outriggers and war canoes pushed off from Kilua to try to stop the invaders. A hundred muskets were spread between seven of his canoes. Twenty ships were mounted with small swivel cannon Kamehameha had purchased, stolen, or captured. An American schooner, the *Fair America,* rode on the left side of Kamehameha's navy. That ship had been captured by a local Kona chief a few months earlier and its crew killed.

Aleta interrupted. "Hand movements told you all that?"

Her mother smiled, "Some of it I remember from a college history course. But some of it I get from the dancers."

An invading army of over fifteen thousand Hawaiians from Maui and Oahu rode hard with the wind to crush him. Kamehameha commanded only seventy ships, four thousand warriors, and two American sailors, Isaac Davis and John Young. Both Americans had been captured from the trading ship *Eleanor,* had been spared by Kamehameha's intervention, and had served him as faithful advisors ever since.

Using flag signals, Davis and Young would direct Kamehameha's cannon fire from the *Fair America.*

A lookout in the *Fair America* crow's-nest first spotted the invading fleet, a thick carpet of shining spears, gleaming swords, and frantically flashing paddles massed across the ocean. The cannon of the *Fair America* spoke first in the great battle. Smoke and fire belched from eight fixed cannon. Screeching shells raced across the water.

Kahekili wheeled his ships in a tight mass to meet this attack.

Kamehameha's plan was simple: First, spread his cannon ships so that enemy cannon fire would be less effective. Second, while cannon from the two sides blazed at each other, Kamehameha's smaller war canoes with musketeers would speed in close to kill Kahekili's cannoneers. Third, once unopposed, Kamehameha's cannon would close in to destroy the enemy fleet.

Smoke and thunder from opposing cannon rolled across the ocean obscuring the distant shore and clear vision of the enemy fleet. Whining, red-hot cannonballs smashed through the thin wooden deck and hull of any ship they found. Dense, black smoke billowed from outriggers that burst into flame from the crashing shells.

The cries of wounded and floundering warriors could be heard above the din of cannon fire. Sharks began to circle.

Kamehameha's musket canoes raced toward Kahekili's massed cannon ships, paddlers straining against the choppy Pacific waters. Rolling smoke and sulfur from exploding cannon made their eyes water, and made it hard to breathe. Still they flew across the waves.

Too late, Kahekili signaled his war canoes to intercept the speeding outriggers. Musketeers rose in the bows of Kamehameha's ships. Volley after volley of musket balls raked across the decks of Kahekili's cannon ships. Blood washed along the decks to tint the waves pink.

One by one Kahekili's cannon fell silent. Davis and Young signaled for an attack. Kahekili's mighty fleet began to dissolve under the withering fire of Kamehameha's cannon and muskets. The tattered remains of the invading fleet came about and limped in desperate retreat for home. Hundreds of ships and thousands of warriors died in the warm, choppy waters that day.

Aleta demanded, "How much of that did the hula really say?"

"The choppy water, the great mass of ships, the cannon and musket fire, canoes skimming over the waves, burning sulfur smoke, circling sharks, drowning and wounded men, thousands of dead warriors. It was all there in their movements."

Now the music changed. New instruments were added. The music felt more regal, more victorious. Extra dancers sprang onto the stage.

"Now what's it about?" demanded Aleta.

"It's telling about Kamehameha's life and about the end of the civil wars in one last battle in Nuuanu Valley here on Oahu."

"Is that where the losing soldiers were driven, screaming, off the *pali* to crash a thousand feet to the rocks below?" *Pali* is the Hawaiian word for a tall, sheer cliff.

Shirley nodded. "We drove up there yesterday."

"That was great," said Aleta. "The wind moaned when you stood near the edge, kind of like hearing the fading screams of the falling warriors."

Shirley grimaced. "I don't know if I'd call hundreds of brave warriors being either slaughtered or driven in droves, screaming over the pali to their deaths, 'great.'"

Shirley held up her hand to stop Aleta's reply. "Now the dancers are telling about how big Kamehameha's army was for that last battle. His war canoes lined the beach at Waikiki as far as the eye could see in either direction."

"That's the beach where all the hotels are?" interrupted Aleta.

"Yes. But back then it was mostly a swampy plain. Kamehameha marched at the head wearing a war helmet of bright yellow feathers and ground-length red-and-yellow flowing cape. Behind him lesser chiefs carried the scepter and banner of the war god and of Pele, the volcano goddess who was said to support Kamehameha. It was so great a force, it took over two hours for the army to all march past a single spot. That day the long civil wars ended. Kamehameha ruled the island kingdom of Hawaii."

The thick crowd applauded as the dancers bowed for their curtain call, and then began to shuffle toward parking lots. Photographers clicked their final shots.

"I liked that story," said Aleta. "Are there any more hulas?"

"Not today."

Aleta stretched and watched the thinning crowd. "So, what do you *do* at the King Kamehameha festival?"

Shirley answered, "Learn about Hawaii and the king. Which, I believe, is what you already did today. Tomorrow we can learn some more. I want to know where he was born, what he liked to eat, what he did as a child … lots of stuff. After the parade and luau at Queen Kapiolani Park, there are more hulas. … Unless you'd rather play on the beach."

Aleta fidgeted and gently kicked at a thick clump of grass. "That's OK. I think I'd rather watch more hula stories."

Follow-up Questions to Explore

1. What's a luau? Would you expect to have something like a luau at every festival?

Answer

A luau is the Hawaiian version of an outdoor, group picnic. On the mainland we call them picnics or potlucks. In Alaska they are called potlatches. In Hawaii it is a luau. Fruits, taro, poi, and roasted pig are typical offerings at a luau. Traditionally, the pig is roasted whole over a bed of hot coals in a buried barbecue pit. The cooking takes ten to twelve hours. When it's done, the pig is dug up and the luau is on!

2. Virtually all celebrations seem to combine five specific elements. Can you name these five? Are they all present at the King Kamehameha festival?

Answer

Before reading on, discuss these questions in class and compare your answers to those of your classmates. The five elements are: food, music, dance, a gathering of people, and remembering. The thing remembered may only be the planting time for a harvest festival. But celebrations always cause us to reflect, to think back. Are all of these present at the King Kamehameha festival? Can you think of any celebrations where some of these elements are missing? April Fool's Day may be one example. Can you find any others?

Suggested Activities

1. Make a chart of the five elements of a celebration: food, music, dance, a gathering of people, and remembering. For each celebration in this book, fill in the chart for those five elements. How do they vary from celebration to celebration? How are they the same?

2. Plan a Hawaiian Day in your classroom. Research the history, culture, celebrations, beliefs, stories, and customs of the Hawaiian people. Make a list of common words in Hawaiian. Find out what common Hawaiian dress looks like. Make a list of common Hawaiian foods, games, and dances. Now plan a day to incorporate these elements into your class with each student sharing and demonstrating the aspects of Hawaiian life they researched.

Juneteenth

An African-American Historic Celebration
of the End of Slavery

At a Glance

THERE IS ONLY ONE EVENT IN THE UNITED STATES to directly celebrate and commemorate the demise of the institution of slavery: Juneteenth.

Juneteenth is the oldest African-American celebration in this country, dating from the early 1870s. Its name is the abbreviated version of a date: June 19, 1865, the day the last slaves in America were notified of their freedom.

Every slave dreamed of freedom, longed for freedom, every hour of every day of their lives. But there were only four ways to win freedom: run away and risk the horrors of bounty-hunting slave chasers; buy your freedom (which often took a lifetime of work and saving); have your master free you in his will (which they occasionally did); or, once the Civil War started, pray that the Yankee army would swoop down and set you free.

President Lincoln signed the Emancipation Proclamation on September 22, 1862. It took effect, officially freeing all slaves, on January 1, 1863. But while the South held on, it was unenforceable.

Robert E. Lee surrendered on April 9, 1865, generally ending the war. But word did not reach the last holdout corner of the slave plantation world in northeast Texas until June 19, 1865. On that day, Army units under the command of General Gordon Granger fanned out across east Texas to notify all slaves that they were free. Slavery was finally ended.

Juneteenth celebrates that day and the final demise of the horrible institution of slavery. For some, Juneteenth represents the general end of slavery. For some it represents the whole struggle for freedom. For some it represents only the day on which the last slave was officially freed.

In any case, it is a significant date in our national evolution, one we should all understand and acknowledge. Few people participate in Juneteenth celebrations anymore. Considering the momentous events Juneteenth celebrates, maybe more of us should.

Juneteenth

"Mamma Bell! Mamma Bell!" Thomas sprinted as best he could into the cotton fields through the midday heat, which felt like a wet, steaming blanket. His bare feet kicked up a thick cloud of dust. His tattered pants, as always, were held up by a rope.

"Mamma Bell! You come quick!" Thomas's arms furiously pumped the air as if—all on their own—they could drag his bad leg faster across the dirt fields. The leg had been badly broken when a cart overturned five years ago. Thomas's right leg ever after dragged behind him like a deadweight.

Mamma Bell stopped her hoeing, shaded her eyes from the fierce June sun that seemed to save all its meanest heat for eastern Texas, and squinted across the bare field toward the tree-lined stream and big house beyond. "Now what's got that boy so agitated today?"

Thomas was twenty-five, but Mamma Bell called every male on the plantation "boy" if they were young enough for her to have been the midwife attending their birth.

Bull shrugged as he hoed the row next to Bell. "Lawd if I know. Ain't nothing worth gettin' excited 'bout on *dis* plantation."

If anyone in Texas was misnamed, it was Bull. A big head on the skinniest body on the plantation, he looked more like a cattail than a bull. Bell said that Bull was so skinny the shadow he cast was too thin to be worth bothering with and should have been thrown back.

Bull was a "runner," having run away three times. Some said it was a miracle he hadn't been killed. The mountain range of welts and scars on his back attested to how close his whippings had come to doing just that. A twelve-pound iron ball and chain welded onto one leg to keep him from running again made him drag his left foot behind him when he walked. He looked much like Thomas.

Gasping for breath, Thomas flung himself into the dirt at Bell's and Bull's feet. "Come ta the big house. Soldiers is here."

"Lawd, what they gwine take dis time?" muttered Bull.

"Naw, Bull. These soldiers are wearin' blue."

"What do you mean blue?" demanded Bell. "You mean *Yankee* blue?"

Thomas pointed toward the hazy, whitewashed sky, like a blue that had been used too much and was now faded like old jeans. "Blue as that sky!"

"Mercy be!" cried Bell dropping the hoe from her callused hands. "The Yankees done come to Texas!"

Thomas rose to his good knee and waved both hands to stop her. "Wait, Mamma Bell. I ain't told you the 'portant part yet. It's mo' what they said."

Bull scowled at Thomas. "*What* they say?" Anyone who had been whipped and beaten as much as Bull was suspicious of all white men.

"They say we's free."

"What do you mean 'free,' boy?" demanded Bell. "Do I *look* like I'm free?"

"They say we's free," repeated Thomas, a churchlike tone ringing in his voice as he said the word.

"I don't believe it," hissed Bull. "Dis a trick by the overseer. He gwine ta whip us good if we leave dis field."

"Not if'n we's free, he won't," said Bell already striding toward the big house.

A crowd of blacks had gathered below the columned front porch when Bell arrived. Bull and Thomas dragged in a minute later. Eight Yankee soldiers, looking bone-weary and dust-covered, slouched on their horses.

A young lieutenant with yellow stripes down his blue pants, gleaming sword dangling at his side, and thick mustache that twitched every time he spoke stood on the porch. Behind him, Master Theodore Turner and his daughter, Mistress Julie, huddled together in chairs, looking confused and frightened.

The lieutenant was reading from a rolled-up piece of paper. "… By order of General Gordon Granger and by Proclamation signed by President Lincoln on 22 September 1862, all slaves in the state of Texas are hereby declared to be free."

The lieutenant paused for the expected cheer. He saw instead a sea of incomprehension and confusion. All he heard was stunned silence. He raised his voice. "I said you're free. Now go on! You're free to go." He added, "The details are on this notice," as he nailed it to a porch column with the butt of his pistol.

Eight-year-old Ellen Mae tugged at Bell's skirt. "What's dat 'free' mean, Mamma Bell?"

"It means we's free to do what we wants and go wherever we wants."

Ellen Mae looked even more confused. "Where do we wants ta go, Mamma Bell?"

Bell shook her head, as if to clear it. "I don' rightly know. I never got to choose before."

"An' what do we want ta *do*, Mamma Bell?"

"Don't know that either, chile." Then Bell began to laugh. "But, Lawd, I am surely gonna enjoy the deciding!"

Master Turner stepped forward. "None of you *have* to leave. You can stay right here and work the land with me. I'll pay you for your services—pay you fair! You know field work's all you're good at, and you know I've always treated you fair. Why, I've always bent over backward to treat you just like family …"

Bull grunted and shook his head.

The Yankee lieutenant remounted his horse. "We'll be riding back down this road at six this evening. If you want, you can leave with us."

Master Turner added, "You all go back to your homes and talk it over. I think you'll agree you'll be better off working here with me."

The slave's "homes" were a double row of flimsy, dirt-floor shacks with mud to cover up the gaps in the walls. Tremors of joy rumbled through the shocked cluster of eighty blacks that milled around the open space between the rows of shacks. Freedom had always been a dream, a distant beacon of light, something for the next life, or at least something you had to work, risk, and plan for. Now this lieutenant had dumped it in their laps, smacked it in their faces. And no one quite knew what to do when some stranger handed them heaven.

"I still don' believe it," muttered Bull.

"Naw, it's true," said Hector. "I heard 'em talkin' 'bout that paper at the big house las' summer. Jus' didn't believe it." Hector was a powerful mountain of a man. He worked at the big house directly for Master Turner and was slow to think, and slow to speak. But when he did speak, what he spoke was true. Hector was the only slave on the plantation who could read a bit.

In a daze, Bell repeated, "'Dat Pres'dent freed us in '62. … All dis time we was free and never know'd it. Almos' three years we've been actin' like slaves when we was really free …"

Thomas sat on a stump that served as both seat and table. "I been savin' fo' seven years to buy my freedom an' I ain't nearly halfways there. Now the bluecoats jus' done give it to us for free."

"What you gonna do?" asked Aunt Pearl, who cooked in the big house.

"I'm gonna burn down the big house an' everyone in it," Bull growled.

"You do dat, an' you get shot real quick," answered Bell.

"I'm gonna burn this here shack," said Thomas, pointing with his thumb at the hut where he slept.

"What you gonna burn your own house fo'?" exclaimed Pearl.

"This is a slave's house. An' I ain't no slave no more."

Wringing her hands as if overcome with the enormity of the decisions now facing her, Pearl repeated, "What you *really* gonna do?"

Hector said, "I hear some is plannin' to go west. But that paper da soldiers tacked on da porch say if we stay, we gits forty acres and a mule. I could do me right nice with my own forty acres an' a mule."

"*Everybody* get that, or jus' forty acres for all of us?" asked Thomas.

"Bluecoats say the gov'ment gwine ta give forty acres to anyone who wants it."

Thomas whistled, "To *anyone?* Lawd! I didn't knows there was that much lan' in the whole worl'."

Aunt Pearl said, "I'm goin' with those soldiers this very night. Anywhere is better than this place."

Bell asked, "What day is this?"

Hector answered, "Massa's wall calendar say June 19."

"June de nineteenth," repeated Bell. "I am surely gonna remember me this date!" Her face spread into a wide grin and she swept forward to the middle of the crowd. "Well, I know what *I'm* gonna do. Right here, right now. I am gonna dance the first free dance of my life. You jus' stan' back an' watch how high a free woman can kick up her heels!"

"Come on and dance with me, Miranda," coaxed Mr. Carl Lewis on June 19, 1995.

"Daaaad," the sixteen-year-old girl whined. "No one else is dancing and it's not cool to dance with your father."

Mr. Lewis and his daughter were two of a thin crowd of several hundred wandering the breezy sunshine of a San Jose, California, park where the 1995 Juneteenth celebration was being held. Food booths advertised Cajun food, barbecue, and soul food, along with hamburgers and fried chicken. Small umbrella-covered booths sold anything that could be called African. A rock band blared its music from a plywood stage.

"Come on and dance, Miranda. It's a good band," repeated Mr. Lewis.

She rolled her eyes as if her father had come from another planet. "It's a *group*, Dad. 'Bands' are from like the sixties."

Miranda said, "You told me about Juneteenth and how the Union Army had to force the plantation owners to free the slaves even after the Civil War was over. Do you think everyone else here knows what Juneteenth means?"

Mr. Lewis cocked his head as he scanned the crowd. "A few probably do. Most probably don't." Then he added, "But somewhere inside, every African American understands the horrible institution of slavery, the ugly face of racial injustice." Now Mr. Lewis laughed, "And that's why my daughter has to dance with me on Juneteenth to celebrate being free."

Again Miranda rolled her eyes. "Daaaad …" But she let him drag her out to join the scattered dancers on the grassy lawn in front of the stage, dancing on Juneteenth to honor the wondrous glory that is freedom.

Follow-up Questions to Explore

1. Juneteenth celebrates the end of slavery in the United States. Certainly, the ending of slavery was a very good thing. But slavery itself was a terrible institution in this country's past. Do you think it's all right to have a celebration that reminds us, in part, of something bad, like slavery?

Answer

We rarely celebrate something evil or bad itself. Usually we celebrate the ending of such an institution, as with slavery (Juneteenth), or World War I (Armistice Day, which evolved into Veterans' Day). Many would argue that it is important to remember evil times and events so that they will not be repeated. Compare your thoughts to those of your classmates.

2. Why do you think most southern plantation owners held onto their slaves as long as they could, even after the Civil War was over?

Answer

Cheap (slave) labor was an essential ingredient of the economic success of the South. Without slaves, most plantations would not have been able to make any profit. Moreover, many plantations housed nearly a hundred or more slaves. Slaves represented a huge investment for the plantation owner. Few would willingly throw away such a great part of their total assets.

Suggested Activities

1. Freed slaves were offered "forty acres and a mule." How much land is forty acres? Is your school site bigger or smaller than forty acres? If the forty acres were shaped as a square, how long would each side of that square be? How much is forty acres of agricultural land in your community worth today? How much was it worth in 1865? How much does a grown mule cost today? How much was a mule worth in 1865?

2. Research freedom celebrations, and make a list of freedom celebrations around the world. Write each celebration on a sticky note and place them on a world map.

Pilgrimage to Mecca

An Islamic Religious Celebration
of One of Its Holy Pillars

At a Glance

SOME RELIGIOUS OBSERVANCES OCCUR ONCE EACH WEEK. A few happen once each month. Many happen once each year. There are a few very special religious celebrations that take place once in a lifetime. A pilgrimage to Mecca is one such celebration for those of the Muslim faith.

Mecca is both a place and a symbol to Muslims. According to their beliefs, Adam lived in a red tent in what is now Mecca after God banished Adam and Eve from the Garden of Eden. Muslim faith stems from Abraham, son of Adam. Mecca is the birthplace of Mohammed, the great prophet. Mecca is also the site of the holiest of Muslim shrines, the Great Mosque.

But Mecca is more than just a place. It is the heart and soul of the Muslim religion. Five times a day, faithful Muslims pray facing toward Mecca. And sometime during their lifetime, Muslims are called to journey on a pilgrimage to Mecca. This pilgrimage may be made at any time. However, if possible, it should be made during the annual holy week, defined by the Koran as beginning on the seventh day of the seventh lunar month, *Dhul-hijja*. Hundreds of thousands of pilgrims pour into Mecca during this week each year to fulfill their pilgrimage. They then return home as heroes and as shining, lifted spirits.

Pilgrimage to Mecca

"Has the plane landed yet, Mother?"

"No, Safu. Two minutes ago the plane had not landed. It *still* has not landed," answered Baraka Binte Jabir Um Hakim. Her seven-year-old daughter sighed and sagged against the chain-link fence.

Both mother's and daughter's shinning black hair was wrapped. Their slender faces were covered from nose down, as was proper. They both wore ground-length flowing dresses—the mother's of brilliant yellow with red trim, Safu's of tan muslin to match the color of the bare, sun-drenched hills.

"Why is the plane late, Mother?" asked Hakim Ben Kamil, her nine-year-old son.

"Planes often are," was all Baraka could think of to answer as she squinted into the scorching June sun at the Adana, Turkey, airport, searching the sky beyond the runway for sight or sound of the two-engine propeller plane her husband was on.

"I've finished," called Musa Ben Dabir Halim Abu Farid Khubb, waving and puffing to catch his breath as he ran out to join them.

"You tied the palm branches securely?" asked Baraka.

"Yes, most securely," answered Musa. "They won't fall off the car no matter how fast I drive." Musa was a tall, thin man with gray speckled hair and beard. His eyes sparkled like black diamonds under the turban he wrapped around his head.

"You tied enough on?" Baraka continued, green eyes probing the familiar face of this family friend.

"Yes!" he insisted. "The car is *covered* in palm branches. I also told Abdul at the market. He will have a sign and palm branches on the store and corner. Last night we tied them across the front of your house and over the door. Now relax, Baraka. Everything will be fine."

The faint hum of engine motors made everyone at the fence shade their eyes and stare into the deep blue sky southwest of the airport and toward the Mediterranean Sea a dozen miles beyond. Baraka nervously chewed on her lower lip.

"I said relax," repeated Musa. He gently nudged her shoulder with his. "And be happy! Your husband has just completed his pilgrimage to Mecca! It is the greatest event in his life."

"But what if something went wrong?" she asked. "What if he didn't complete all ten stations? What if he isn't wearing a green *hajj* (long scarf) as he steps off the plane?"

"Kamil?! My friend and your husband? Not complete his pilgrimage?" laughed Musa. "Ridiculous. You'll see."

"But if he didn't finish," pressed Baraka, "then the palm branches and reception will be an embarrassment to him."

"Relax and put a smile on those green eyes of yours. All will be well."

"I see the plane!" shouted Hakim, raised finger jabbing at a silver speck in the distant sky. "Father's home!"

"I see it, too. I see it, too," chanted Safu, bouncing as her fingers gripped the chain link separating her from the shimmering tarmac.

The plane taxied to its gate and the propellers stopped with a final cough of gray smoke. Baraka turned her head away. "I can't watch. I'm too nervous. Tell me what you see."

Musa reported, "They've pushed a ramp to the plane. ... They've opened the door ... People coming out ..."

"Father!" cried Hakim and Safu.

"Kamil, my friend, over here," called Musa, waving both arms.

"The *scarf*. Does he wear the green scarf?" hissed Baraka.

"Of course he does," smiled Musa.

With a wave of relief Baraka rushed toward her husband, who still wore the two white linen sheets of his pilgrimage. A long green scarf was proudly draped over his shoulders. Two other green-scarfed pilgrims stepped off the plane to be greeted by other cheering clusters of family and friends.

A jumping mass of arms and eager smiles, family and friends crowded around Kamil ben Kasib Fadil. He returned each smile, hug, and backslap as enthusiastically as it was given, his blue eyes sparkling as bright as the sky under his curly shock of black hair.

Kamil's voice squeaked out in a hoarse whisper. "We chanted and sang for two whole nights. I can barely talk."

"How was Mecca?" demanded Musa. "Your eyes, my friend, they glow with holy fire!"

"Ah, the sights these eyes have seen in just one week," answered Kamil, "a lifetime of wonder and glory! But, praise be to Allah, I am very glad to be home."

Kamil stood a good head shorter than his friend. But his arms and shoulders were thick and powerful from years of factory work. Kamil's teeth were straight and white so that his smile shone like the summer sun.

As the family cluster made its way through the Adana airport with Kamil's meager baggage, other travelers cheered the green-scarfed pilgrims as if they were national heroes.

At the front curb Kamil laughed, "What has happened to my car? It has become a jungle."

"For the returning hero who has made his pilgrimage to Mecca during holy week," beamed Baraka at his side.

"I'll drive," said Musa. "You ride and tell us stories of Mecca." Musa blasted the horn as they pulled into thick traffic on the two-lane highway toward Adana. Heat waves shimmered off the brown and barren hills above the green, irrigated fields on both sides of the road. Dust swirled in the hot winds, leaving the car with a thin brown coat.

Over and over, Musa honked, laughed, and cheered out the window. On seeing the palm branches and Kamil's green scarf, other drivers honked back and waved as they might for a famous celebrity.

"Enough, Musa!" cried Kamil. Then reached up to hold his raw throat.

"Then talk," urged Kamil's friend.

Kamil shifted in his crowded seat searching for the right words before he began. "It was indescribable to be part of a sea of five hundred thousand chanting pilgrims…"

"What's a pilgrim, Father?" asked Safu.

Hakim said, "A pilgrim is someone who travels to a sacred place to open their heart and mind to Allah." Then he nodded and leaned back in his seat.

"Very good, Hakim," smiled his father before continuing. "Six miles from Mecca there were long rows of tents where we removed shoes and turbans."

"You didn't wear the new sandals I gave you?" asked Baraka.

"The Koran says that all men must complete their pilgrimage with bare feet and bare heads," said Musa.

"I put on my two white linen sheets and joined a river of pilgrims flowing down the long sand and dirt slopes to Mecca. The Great Mosque rose before us, towering over the desert. Some wept with joy at the wondrous sight. Many cried out, 'I am here, oh my Allah. I am here!' The sound echoed back from the massive mosque, 'I am here.'

"And so our barefoot river swirled to the gates of the Great Mosque itself."

"Is there more than one gate, father?" asked Hakim.

"Nineteen," he answered. "But all pilgrims must enter through the Bab a-Salam, the Gate of Peace—wide enough for two cars to drive through side by side. There were so many pilgrims I had to wait over an hour for my turn to squeeze through.

Baraka asked, "Was it really that crowd—Ouch!" Musa skidded the car through a sharp right turn. Safu was flung across her mother. Both banged their heads on the side window.

"Sorry. Sorry. But this side road will have less traffic. Too many trucks on the highway."

"Was it really crowded?" repeated Kamil. "The courtyard of the Great Mosque is five hundred fifty feet long and three hundred sixty feet wide (the size of four football fields). In the center stands the Kaaba, a reddish building on the site of Adam's red tent. After entering the Gate of Peace the second task is to touch the Black Stone set into the wall near the eastern corner."

"What's the Black Stone?" asked Safu.

"The Ruby from Heaven," answered Kamil. "The only thing Adam carried from the Garden of Eden. It is a part of Heaven itself. Half a million white-robed pilgrims were all jammed into the courtyard wanting to touch that stone. I struggled for five hours to worm my way to the wall and with these two lips I kissed the Black Stone."

"Is that all you had to do father?" asked Hakim.

"Why were you gone a week?" added Safu.

"Those are only two of the ten tasks, or stations. I ran seven laps around the Kaaba—from above we pilgrims must have looked like a giant white-robed whirlpool circling closer and closer to the sacred Kaaba as we ran. I prayed at the Mosque of Abraham. I drank from the well of Ishmael—I could feel each drop flow down my throat as if they were pure specks of holy light."

All in the crowded car were silent with awe as Kamil described the sacred tasks.

"I climbed Mount Safa and Mount Maret. There were seven hundred thousand of us by now. The dust cloud rising from one and a half million shuffling feet rose thick and dark as a sandstorm.

"We heard sermons. We chanted all night in the mosque at Muzdalifa. I Stoned the Devils with seventy pebbles …"

"You did what?" asked Baraka.

"The ninth station. It was late on the seventh day when I made it through the long line and broke into the village of Mina. Here, there are three tall pillars. Each pilgrim throws their pebbles at the pillars, shouting with each throw, 'There is no god but Allah!' It is called 'Stoning the Devils.' Can you imagine the sound? Over ten thousand voices at any given moment crying, 'There is no god but Allah!' Thousands of pebbles crashing like a thunderous hailstorm into the pillars. The sound throbbed through the desert until it seemed to cover the whole world."

Hakim asked, "If you had to wait so long in lines, Father, didn't you get bored?"

"No, my son," laughed Kamil. "I was not bored one second. These are sacred tasks. Each requires devotion, concentration, and obedience. My heart was so full of joy and wonder there was no time to think of being bored—or tired, or thirsty—which, by the way, I am now."

"Perfect timing," said Musa, squealing the palm-covered car around a tight turn in a narrow neighborhood street. "We are home."

A throng of neighbors waved palm branches from the curb. Banners were draped crisscross over the street. People cheered. "Kamil is back! Kamil is back!"

A shining star had returned to a simple neighborhood in the middle of an ordinary city in Turkey, and for a moment every person was touched by the glorious light of Mecca and shone brighter and happier themselves.

Follow-up Questions to Explore

1. A Pilgrimage to Mecca is a once-in-a-lifetime celebration. Are there celebrations and events you observe once in a lifetime?

Answer

We have many such events. First are the whole group of "coming-of-age" events: first driver's license, first kiss, being old enough to vote, etc. Second are religious events: bar mitzvah, baptism, confirmation, etc. Finally, there are those events that mark milestones in our lives that we expect to be once-in-a-lifetime events: high school graduation, college graduation, marriage, etc. Can you find others?

2. Islam associates great religious importance and power to the city of Mecca and to many squares, buildings, pillars, and hills in Mecca. Judaism and Christianity attach similar significance to parts of Jerusalem. Do you think it is wise to associate beliefs and concepts with a physical place? Wouldn't the beliefs be the same even without a specific geographical reference? Are there special places for your beliefs? Which is more important to you, the place or the beliefs?

Answer

Discuss these questions in class and compare your answers to those of your classmates.

Suggested Activities

1. Locate Mecca on a map. What country is Mecca in? Over the last three thousand years, has the name of the country around Mecca changed? How often? Find pictures of Mecca and the land around it. What do the buildings and people of Mecca look like? What is the climate like? Find pictures of the places in Mecca pilgrims visit.

2. Research other sites pilgrims visit around the world. Find out what group makes pilgrimages to each site, and what the purpose of their pilgrimage is. What at this site draws pilgrims? What do pilgrims do at the site? Do pilgrims visit the site anytime, or is there a special date, season, or period for pilgrimages? Locate each of the sites you discover on a world map.

JULY

United States
Independence Day

A Celebration
of National Independence

At a Glance

TO WHAT DATE OR EVENT WOULD YOU TRACE THE ORIGIN, the founding of the United States? To the Boston Tea Party? To the first shots fired at Lexington and Concord? The first real battle, the Battle of Bunker Hill? To the moment when the Continental Congress resolved to become an independent nation? The date the Declaration of Independence was signed?

Our July 4 celebration honors none of these events. The great vote was taken on the stormy afternoon of July 2, 1776, in Philadelphia by the Continental Congress. That is when they voted to break away from England and become the United States of America. July 2 is the first time the words "United States" were officially spoken or written.

However, it took two more days for the delegates to agree on the specific wording of the declaration announcing their decision to the world. The final document, the Declaration of Independence, was announced to the public on the afternoon of July 4. The document wasn't brought back to Congress for signatures until August 4.

John Adams predicted that future generations would honor and cherish the date of July 2, when the decision to become a free nation was made. He was wrong. We chose to honor and celebrate the date of the completion of the document. The most interesting story of all, though, is how close the vote on July 2 was, and by the razor-thin margin that we agreed to become a unified country of thirteen states.

United States Independence Day

Unanimous … Why did Mr. Adams say it had to be unanimous?

My name is Andrew McNair. I've been the one and only doorman for the First and Second Continental Congresses. Some say I'm too old for an important job like this. But then they see what happens when someone tries to sneak past me without proper credentials, and they don't say that anymore. No, I don't just open the door. My real job is to make sure no one gets into the redbrick State House here in Philadelphia without proper credentials. No assistants, pages, messengers, or visitors. *No one* gets in except the delegates themselves, and they have to have proper credentials from their state.

Now, it's always exciting, listening to official Congress business, watching President John Hancock with his aristocratic airs run the debates from his raised presidential platform. But now, now this vote on independence has got me in such a lather I can scarcely sleep! When the vote on independence first came up on June 10, it was defeated—couldn't even get a simple majority. So it got postponed for three weeks.

Now today, on Monday, July 1, 1776, it comes up again. And Mr. John Adams went and declared that it had to be a *unanimous* vote for independence! Ha! A month ago they couldn't even win a majority of the thirteen colonies and fifty-six delegates! But if it looses now, I fear the tide of freedom will be lost forever.

Oh, I understand Mr. Adams's reasoning. If the thirteen colonies aren't united, he's afraid they'll tear apart from within. We'll wind up in a civil war instead of a united fight against England. But how can he hope to get a unanimous vote of all thirteen colonies when he couldn't get seven to vote "yes" a month ago?

I couldn't lie in bed past 5:00 this morning. I walked the five blocks down Chestnut to the meeting house and arrived by 7:00, a full hour early. Sessions start at 9:00. I am usually here by 8:00. I check the Congress meeting room, loaned to Congress by the Pennsylvania legislature. I open the curtains to flood light across the white-paneled walls. I make sure the high-ceilinged room is ready. If there is a chill, I light the fireplaces. Then I take my post by the heavy, carved door to greet and admit the delegates.

But every action seemed charged, and extra-significant today. Even the weather seemed to feel the tension. By 8:00 the thermometer reached seventy-eight degrees. It was frightfully muggy. Swirling clouds were gathering. A summer storm was brewing—as if even the sky knew that today was the day—either we commit to freedom (and war) or we remain forever a servant of England!

Such a momentous decision for fifty-six men to make all on their own, isolated here in this room. One way or the other they will commit the lives of a hundred thousand Americans!

It will be difficult enough to get a majority. But John Adams insists on a unanimous vote!

Last Friday I overheard Adams and Benjamin Franklin talking outside the meeting hall while Dr. Franklin waited for his "sedan chair." He suffers from gout and can't walk much, so has hired two stout men to carry him around Philadelphia in a chair mounted on poles.

As I passed by I heard Adams mutter as he rummaged through his green cloth satchel, "The four New England colonies are solid. So are Virginia and Georgia."

"That's only six," cautioned Franklin, peering through his spectacles.

"Two weeks ago New Jersey appointed new delegates. The new group is solidly for independence."

"That's seven," answered Franklin.

"Both Carolinas are wavering. I think they could be talked into voting yes."

"That's nine."

Adams rubbed his forehead for a moment. "The Delaware delegates are split. Maryland delegates are in favor. But their legislature back home won't allow them to vote yes."

Franklin's chair arrived and he climbed in, his long gray hair straggling across his shoulders. "That still leaves New York and Pennsylvania's 'cool considerate men.' "

New York was thick with Tories, supporters of English rule in America. No one believed New York would ever vote to split from England. Pennsylvania delegates, led by the tall, beanpole-thin Quaker, John Dickinson, were opposed to any drastic action and especially to war. They *were* in favor of pressing the colonies' case with England, but firmly against anything so radical as a declaration of independence. They were now called the "cool considerate men." Those favoring independence and war were dubbed "the violent men." Most of these were rash New Englanders.

As two thick, seaman-looking porters hoisted Franklin's chair and started toward his home, Adams called, "Has your committee of five finished the declaration yet?"

Franklin shook his head. "It's really a committee of one. Tom Jefferson's doing all the writing. He has a wonderful start on the first two sections. But the last two are going more slowly."

"Tell him to hurry. If the vote goes for independence on Monday, we'll need a document to present to the delegates for their approval."

After hearing *that* conversation, how could I sleep over the weekend? So much rides on one roll call of the colonies today. Each colony casts one vote. If a colony's delegates disagree on an issue, that colony's vote goes with the majority of its delegates.

By 8:30 A.M. delegates began to file in, wigs carefully combed, knee breeches and white hose, satin waistcoats, broadcloth overcoats, stylish pumps. Southern drawls clashed with Yankee twangs. A subdued rumble grew across the room as delegates in small groups discussed the day's decision in urgent tones.

I cleared every delegate through the great front door by 8:50, a record. Outside the temperature climbed over eighty-four degrees. The first rumblings of a distant storm crept down Chestnut Street.

President Hancock gaveled the meeting to order exactly at 9:00. Delegates expectantly slid into their seats. Hancock raised a stack of mundane business that needed attention before bigger matters could be addressed. Many groaned openly. There were two letters from General Washington concerning new British troop ship arrivals in New York Harbor. There were army supply requests—mostly for food and shoes this day.

On and on the business of Congress droned until 12:30 P.M. when Hancock announced that Congress would now consider the proposal by Richard Henry Lee. This was it! Richard Henry Lee was the Virginian who first moved to declare independence back in June. An electric tingle surged through the room matching the growing rumble of thunder from gathering clouds outside. Delegates straightened in their chairs. Attention focused on every word of the debate.

John Dickinson, the Pennsylvania Quaker and leader of the "cool considerate men," leapt to his feet asking to be heard. Apparently he had been up most of the night preparing for this all-important plea. Once he had been considered the leader of Congress. But his power had fallen away in recent weeks as independence gained support. Besides pleading to defeat this measure (which he called "far too extreme"), he seemed to be making a final plea for his own position of authority in Congress.

Dickinson spoke for over four hours. Through his impassioned speech we again and again heard the arguments against independence. Mutters of support drifted through the chamber as he spoke and respoke each one. So did louder grumbles of disagreement.

"A lack of prudence will cost the lives of thousands of Americans."

"France's friendship and support are still unknown. But we cannot hope to win a war without them."

"We can still make gains through negotiation."

"Declaring independence now is rash and is a blind and precipitous measure!"

"We are in a wretched state of preparation for war."

At 5:00 an unofficial, straw vote was taken as the first jagged lightning bolt knifed to the ground nearby. Hancock wanted to see how the votes would fall. Thunder rattled the windows as New Hampshire, the first colony, shouted, "Yes!"

The declaration for independence won that straw poll. But only by a vote of nine to four. New York, Pennsylvania, Delaware, and South Carolina voted "no." Edward Rutledge of South Carolina quickly called for a one-day postponement of the official vote.

John Dickinson paled and seemed to shrink. His lengthy plea hadn't swayed anyone. Independence won the day. He was defeated.

I glanced at John Adams. He looked, if not defeated, worried. Only one day left to the official vote, and still four colonies to convert if the vote was to be unanimous.

Before I could lock the doors, rumors were flying. The real key, it seemed, was Pennsylvania. One of Delaware's delegates, Caesar Rodney, was absent, but had been sent for. If he arrived in time, Delaware would swing to the "yes" side. New York voted "no" because their delegates had not received new instructions from the colony legislature, even though they had repeatedly requested them. Early on the evening of July 1, the New York delegates agreed to abstain from voting at all unless they received new orders from home. South Carolina delegates agreed to vote "yes" for the sake of unity if no one else voted "no."

That left Pennsylvania. Their delegates had voted five to two against independence. But I heard John Dickinson say he would not even attend the session tomorrow as a protest over losing the unofficial independence vote. One of his strongest supporters decided to do the same. That meant that their vote tomorrow would be *three* to two against. But one of the three, John Morton, was wavering. I heard Sam Adams tell Hancock that he planned to take Morton out for dinner and a talk that night.

Suddenly quiet, John Morton of Pennsylvania was the key. How this one man voted tomorrow would decide the fate of all thirteen colonies! If he voted "no," Pennsylvania, followed by South Carolina, New York, and possibly North Carolina, would vote "no." Any thought of a united front of colonies would be destroyed. But if he voted "yes," everyone else would swing in behind.

Morton had been a long supporter of John Dickinson. His family, friends, and colleagues were all "cool considerate men." Though he had lately begun to see the value of independence, could he possibly vote against family, friends, and his own history tomorrow when so much rode on his one vote?

I shuddered as I walked back home. What an awesome responsibility for one delegate! Then I shuddered again. Independence seemed to hang on a thin and tenuous thread of "ifs." *If* Rodney of Delaware arrived in time, and *if* no new instructions arrived from New York, and *if* South Carolina held true to their word, then, *if* Morton voted "yes," independence would be declared.

What a day the second of July would be!

I arrived by 6:30 on the hot, rainy morning of July 2. Somber delegates also arrived early. Hancock gaveled the session to order at exactly 9:00 A.M. Several bits of congressional business had piled up overnight. It was after 11:00 when Hancock turned back to the final vote on Richard Henry Lee's motion to declare independence.

After final debate the roll call began. Massachusetts, Rhode Island, New Hampshire, and Connecticut all voted "yes," as expected. New York abstained, having received no new instructions overnight. I nervously scanned the room. Caesar Rodney had not yet arrived. I stood by the front door, looking into rain-soaked Chestnut Street, listening to the voting inside.

New Jersey voted "yes." So did Maryland. The clerk called, "How does Delaware vote?" My heart sank. Rodney didn't make it. Just as fast my heart bounced into my throat. I heard the hard clatter of pounding hooves on the cobbled street.

"A rider approaches!" I yelled into the meeting room.

Splattered with mud, soaked with rain, gaunt and pale from having ridden all night through the storm, Caesar Rodney slid from his horse and handed me his credentials. One minute later Delaware officially voted "yes."

I sagged, panting against the great front door. We think such drama only happens in stories. But here it was in real life. Rodney arrived with only seconds to spare! And all our independence had hung in that narrow balance. But the drama was not over yet. The clerk called, "How does Pennsylvania vote?"

Through the first four delegates, two voted "no," two voted "yes," as expected. All eyes turned to John Morton. John remained seated for over a minute, eyes down toward the floor. He neither moved nor uttered a sound. I could see the doubts, the uncertainty, the inner conflict written across his face. Slowly, ashened-faced, he rose and said simply, "I vote yes," and slumped back into his chair.

Quickly Virginia, Georgia, South Carolina, and North Carolina added their "yes" votes. The clerk reported the vote, "Twelve for, one abstention, none opposed."

Adams had done it! I expected cheers to explode across the room, and for delegates to jump and dance, tossing papers into the air.

Instead there was silence. The moment was too solemn, too important for cheering. The delegates simply sat in silence, almost stunned.

Hancock adjourned the session with an agreement to take up the wording of Mr. Jefferson's Declaration of Independence in the morning.

The delegates filed quietly into the late afternoon as the rain faded to drizzle and streaks of golden sunlight broke through from the west.

As he pulled his broadcloth coat over his shoulders, Mr. Adams said, "The second of July will be the most memorable date in the history of America. It will be celebrated by generations to come as the day of deliverance for our new nation."

I smiled and nodded in agreement as I locked the door. The second of July. What a day! I was sure Americans would celebrate this date as long as there was an America.

Follow-up Questions to Explore

1. Why do we celebrate independence on July 4 instead of July 2?

Answer

The American public didn't hear about the vote in Congress or about the declaration on July 2 when the vote was taken. Congress decided not to announce their vote until the wording of their declaration was finalized. It took two more days of debate and compromise to agree on that wording. No one knew of the vote or of the declaration until the afternoon of July 4. That became the date we remember and celebrate even though Congress voted to declare independence two days earlier.

2. What do you do to celebrate our independence? Why?

Answer

Discuss these questions in class and compare your answers to those of your classmates. Typically, Fourth of July celebrations include picnics and barbecues, parades (often neighborhood or small local parades), wearing (and eating) of red, white, and blue items, and fireworks. For us it is mostly a family celebration filled with very general celebratory stuff.

3. Why do you think we shoot off fireworks during our Fourth of July celebration?

Answer

Some say we shoot off fireworks just because it is pretty, exciting, dazzling, and has always been part of special celebrations. But many others argue that fireworks were incorporated into our Fourth of July celebrations after the War of 1812 to commemorate the British bombardment on Fort McHenry in Baltimore Harbor during which Francis Scott Key wrote our national anthem, the "Star Spangled Banner." What do you think?

Suggested Activities

1. Research fireworks. How and where are fireworks made? How are different colors and patterns created when they explode overhead? Are fireworks really dangerous? Develop a list of safety rules for using fireworks.

2. Research the history of the Declaration of Independence. Who first proposed the idea? Where did the ideas of the declaration and its wording come from? Who was in favor of it? Who was opposed? Why? How many votes were taken? When and what was the outcome each time?

Tanabata Matsuri

A Japanese Cultural Celebration of a Myth

At a Glance

SOME CELEBRATIONS HONOR RELIGIOUS BELIEFS, common history, or common values. There are a few that were created specifically to honor myths. Japan's Tanabata Matsuri is such a celebration. Now a major tourist attraction to the northern Japanese city of Sendai, the celebration is conducted in villages and neighborhoods and households all across Japan to honor the Japanese version of an old and common myth to explain why, for one day a year in early August, the star Vega seems to jump across the Milky Way and rest near Altair.

Tanabata Matsuri (*Matsuri* is the Japanese word for celebration) is a day of wishes, of making them and of pledging to keep them—like our New Year's resolutions. It is also a day of incredible decorations, hanging like a forest of streamers and flowers above the streets. The decorations are not the sole focus of Tanabata, but they are certainly what draws the great crowds to Sendai.

Tanabata Matsuri

"Aren't you coming with us, Mother?"

Suniku Aiyaki smiled and shook her head, but did not break her concentration on her needle as it sped in and out of the cloth of her needlepoint.

"But it will be *pretty*," said nine-year-old Yokira, tossing her short black hair so that it swished across her face.

"Far more than pretty," answered her mother. "The decorations will be breathtakingly beautiful."

"Then why don't you want to come and see?" demanded Yokira, not understanding how her mother could choose to skip one of the most glorious spectacles of the year. "… It's a beautiful day," Yokira added, hoping that would convince her mother.

Her mother paused in her sewing. "Summers in Sendai City are always beautiful." Then she pointed at a fluttering strip of white parchment paper with Japanese characters drawn in bright red paint. The strip hung from the top end of a long bamboo shoot tied just outside the front door of their house. "I made a wish to the *kami,* and I must practice."

Kami (literally, all deities, but usually taken to mean minor deities who watch over a certain neighborhood or village) are believed to descend to visit and check on the village on celebration days. If, on Tanabata, the kami see a woman working to better herself and achieve her own wish, they will use their power to assist her.

"Practice *tomorrow*. Come and *look* today."

Now her mother softly laughed as she resumed her needlepoint. "Of all days, I must practice *today*."

Yokira stubbornly crossed her arms and scowled. "I don't understand why you won't come."

Ichiro Aiyaki, Yokira's father, stood in the doorway behind Yokira. "When a woman is serious about improving her skills in one of the arts, she makes a wish on the day of Tanabata to the kami for help. The kami will only respond and help make the wish come true if she devotes herself to the practice of that art throughout the day of Tanabata Matsuri."

Yokira slowly nodded in thought. "And you want to be better at needlepoint?"

"I do." Again Suniku paused and smiled at her daughter. "You will have to enjoy the Tanabata spectacle for both of us."

"I will!" And, beaming with pride at having been given such an important mission, Yokira lead her father out the front door.

Sendai City lies near the northeast coast of Japan's Honshu Island. Summers run mild with pleasant breezes flowing in off the Pacific. Even the hottest days feel more pleasant in Sendai. Sendai is called the "City of Trees," and the waving boughs of countless shade trees seem to soak up the heat and leave a soft coolness on the ground beneath.

This day of August 7, 1993, promised to blossom magnificently. A cacophony of birds sang its praises in the trees. Above, lazy white puffs drifted across an azure blue sky. The splashes of sunlight sifting through the trees felt warm and inviting on Yokira's back and shoulders.

"Downtown will be crowded today," warned her father. "So hold my hand."

"I've been downtown before," Yokira laughed in reply.

"Never when it is as crowded as today."

Hand in hand they walked the residential streets leading to downtown Sendai. Almost every house hung decorations of flowered balls and paper streamers on tall bamboo poles. They fluttered in the warm morning breeze. Many doors were draped with bamboo and streamers. "They are so lovely," sighed Yokira.

"These?" laughed Ichiro. "These are nothing. Wait until we reach Tanabata-dori Avenue! Then you will see what makes Sendai Tanabata displays so famous."

"They're still very pretty," insisted Yokira, not wanting to admit she had been impressed by a mere trifle of decoration.

Near the doors of most houses, Yokira also saw white "wish streamers" flapping on thin bamboo shoots. "Does everyone make Tanabata wishes, Father?"

Ichiro frowned, hands now clasped behind his back as they walked. "Many of the wishes you see are put up just for decoration. Many people do not take the wishes or the kami seriously."

"Can I make a wish on Tanabata?" asked Yokira.

"You? Yes. You are a woman." Her father explained. "Making wishes to kami doesn't work for men. Women have a special close connection to kami that men can never possess."

Yokira paused in her walk, brow furrowed deep in thought. "I like that, Father. It's good that women have the stronger connection to kami."

Ichiro shrugged. "Good or not; that's how it is. Now we must hurry to beat the worst of the crowds. I want to show you the decorations we have put up at my store. We will win the merchant division competition this year. I know we will!"

Again Ichiro insisted on holding his daughter's hand. Yokira rolled her eyes, thinking he was being overprotective and overdramatic.

Then they rounded the corner onto Tanabata-dori Avenue.

Yokira couldn't see the street. Every square inch of it was covered by people. Cars crawled through the human sea honking their horns to move the solid wall of strollers out of their way. Often the cars would stop altogether as passengers hopped out to snap photos. Then cars behind them would lay all the harder on their horns. Endless crowds milled in the street, gazing and pointing up in wonder. Uniformed police blew on whistles at every corner, trying in vain to keep the traffic moving.

On any other day of the year, open air—sky—occupied the wide space above Tanabata-dori Avenue between the two- and three-story stores and office buildings. But not on the day of Tanabata!

Thick bamboo poles arched high above the street every fifteen or twenty feet. From these poles spread an endless forest of rustling paper streamers in every color and hue imaginable. The streamers flowed from giant bamboo and flower balls often fifteen feet high and twenty feet around. Brilliant flowered streamers hung intertwined with the paper ones. The patterns were dazzling. The brilliant colors seemed to pulse and throb as they waved back and forth like an endless thick forest of kelp washing in and out with the waves. There was no sky. There was only dazzling color waving everywhere overhead with the gusts of wind.

Yokira was staggered by the incredible majesty of the sight as if, like a giant mallet, the visual spectacle smacked her on the head. Her mouth forgot how to close. Her eyes struggled to soak in the most wondrous sight she had ever seen. Yokira had been on Tanabata-dori Avenue hundreds of times to visit her father at his fish market. This was not the street she knew. This was some magical garden of the gods, a fairyland of waving color and form that belonged to some other, magical world.

"Oh, my!" she gasped. "Oh, my!"

Ichiro proudly smiled. "You like our little decorations, Yokira?"

Her glazed eyes turned toward her father. "Oh, my!"

It took them fifteen minutes to shuffle the block and a half to Ichiro's fish store. Over all that walk Yokira repeated, "Oh, my!"

In front of his store Ichiro pointed up. "Look at our decorations this year. Don't you think they'll win the competition?"

An intricate bamboo frame of massive size was covered in fuchsia and yellow streaks of flowers. Below twirled a pinwheel of bamboo strips and bright flowers, a spinning rainbow floating in the sky. A vast horde of streamers seemed to explode from it in all directions.

"Oh my, Father!" It was the most glorious sight Yokira had ever seen.

Heideki Kiro, owner of another fish shop, stopped beside them.

"I will beat you this year," said Ichiro with a fierce gleam.

"With this?" laughed Heideki. "Ha! You must see the street in front of *my* shop!"

"How can yours be better than this?"

"You'll see," laughed Heideki over a shoulder as he continued his walk.

Ichiro began to worry.

Yokira interrupted his thoughts. "This is a celebration, isn't it, Father?"

"Of course."

"What are we celebrating? Why do we decorate our city? Just for the competition?"

"Tanabata honors the sad story of two stars," answered Ichiro.

"Two stars?" repeated Yokira.

"I will show them to you tonight, Yokira. Here is the story of the Weaver Princess Star and the lowly Herdboy Star. The Celestial Princess Star, highly skilled in the art of weaving, was the daughter of a heavenly king. But she fell in love with the Herdboy Star, a lad of lowly birth. Her father, the king, was a kindly man and allowed them to marry because they were so much in love.

"So *much* in love were they, however, that they neglected their duties. Cloth was not woven. Herds were allowed to wander, unattended, across the sky.

"The king grew angry and separated the sweethearts so that they would attend to their jobs."

"How did he separate them?" asked Yokira.

"He spread a river of stars between them, the Milky Way. Neither was able to cross, and both wept countless tears as they gazed at each other from opposite sides of that vast river.

"But the king took pity on his daughter and, forever after, has allowed her to cross the Milky Way on one night each year to be with her husband.

"That night is Tanabata. And on that one night each year, Vega, the Weaver Princess Star, crosses over the Milky Way to be with her Herdboy Star, Altair."

Yokira's eyes softened with the tragedy of the story. "They only get one night together every year? That's a very sad story, Father. I want a happier ending."

Ichiro took his daughter's hand. "Maybe that is why we celebrate today—to honor their unhappiness and to hope that our fate will be better. Now let us see just how good the decorations of Heideki Kiro are."

Outside of Heideki's shop Ichiro and Yokira gazed up in wonder.

"Oh, my!" gasped Yokira.

"Oh, no!" groaned Ichiro. "His decorations are spectacular."

"They're wonderful," whispered Yokira. "They're the most beautiful I have ever seen …"

"Enough!" growled her father. "Next year I will outdo him. You'll see!"

As they started home Yokira said, "Next year I will watch the stars and make a wish to the kami that they can be together longer."

Follow-up Questions to Explore

1. Tanabata is about celebrating a myth based on celestial movement. How and why do you think wishing for better skill in the arts became a part of this celebration?

Answer

Feudal Lord Masamune, during the Edo period, wanted to improve cultural awareness and skill among the women of his region, which he feared were sagging. He decreed that all women should set aside time on

Tanabata to improve their arts-related skills. The activity caught on, and was, over time, woven into the fabric of Tanabata Matsuri and the Japanese beliefs about kami. It has survived this way over the centuries.

2. Do you think it's all right to have a celebration based on a myth, a fictional event that never happened, a fictional person who never existed? Do you celebrate any myths?

Answer

Discuss these questions in class and compare your answers to those of your classmates.

Suggested Activities

1. What skill would you choose to improve? Make a list of the students in your class and the skill they would choose. Plan a half-day devoted to practicing and improving each student's chosen skill. After this practice period, discuss its effectiveness. Is practice more effective than wishing for improved skill? Is a one-time, half-day intensive practice session more effective than regular, shorter practice periods each day?

2. Tanabata Matsuri is woven around a myth about stars. Research stories that explain how the sun, moon, planets, and stars came to be, and why they are as they are. How many cultures have such stories? In what ways are the stories from different cultures the same? In what ways are they unique? Why do you think humans create such stories and myths?

AUGUST

Boyaca

A Colombian History
and Independence Celebration

At a Glance

MANY OF THE EVENTS CELEBRATED AROUND THE WORLD seemed like anything but noteworthy events at the time of their occurrence. Often an event's significance can only be seen in hindsight. One such event was the desperate struggle of a small band of soldiers in South America under the command of Simón Bolívar. A ragtag band of fighters, they seemed hardly worth noticing as they passed by. The sight of Bolívar's army did not stir the soul and quicken the heart. It did not seem to be the stuff from which legends are born. It seemed more likely they'd collapse and disintegrate during the long march to battle.

Bolívar's goal was to drive the Spanish out of New Granada (now Colombia). But in early 1819, it seemed most probable that he would never march an army to New Granada. If by some miracle he did, any sage betting man would have given fifty-to-one odds he'd be crushed like an annoying bug by the Spanish.

It didn't seem like the time was right for the bells of freedom to ring in South America, for the yoke of oppression to be cast off. But then, things do not always turn out as they seem.

Today in Colombia the seventh of August is Independence Day, a national holiday to commemorate Simón Bolívar's victory over the Spanish at the Battle of Boyaca. The day is so important to Colombians that they hold their elections on this Independence Day—the act of freedom on the day of freedom.

But in 1819, it did not seem that anyone would remember.

Boyaca

Two bleak forms huddled next to each other on a small rock outcropping on the craggy mountain ledge. Their heads lay hunched into their folded arms, their arms wrapped around bent knees, their backs pressed to each other for warmth and shelter from the driving sleet. Their long muskets were carelessly laid on a rock just out of arm's reach. It was the bitter winter night (in South America) of June 30, 1819.

Pitch-black darkness hid the plight of these miserable soldiers from their eyes. Sheer granite cliffs fell away below them. Jagged mountain peaks pierced the heavens two thousand feet above.

One man unfolded one hand and held it out from under the thin, cloth poncho that served both as jacket and blanket. "Miguel, I think it's changed from sleet to snow."

"Either way I'm frozen stiff," grumbled his mate. After a moment he snarled, "Guard duty! What could there possibly be to guard against in these horrid frozen Andes?"

The first man, eighteen-year-old German-born Hans Wertling, shook his head in bewilderment. "This is not soldering. We'll be swallowed up by these mountains and no one will ever know. I signed on with General Bolívar to drive the Spanish out of New Granada, to face Spanish soldiers on the field, not death by freezing. Why are we doing this? Will anyone ever care?"

They both fumbled for their muskets at the sound of footsteps approaching along the ledge. "You're in these mountains 'cause the general said this is the way we'd go." Burly Sergeant Hernandez towered over them. His voice blasted into them like a snarling sledgehammer. "And you're on this ledge 'cause I put you on guard duty. Now keep your eyes pealed or I'll leave you out here for a week!"

"Yes, sergeant!" Hans and Miguel mumbled.

"And no sleeping!"

"How can we sleep in this freezing nightmare?"

The sergeant started to leave, then stopped. "The main army's holed up a quarter-mile down this trail. We'll be pulling out in the morning, so rejoin your units at dawn."

"If we haven't frozen by then," muttered Miguel.

Hans giggled.

"What was that?" snarled Sergeant Hernandez.

"Nothing, sergeant."

"Do either of you have any supplies?"

Both men shook their heads. Sergeant Hernandez stomped in frustration. "Blast! You tossed everything on the climb like everyone else, didn't you?"

Hans shrugged apologetically. "Climbing hand over hand up the cliffs in the ice and snow, I couldn't carry the supply bags any farther."

Hernandez's finger jabbed through the black night at the two guards. "That's what everyone says. So now we're almost out of food, and most of the ammo's been tossed." Hernandez sighed and softened. "See that mountain peak above us, boys?"

"It's too dark. I can't see a thing," answered Miguel.

"Except for the ice on my mustache," added Hans.

"Well, it's Mount Pisba, over thirteen thousand feet. Tomorrow we cross the pass and start back down. It'll get better."

"It can't get worse," muttered Miguel after the sergeant had left.

Simón Bolívar had started up the mountains two weeks earlier with an army of thirty-five hundred soldiers, five hundred horses for cavalry, fifteen hundred mules to carry supplies, and about one hundred women, all wives of soldiers who had elected to trek with their husbands.

The climb had been brutal and treacherous, often climbing hand over hand up ragged cliff faces and crossing steep, slick ice fields. Three of the women were pregnant and suffered most of all. Still, every person had to carry their own weight. Not even the general got to ride in relative luxury.

Now at the summit, the army seemed shriveled and diminished. Only eighty horses and fewer than a hundred mules had survived the climb. As the mules were lost, supply packs were shifted to the soldiers, making their climb all the more dangerous. Over two hundred men and eight women had died from falls, injury, or cold.

Soldiers who had swaggered so bravely in the lowlands and savanna (plain) now whimpered like frightened children in the howling winds and relentless pounding of the storm at this Mount Pisba camp. Many muttered that they would rather fight buffalo and crocodile bare-handed than set foot in the mountains again.

By Mount Pisba, all the tents had been lost, as had most of the food. They were above timberline and there was no wood for fires. One woman, Sylvia Sanchez, went into labor shortly after dark. In the middle of the night she gave birth to a girl, lying on a bare rock in the swirling sleet. Sylvia lay that night on the stone, rocking her baby, wondering if anyone would survive to remember how this babe came into the world. Her baby was four hours old before there was enough light for her mother to finally see the face of her new daughter.

Sergeant Sanchez had saved three cigars for this occasion. He gave one to General Bolívar, one to the colonel leading his regiment, and one to the captain of his company. But all three were far too soggy to light and disintegrated before the army escaped from the pass.

In the morning, mother and daughter had to continue the march like everyone else. Both survived.

One week later, on July 6, the army staggered below the snow line on their march down the far side of the Andes. No horses and no mules remained. Eighty more men had died, mostly from the cold. Miguel Huerta lost four fingers to frostbite. He had to learn to shoot with his left hand. Hans Wertling lost all the toes on one foot. He limped ever after and called it his "Pisba limp."

Gazing back up at the snow-covered peaks from the warmth of a fire, Hans wondered, "So much terrible loss. Will anyone ever care or remember?"

On August 2 the army of less than three thousand finally crossed into New Granada, tattered, gaunt, bedraggled, but fiercely determined. General Bolívar had said that, if they lost the fight, the only way out was to cross the mountains again.

Spanish General Barreira heard of Bolívar's band of rebels marching so brazenly across his lands. He sent a well-armed force of sixty-five hundred Spanish regulars to squash Bolívar like a worthless bug. These were the same troops who had defeated Napoleon in his attempt to cross the mountains into Spain. These were some of the finest fighting troops in the world.

Sixty miles from the capital of Bogotá at the small village of Boyaca, the two armies met on the sloping fields of Venta Quemada's rambling farm on the morning of August 7. In the thin, cold light of dawn, General Barreira saw a puny line of rebel infantry advancing up the slope.

He ordered a thousand cavalry to ride them down with lances. He ordered three thousand infantry to follow behind with fixed bayonet and kill every last rebel. So grand the Spanish soldiers looked, in long mounted lines, all in perfect blue and white, lances gleaming in the sun, steam snorting from horses' nostrils. At a trot, they started for the helpless rabble at the bottom of the hill.

But halfway down the hill everything changed. The bushes along both sides of the hill exploded in rifle fire. Bolívar had hidden half his force in these lines of bushes with the long, powerful Baker rifles the English and Germans had given him to aid in his fight against their longtime enemy, Spain. Baker rifles were the most accurate long-range rifles in the world.

The perfect lines of advancing Spanish cavalry melted into chaos. Horses and riders fell faster than they could regroup or identify new leaders to replace fallen officers. The Spanish infantry fared little better. Great holes were torn in their lines by volley after volley from the hidden rebel riflemen.

Steadily the small lines of Bolívar's infantry advanced up the slope. Bolívar gave a signal and the concealed riflemen rushed out, fixing bayonets, and swelled his line of infantry. Some of the wives ran onto the field to pick up rifles of the dead and join in the attack. They rushed up the slope into the crumbling lines of Spanish foot soldiers. Retreat for the Spanish soon turned to rout. The mighty Spanish army dissolved.

Bolívar and his men celebrated at Venta Quemada's farmhouse at the top of the long slope that had been the Spanish headquarters. Within a week every Spanish official and soldier had fled New Granada. It was again Colombia, a free nation.

But many bodies lay crumpled and broken on the long slope at Boyaca. Sylvia Sanchez, holding her five-week-old daughter, wept over the body of her slain husband. Hans Wertling limped back down the slope until he found the fallen body of Miguel Huerta.

Kneeling over the body that had been his friend, Hans cried out to the sky wondering if anyone would ever remember the hardship, the suffering, and the sacrifice.

:ʘ ʘ ʘ:

"We will never forget!" Two thousand watts of power blasted the words through huge banks of speakers and across the Bogotá city center plaza. A hundred thousand people heard and cheered on this Independence Day celebration on August 7, 1986.

A political candidate hoping to win election during the voting on this national holiday to celebrate Colombia's independence was making this speech. He had to speak slowly because the huge crowd cheered at almost every phrase. "We will never forget their sacrifice, ... their courage, ... the glorious spirit of Bolívar's small army of freedom fighters. ... Their very names are precious to us. ... Their memory is sacred."

The speeches finished. The voting was completed. The parades were held. Fireworks followed. Another Independence Day celebration was over. And once again, in answer to Hans Wertling's prayer, a grateful and proud nation remembered.

Follow-up Questions to Explore

1. Boyaca commemorates a battle. Can you think of any other celebrations created to honor battles? How else do we honor and remember major victories and defeats in battle and war?

Answer

American celebrations honoring battles and war victories include Cinco de Mayo, Memorial Day, Veterans' Day, and Thanksgiving. Such celebrations remember the events and participants. We also remember by preserving the site of a battle, by erecting monuments, and by turning the sites into parks. U.S. examples include: Gettsyburg in Pennsylvania, Antietam in Maryland, and other Civil War sites; Cowpens Revolutionary War site in South Carolina; the sunken battleship *Arizona* in Hawaii; Custer's Last Stand along the Little Big Horn River in Montana; and hundreds of others. How many such monuments have you seen?

2. Few people thought Simón Bolívar's small, ragtag army would defeat the well-equipped and trained Spanish army. Do you think his accomplishments were unique? Can you think of other countries that have started on underfunded, ill-equipped, shoestring revolutions?

Answer

The United States started with such a revolution. So did the current Cuban government. So have other Central and South American countries. Can you find others?

Suggested Activities

1. Research American battle monuments. Use the library and the Internet to locate as many as you can. Download photos of the monuments. Collect descriptions of the battles and pictures of the participants. Research the history and significance of each battle and battle monument you find.

2. Simón Bolívar won a great victory over a much stronger opponent. The Battle of Boyaca was a classic underdog victory. Research major underdog victories throughout history, both in individual battles (from David versus Goliath on) and in wars (including the American Revolutionary War). List each underdog victory on a sticky note and place them on a world map. In what ways are the underdogs all similar?

Green Corn Festival

A Seminole Nation
Harvest Celebration

At a Glance

EACH OF THE SOUTHEASTERN AMERICAN TRIBES (Creek, Choctaw, Chickasaw, Cherokee, Timucua, and Calusa) have always held a major ceremony as the new corn crop ripened. These are not typical harvest festivals held after harvest has been completed. Rather, the Green Corn Festival is held as corn first ripens ready for picking, but before even one ear has been picked and eaten.

These Green Corn Festivals have served several important purposes besides giving thanks for a successful harvest to come. They have acted, in effect, as New Year's celebrations, since the tribal year is marked from one Green Corn Festival to the next. They served as the annual principal opportunity for the conduct of tribal business, both internal and external. Finally, they served a spiritual purpose. The Green Corn Festival was a time for each individual to purify him- or herself, to seek and bestow forgiveness, and to reestablish harmony within the tribe.

As tribes have integrated into American life, much of importance in festivals such as these has been lost. Business is now conducted by phone, fax, and e-mail. Meetings are only a few hours' flight away. Spirituality is handled through the practice of weekly religious services. Unemployment and economic pressures have changed tribal attitudes toward traditional celebrations.

But until the last forty years, festivals were the foundation of tribal life, the storehouses of the customs and lore, the avenue to tribal roots, heritage, and tradition. This is nowhere truer than for the Seminole Nation of Florida. The Seminole Green Corn Festival is not held every year anymore. Attendance lagged. Many complained that attendees came just for a party and ignored the traditional purpose and significance of the festival.

There is now a move to revive and restore the Seminole Green Corn Festival to its rightful place of importance to the tribe, to each tribal member, and to us all, for we are all made stronger by understanding and honoring each of our many diverse ways to celebrate. Certainly, the Seminole Green Corn Festival is a celebration worth understanding.

Green Corn Festival

One step forward, one step back. Hop-turn. Hop-turn. Shuffle …

"What are you doing?"

"Go away. I'm practicing."

Myron Osceola stood in the doorway watching his friend Billy Wingfeet kick up dust in the long council ceremonial lodge. A thick streak of heat and sunlight stabbed into the cool, dark interior of the lodge through the open doorway. With everyone else in the tribe outside watching the Seminole Nation chief say the prayers of thanks to open the annual Green Corn Festival, the lodge stood empty.

"I'm twelve," said Billy, trying to sound much older as he brushed his dark brown hair out of his face. "It's my year to be named. But I don't have the steps right for the Naming Dance."

"*That* was the Naming Dance?" guffawed Myron. Eleven-year-old Myron Osceola was lanky and quick. A natural runner, jumper, and dancer, he had the speed and agility of a gazelle.

Billy grunted. Myron would never have to worry about what name the council gave him next year.

"Your rhythm is all wrong," added Myron. "Dance the Name Dance that way and they'll name you 'Leadfoot.'"

"It's not funny! The name they give me will be a part of me for all my life."

The lodge, like the surrounding Seminole *chickees* (houses), was built of cyprus poles with interwoven palmetto fronds. Most chickees had open sides. The council lodge, because of the important meetings and ceremonial dances, had closed sides of closely woven palmetto. Over eighty feet long, the lodge had two flap-covered entrances—the women's entrance at the northeast corner, and the men's at the southwest where Myron now stood. Four long rows of wooden benches, raised like minibleachers, stood against the north and south walls. Unraised rows of low, backless benches were stacked against the shorter east and west walls.

"Don't worry so much," said Myron. "Or they'll name you 'Black Cloud.'"

"I said, no name jokes!" snapped Billy.

Myron shrugged. "Sorry. But this is the Green Corn Festival. It's supposed to be a happy time."

Billy said, "My uncles in my mother's clan said it's a solemn time for giving thanks and for becoming pure."

"I say it's a time to play ball. Come on. We haven't had this many kids to play with all year!"

"No," insisted Billy. He was short for twelve and tried to stretch as tall and proud as his lanky friend. "I have to practice. Besides I'm not a kid anymore. I'm going to get my real name tomorrow."

Still standing at the open flap doorway of the lodge, Myron crossed his arms. "It's spooky in here with no fire. I've never been in here before on the first day of the Green Corn Festival when the shaman has rubbed out the old fire."

Billy Wingfeet returned to his halting practice. *One step forward, one step back. Hop-turn. Hop-turn.* "Don't stand there gawking. Either go play or help."

One hour later, dripping sweat on this muggy August afternoon at the Big Cyprus Swamp Seminole Reservation in southern Florida, the two friends threw back the cover flap and stepped outside into the happy atmosphere of a festival, an important council meeting, and a family reunion.

Scattered from Florida to Oklahoma, the Seminole tribe gathers each year at Big Cyprus Swamp Reservation for the Green Corn Festival. Over eight hundred had gathered in this year of 1954, crowded into domed clan chickees fanned out from the council's ceremonial lodge. A small ball field where the grass had been trampled down sat on the south side of the compound.

Beyond in every direction stretched a sea of sawgrass swamp and scattered clumps of cyprus trees with snaking channels of creeping water everywhere. Most of south Florida is a river, a few inches deep, hundreds of miles wide. Occasional raised islands of land, such as the Big Cyprus Swamp Seminole compound, force the water to flow around through deeper channels.

A great crowd of Seminole from the three Florida reservations watched as a shaman lit a new fire and gave thanks. The spark caught, spreading into flame. The flame fanned into fire, the first of the tribal new year. All fires on the reservation had been put out early that morning to mark the end of another year—house fires, the ever-burning council fire, campfires. Now a new fire had been lit, a new beginning, a pure fire to symbolize a renewed purity for the people.

Wearing traditional Seminole dress, the crowd looked like a great rainbow sea of patchwork color to Billy and Myron. Seminole dresses, shirts, and pants were stitched from bands sewn from a colored patchwork of light cotton cloth. Reds, blues, yellows, greens, all in tight, repeating patterns. Many wore wide-brim hats to block out the fierce summer sun. Many of the hats sprouted brilliant heron feathers from their tops.

The Seminole chief was offering a prayer of thanksgiving over the new fire. He chanted thanks to the land for sustenance and life, and sprinkled ground tobacco leaves over the fire. Thick, pungent smoke billowed up and spread across the gathering. He chanted thanks to the crops and to the sun for their good growth, and tossed the first four ears of that year's fresh green corn onto the fire to roast.

Billy could feel the strong pride in the adults at this, their biggest annual gathering. He could feel their sense of community, their excitement at another reunion. But he knew there was a serious side to the festival. The council would conduct important tribal business—policies for dealing with state and federal governments would be decided, past wrongs would be addressed and righted, forgiveness would be bestowed, complaints would be forever settled. All would strive to regain a sense of purity, of balance with nature and for the tribe.

"Come on. Let's play ball," begged Myron.

"You go ahead. I'll be there in a minute," replied Billy. But Billy Wingfeet could not concentrate on ball games or even on the meaning of the festival. *One step forward, one step back. Hop-turn. Hop-turn.* Tomorrow he would be given his tribal name!

As the chief's opening prayer finished, burning coals were carried to each chickee. The shaman carried a flame inside the lodge to relight the council fire. Fires blazed in the shimmering summer heat and festival cooking began. Mounds of corn were roasted and boiled; alligator and beef were roasted for stews; *sofki*, a mashed corn drink, was passed in tall glasses to the men who had fasted in preparation for the dances of the Green Corn Festival. Pots of squash and swamp cabbage were heated and stirred.

As the sun set fiery red over the western swamp, the drums and rattles began to play. "Billy!" called his mother. "Come and eat before the Stomp Dances."

Billy shrugged. How could he eat when tomorrow was such an important day, and when he still feared his clan would be shamed by his dancing?

Rather than watch the twirling dancers with their rattles and elaborate headdresses and costumes, rather than sit with his family and clan and listen to the driving beat of the many pounding drums, Billy sat alone and cross-legged in his mother's chickee.

He sat and he prayed and he concentrated as he had seen his uncles do. He no longer tried to picture each individual step of the Naming Dance; now he tried to picture himself with winged feet flying, soaring across the dance floor, tried to picture smiles and nods of approval on every face on the council and in the watching crowd.

But try as he might, Billy didn't think it was working. He still felt like Billy Leadfoot.

When Billy awoke in the morning, council meetings had already started. The feather dance was about to begin with two rings of dancers spaced around the outside sacred fire. Mosquitoes buzzed in thick swarms. The day felt hot and muggy with no breath of stirring air.

"I made some frybread for you," called his mother as she left to watch the dancers. Billy hungrily stuffed a first bite of the thick, round bread into his mouth.

Then he remembered. Three hours to the Naming Dance. There were only eleven twelve-year-olds this year for everyone to watch. He would never be able to hide in the middle of a dancing crowd. Billy's appetite vanished.

One step forward, one step back. Hop-turn. Hop-turn. Again he tried to picture the steps in his mind and send the message to his feet.

In what felt like a blink, the Naming Dance was announced. The twelve-year-olds were summoned. Billy's heart pounded against his ribs. He didn't dare look at any of his watching clan members or at the other dancers as he stood in the middle of the lodge, waiting. The shaman said prayers for these eleven youngsters who were about to join the tribe as adults and explained the importance of the dance and of the names they would be given by the council.

Quite talking and let's get it over with! shouted Billy inside his head.

The drums began to pound. The rhythm seemed to beat inside Billy's chest and calm his heart. The jangling rattles seemed to lift his troubled spirits.

One step forward, one step back. Hop-turn. Hop-turn.

Eyes squeezed closed, Billy began to dance. He started at the northeast corner of the open lodge floor to honor his mother and her clan. He danced to the southwest to pay respect to his father.

One step forward, one step back. Hop-turn. Hop-turn.

With surprise, almost with shock, Billy realized the dance felt good, that *he* felt good dancing. He cracked open one eye to see if his clan were laughing or turning away in shame.

No! They were nodding approval. Myron cheered from a thicket of watchers on the benches of the lodge's west end. Even Billy's mother and uncles smiled and clapped!

Now Billy felt like a Wingfeet! He sprang into the middle of the dancers feeling like his feet really had sprouted wings. His arms flew with wild triumph, his body and heart soared.

The council elders nodded in recognition and smiled. Another Wingfeet had earned his name. They knew he would. His clan had always been good dancers. A good harvest, good dances, good meetings. It would be another good year.

Follow-up Questions to Explore

1. In this story, a boy worries about the adult tribal name he is going to be given. Would you like to have others give you a name that could never be changed and would always be considered a part of your personality, your very being? Has it already happened to you?

Answer

Didn't someone else (your parents) give you the name you now have? Who created any nicknames you go by, you or friends and family? Discuss these questions in class and compare your answers to those of your classmates.

2. Do you think it is all right for one group of people, such as the Seminole Nation, to have their own celebration where nonmembers are not welcome or allowed? What other ethnic, religious, national, or geographic groups have such celebrations? Are you a member of such a group?

Answer

Discuss these questions in class and compare your answers to those of your classmates.

Suggested Activities

1. Create class names for each student. Make a list of what a name tells us about a person, and why a name is important. Research the meaning of names at the library and on the Internet. Have each student research their own name. Interview parents to learn why and how their first and middle names were picked. Research the family history of your name and other family members who had it before you. Research the general meaning and origin of your name.

2. Have each student create a new name for themselves and explain both why they chose that name and what the name says about them. As a class, pick a name for each student that the class feels best captures the essence of that student. This is what the Seminole people do. Which name do you like better and value more, the one you create yourself or the one given to you by the class? Why?

September

Onam

An Indian Celebration
of a Myth

At a Glance

THERE ARE CELEBRATIONS AROUND THE WORLD based on a legend or myth from a country's distant past. One of the most interesting is Onam, a celebration from the state of Kerela in southwest India. Onam is a time of joy and happiness, of eager anticipation, as are the weeks before Christmas for most Americans. New clothes are bought and worn. Houses are spotlessly cleaned. Bright floral displays are laid out at the doorstep each day.

The source and purpose of all this activity is a legend about a demon king who once ruled Kerela. The people loved their king, but the god Vishnu forced him to leave the lands of the living forever—except for once a year, on the last day of Onam, when the king is allowed to return to his beloved people.

The king's return is the source of the Onam excitement. But more than that, they believe that the king seeks out houses that are the most happy, the most spotlessly clean, the most generous, and (in spirit) visits and blesses these houses. The personal blessings of the king bring peace, joy, and prosperity over the coming year.

 Onam

The wood and glass door of the spice shop opened, clanging the bell mounted above it. For a moment the noises of a busy commercial street crept into the quiet shop and the intense smells of fresh spices crept out.

"Mr …" The primly dressed woman at the door thumbed through her appointment book to make sure she had the name right. Her finger paused at 10 A.M. on the page for September 4, 1977. "Ah, yes. Here it is. Mr. Kistna?" She breathed in the pungent aroma as she stepped forward and extended her hand. "I am Penny Dunsworth."

A slight, wiry man looked up from his ledger book behind the counter. His thick mustache seemed to be held up by a broad, warm smile. His eyes, hiding behind thin, wire-rimmed glasses, seemed far too big and piercing by English standards. "Ahh, hello, Mrs. Dunsworth. I received your letter. Welcome to India." He rose and took her hand.

"I had expected jungles and towering mountains. But this region reminds me more of my visit to the Hawaiian Islands."

"Kerela is a unique region of India, Mrs. Dunsworth. The warm Arabian Sea controls our climate. Our beaches are wide and framed by palm trees. Is this your first trip to Kerela?"

"My first time anywhere in India. I have come to purchase spices."

Stepping from behind the counter, Mr. Kistna stood a good three inches shorter than his new customer. "As you have guessed, I am Raktim Kistna, at your humble service. Do you not find our corner of India a beautiful paradise?"

"Yes, I suppose. But that's not what I noticed most."

"What? Did you not see the sparkling beaches with the towering lighthouse at one end and a grove of over five hundred magnificent palm trees at the other? Did you not see the endless maze of canals and backwater inlets that has earned our city of Alleppey the title of 'Venice of the East'?"

Penny Dunsworth fidgeted, not wanting to offend the man she had traveled five thousand miles to buy from. "Yes, it's all quite lovely, but …"

"*But?*" Raktim repeated. "Didn't you see the brilliant green rice paddy fields surrounded by blue lagoons, like emeralds lying on soft blue velvet? Kerela is the loveliest country on earth!"

"Yes, I'm sure it is," she stammered. "But it was the people that amazed me. I've never seen a place where *everyone* looks so happy."

Mr. Kistna laughed and bowed. "Ahh. Welcome to our Onam celebration, four days of exuberant bliss and joy! The people are happy because they have to be."

"*Have* to be happy?" repeated Mrs. Dunsworth. "I don't understand."

Mr. Kistna motioned to two of his workers. Both bowed with gracious smiles and hurried down a flight of stairs at the back of the shop. "While my assistants bring up the rest of the spice kegs, I will explain Onam.

"Onam is a time of joy and happiness for us. The monsoon rains are over. A bountiful harvest is about to begin. But there is more. Onam is the celebration of a legend. Many centuries ago a demon king, Mahabali, ruled Kerela. He brought peace and prosperity and so was loved by the people.

"But the gods, and especially the great god Vishnu, grew jealous. Vishnu cast Mahabali out and banished him from the lands of the living. But the people of Kerela wailed and lamented for their lost king. Vishnu took pity on them and ever after has allowed Mahabali to return to Kerela for one day each year—Onam."

"But why does that *force* everyone to act happy?" asked Penny Dunsworth.

"Ahh, yes. How shall I put it?" muttered Raktim, tapping one finger against his chin. "Ahh! To us, King Mahabali is much like your Santa Claus. But he doesn't bring physical gifts. His gifts are blessings of peace, joy, and prosperity. And his gifts don't go to everyone each year. Each year, the king is drawn to the cleanest, happiest, most gracious homes. The homes he visits are touched with his blessing.

"During Onam every family tries to present to the world their most cheerful, gracious manners and the cleanest house with the most beautiful floral patterns. Every person wears new clothes—do you like my new madras shirt? We spend money on decorating ourselves and our homes at Onam like you spend money on buying Christmas presents. All to draw the attention of King Mahabali, and receive his blessings."

Mrs. Dunsworth frowned. "The shirt is very nice. But it sounds like you're putting on an act to fool the king."

"Oh, no. Onam is a truly joyous time. But if we remember to share our joy and bounty, the king may visit us. Of course, he doesn't come down the chimney. He is from the spirit world. But when he enters and blesses your house and family, you know it and feel it."

The assistants rolled two kegs off a small lift and pried off the tops. The strong scent of ginger and turmeric flooded the shop.

"Lovely," sighed Penny, breathing deeply. Then she added, "Onam sounds joyous, but very private."

"Much of it is," answered Raktim. "But what would be a celebration without some spectacular public events?"

Penny's eyebrows arched in anticipation, "Such as …"

Raktim's great eyes twinkled behind his glasses. "We'll show you. You have arrived on the perfect day to experience the thrill of Onam!" Then he waved his hands to signal a mistake. "I cannot leave the shop today. Ahh. My daughter will show you. Indiri!"

"I don't want to be a bother."

"No bother at all. Besides, we, too, must do our gracious good deeds. I would like Mahabali to grace *my* house this year."

A twelve-year-old girl with dark skin, straight black hair, and almond-shaped eyes climbed the stairs wearing a brilliant yellow and red sari.

Raktim said, "Indiri, meet Penny Dunsworth. She has never seen the Snake Boat races …"

"I'd love to take her!" interrupted Indiri.

"*Snake* boats?" repeated Penny.

"Indiri, this will give you a good chance to show off your new dress."

Outside on the crowded, narrow streets of Alleppey, Penny asked, "Shall we take my rental car?"

"This is Alleppey, the city of canals," laughed Indiri. "We'll take our boat."

Indiri threaded the small outboard through a maze of canals and backwater channels, some edged by stores and offices and jammed with traffic, like Venice. Some were lined with wide overhanging trees and carpets of emerald green grass and completely empty, like a deserted island paradise.

"How can you remember where you're going?" Penny asked.

"I grew up on the canals," answered Indiri.

Several canals merged into a river. The river emptied into a wide lake. "Lake Vembanad," said Indiri. "The largest lake in all India."

Ahead on the lake Penny saw thick clusters of boats. Back along the shore she saw an endless crowd of people, thick as army ants on the move. Indiri wormed her boat through to the front of the boats gently bobbing on the lake.

Penny stood as tall as she dared in the rocking boat. "What is everyone watching?"

Indiri glanced at her watch. "We are just in time. You will hear them before you see them."

"Hear *what?*"

"The Snake Boats."

"*Snake* boats?" gulped Penny.

For a long moment all was quiet except for screeching gulls and the soft slapping of water against boat hulls. Then, far off, Penny heard muffled singing roll across the lake. "*Kuttanadan punchayile. ...*"

"What are they singing, Indiri?"

"It is the 'Song of Vallamkali,' the song of welcome to the king. The racing rowers are singing. You will see the boats soon—from the left."

The crowd onshore and in the boats either picked up the song, chanting with the rowers, or cheered and waved scarves.

Soon Penny saw tiny dots far off down the lake. "Are those the Snake Boats?" Indiri rose in the boat, chanting, cheering, waving with the rest of the crowd.

In a flash the speeding boats were on them. Thin, sleek, carved-wood hulls with the heads of great serpents carved into the front. Over a hundred rowers were in each boat, each singing at the top of his lungs and straining at the oars. As many as a dozen musicians on each boat were pounding out a rhythm for the rowers with drum and cymbal. The boats seemed almost to fly, skimming along the wave tops.

The crowd went wild, cheering, waving, chanting. The song of welcome seemed to reverberate through the water itself. Penny was thrilled by the dazzling sight of these ten beautifully carved boats hurtling past. The throng of watching boats rocked violently in the wake of the racing ships.

Penny shouted back to Indiri, in order to be heard, "Shouldn't the rowers just row? They'd row faster and win."

After the boats had sped past on their four-mile race down the lake, Indiri said, "They are racing to the far end of the lake. Legend says that is where King Mahabali reenters Kerela each year. They are racing to see who will be first to greet the king. They must be fast, but what is the point of being first if you aren't joyously singing the proper greeting song when you greet the returning king?"

The crowd slowly drifted away from the lake. Indiri guided their boat back into the heart of Alleppey. "There is another sight you should see. If we hurry we will make it."

"Another water show?" asked Penny.

Indiri laughed, her almond eyes dancing with delight. "Elephants do not ride well on the water."

"Elephants?!"

They docked at a downtown side street. A thick mob of people lined the street above them. "We're too late for a good spot here. Come. I know another way."

They skirted along the back of the thick crowd, stacked twenty deep along the wide boulevard. Indiri led the way down a narrow, crooked alley and under a loose board in a fence. "I have a friend who lives in this neighborhood."

Through the loading docks of a warehouse and down another alley, Indiri and Penny emerged onto the wide plaza of a temple—and ran smack into the first of three rows of ten towering elephants. The corner elephant reared back and blasted a mighty trumpet, its trunk accidentally knocking Penny to the ground as it bucked.

"Oh, my! Elephants!" Penny stammered, gazing at the woven gold head plate of the massive animal towering eight feet above her as she scrambled back to the alley entrance.

"Most people line up along the parade route," explained Indiri. "Very few come to the Temple of Pooram to see the elephants get organized. But I like this better."

"Oh, my!" whispered Penny, reliving her close encounter with four tons of gold-plated pachyderm. Each of the thirty elephants wore elaborate gold, silver, and brocade head plates that twined partway down their trunks. On top of each was an ornate saddle. Behind each saddle stood a robed man holding a tall, carefully designed parasol.

"Who rides in the saddles?" asked Penny, brushing the dirt off her knees.

"The king in the middle one, deities in the rest," answered Indiri.

Three five-member bands, called *Panchavadym*, formed in front of the elephants. Each had a trumpet, symbols, and three kinds of drums. On a signal from the center band, all three began to play and the parade lumbered off down the wide boulevard to the wild cheerings of the waiting crowd.

Standing in the street gazing after them Indiri said, "There will be fireworks tonight. But I can't go with you. Our family will be praying at the altar in our house."

"Thank you for a spectacular day," said Penny. "And I hope the spirit of Mahabali visits your house tonight."

Indiri smiled, her wide eyes dancing with delight. "I will let you know."

Follow-up Questions to Explore

1. During Onam, people in Kerela try to be extra happy, extra generous and kind, and extra clean to make the king visit their house. Do you think this is trying to deceive, to fool the king by making him believe they are this way all year long? Do you think you can fool the spirit of an ancient king? Do you try to similarly fool anyone as part of your celebrations?

Answer

Some would say it is an attempt to falsely trick the returning king and shouldn't be done. Others would say Onam gives them a once-a-year excuse to try to be their best, and that it is valuable for them to have a reason to practice being kinder and more generous. Still others would say it doesn't matter what the motives of the people are. It is a good unto itself that, for several weeks each year, people do act better. Which do you believe?

Doesn't acting nice for a couple of weeks to fool the king remind you of American children being on their best behavior in December to fool Santa Claus into bringing more presents?

2. Do you think anyone really believes that there ever was a demon king who ruled Kerela, or that his spirit actually returns once a year to bless a few of the modern citizens? Can you find similar beliefs in other celebrations?

Answer

Many in Kerela do believe. It is part of their faith. In your faith, whatever that faith may be, you have to believe things with no real proof. You accept them on faith and believe that they are true. For you, that makes them true.

A good example is the Japanese celebration, Tanabata Matsuri, the celebration of the myth about the star Vega. Everyone knows that the myth about Vega is a fictional story, but one with important moral truths for them to understand and follow. But most of those same people believe that the household gods, the kami, are real.

Do you believe in Santa Claus? Did you used to? Would you be surprised to learn that many adults believe in Santa Claus—not as a physical person, but as a spirit, as the embodiment of the spirit of Christmas? In this same way, many in Kerela believe in the continued existence of their demon king.

Suggested Activities

1. The Onam myth explains what behavior the people of Kerela value: friendliness, generosity, and cleanliness. Research other mythic stories from other cultures. Can you find myths that support and advocate certain behavior? Make a chart of the myths you find and the attitudes and behavior those myths promote.

2. Research myths. What is a myth? What makes a myth a myth instead of just a story? What are the common characteristics of all myths? How is a myth different from a legend or a history?

3. Create a new myth. Choose one or more behaviors or attitudes the class feels are beneficial and important. Create a myth to support and explain those behaviors and attitudes.

Sukkot

A Jewish
Harvest Celebration

At a Glance

THREE THOUSAND YEARS AGO, Sukkot was the main Jewish holiday. It was then called *he-Hag*, which literally means "the holiday." Back then it was primarily a harvest festival, coming at the end of the growing season. During that long-ago version of Sukkot, farmers set up temporary booths in the fields to stay close to their work during harvest.

Over time, Sukkot and the booths have taken on expanded significance. The booths are now built as temporary "dwellings" in almost every Jewish house for the week of Sukkot. Some actually camp out in these booths. At least two meals must be eaten there during the week.

But modern Sukkot booths, called *sukkah*, remind the family not only of ancient agricultural harvests, but also of two added concepts. First, they are reminders of the forty years the Jewish people wandered the desert after successfully fleeing bondage in Egypt. That was a time when all dwellings were, by necessity, temporary and flimsy, and a time that ended with the Jews' arrival in the fertile lands that are now Israel.

Second, the sukkah reminds the family that we are all part of nature and there is value and joy in simple lives lived in close harmony with nature.

In this way, Sukkot has become both a harvest festival and a time of joyful thanksgiving for the salvation of the Jewish people, like Thanksgiving in America. Its activities revolve around happy family celebrations in and around the sukkah, and equally enthusiastic services in synagogues. Above all, Sukkot has become a time for joy when all other emotions seem to be swept away by feasting and fellowship.

Sukkot

"Papa, can we build the sukkah this year?" Eleven-year-old Erin Mindel stood, fists on hips, feet spread, as if ready for battle, before her father as he read the morning newspaper. Her nine-year-old brother, Ethan, stood behind her, wishing he was as resolute and strong as his sister.

It was the morning of Sunday, September 27, 1981. The leaves were showing their first hints of coming fall colors. The Mindel family lived in a western suburb of Boston. Erin was short, with straight black hair and fiery green eyes. Ethan was taller with curly black hair. But his brown eyes lacked Erin's fire. So she was always the leader. He was always the assistant.

Mr. Mathew Mindel folded his newspaper and cleaned his glasses with a handkerchief as he studied his two children. "So, you want to build our family's sukkah for the Sukkot celebration?"

A sukkah was a light, temporary structure, like a booth, for the family to eat in during the eight-day Sukkot celebration.

Erin nodded, "We do."

After a glance at his sister, Ethan also nodded.

"Do you think you *can* build a sukkah?"

Erin's eyes flashed with determination and pride. "I *know* we can."

Ethan added, "We've helped you build one for the last two years." While Erin bulled her way through life on determination and passion, Ethan relied on cautious logic.

Mr. Mindel slowly nodded, weighing his response. "It's an important job."

Both children nodded.

"You'll have to use real tools and be very careful."

Again they nodded.

Mr. Mindel sighed. "All right. But I want to see your plans, and either your grandfather or I must supervise your work."

"But, Dad," complained Ethan, "you didn't draw any plans last year."

"Agreed," said Erin, quieting her brother's protests. "We'll have the plans ready by lunch." She turned to leave, then stopped. "And this will be our best sukkah ever!"

Mrs. Mindel's father, Grandpa Isaac Herzhaft, pointed at his son-in-law. "That was good, Mathew. That was a good thing you did there." Grandpa Isaac was a short, stooped man with a thick mat of snow-white hair and round belly from years of no exercise. Still, his eyes were sharp and bright, and his mind was quick.

Mr. Mindel shook his head. "I'm not so sure. Building a sukkah is important for Sukkot."

For three thousand years Sukkot had been an important Jewish holiday. In the home, Sukkot revolved around the sukkah. The family would eat in the sukkah, entertain in the sukkah, sometimes even sleep in the sukkah. If the sukkah wasn't built well, Sukkot could be ruined.

Upstairs, Erin and Ethan huddled in Erin's room with paper, calculator, pencils, and ruler. "What do we do?" asked Ethan.

"Design a sukkah," answered Erin.

After a long pause Ethan asked, "How?"

After another pause Erin answered, "Let's get some advice."

Downstairs they found Mrs. Mindel and her father in the kitchen. She said, "I think it's wonderful that you two are gong to build the sukkah this year."

"That's what we came to talk to you about," answered Erin.

Behind her Ethan nodded.

Mrs. Mindel continued. "Building a sukkah is the first of the three great commandments for Sukkot. Since you're doing the first one, Grandpa and I will get the *lulav* and *etrog*."

Erin asked, "Since I'm in charge of ..."

"*We*," corrected Ethan.

Erin sighed. "Since *we* are in charge of the sukkah this year, it's made me think more about the things we do. We've always carried a *lulav* and *etrog*. But why?"

Mrs. Mindel answered, "That's the second commandment for Sukkot. Carry together the four goodly species of plant. Those four are the bitter fruit, *etrog* ..."

"They look like lumpy lemons," interrupted Ethan.

"You're right," laughed Mrs. Mindel. "But *etrog* is supposed to be the fruit of knowledge from the Garden of Eden. The other three are the palm branch, myrtle, and willow. Those three we wrap together to form a *lulav*."

"But what are they for?" asked Erin.

"They are symbols of the harvest. The palm has no fragrance, but has taste in the palm dates. Myrtle has no taste, but a strong fragrance. Willow has neither. *Etrog* has both. They are like the four kinds of people: those who posses knowledge but do no good deeds, those who are ignorant but kind, those who are neither learned nor kind, and those who are both. We hold them together during Sukkot to remind us that the world needs all four kinds of people."

"If those are the first two Sukkot commandments," said Ethan, "what's the third?"

"To be joyful!" answered Grandpa Isaac. "To be filled with joy!"

Both children rolled their eyes. "Grandpa!"

"It's the truth. Look it up in the Torah."

Mrs. Mindel nodded. "That's what the Torah says."

Grandpa Isaac added, "That's what Sukkot is all about. Be kind and generous and joyful—and do good works and deeds; *mitzvoth* we call them."

Erin asked, "But how do we build a sukkah?"

Grandpa Isaac said, "Build a flimsy, temporary home to remind us both of the forty years the Jewish people wandered through the desert and of the farmer's temporary booths for the original Sukkot celebrations."

"Build the walls of any material," said their mother. "But the roof must be of leafy branches. It must provide shade, but still let us see up to the stars at night."

Grandpa Isaac added, "Remember that the sukkah reminds us that a plain, simple life is best."

Their mother continued, "The sukkah must be built where no tree or roof is above it, and it must be single-story." As Mr. Mindel stepped into the kitchen she added, "Oh, and the sukkah must be at least five feet high."

Mr. Mindel muttered, "I must be out of my mind letting them build this alone."

In the garage Erin and Ethan gathered all the scrap lumber they could find. "Since we already have our materials, we'll skip the planning part and just start building and see how far we get," Erin decided.

Stacking two-by-fours, one-by-fours, and wood scraps of different sizes in the backyard, Ethan said, "I feel like the desert nomads of three thousand years ago, building what we can with what we have. Makes me feel like part of history."

They began to hammer, pound, and assemble their structure. At noon, Grandpa Isaac wandered out to inspect their progress.

"Very ... original," he said, hands clasped behind his back as he circled the wobbling structure. "Most people make a rectangular sukkah. Is yours a triangle? No, I see there is a fourth side tucked in over there."

"It was supposed to be a square," explained Ethan. "But the last two sides didn't exactly meet."

"That's not a criticism," said Grandpa Isaac. "I think original is good. And it's fragile—as it's supposed to be." He continued to circle the growing sukkah and nod. "Good and open, too. But you might consider adding a couple of braces."

"What are braces?" asked Erin.

"Angled lengths of wood to keep the vertical poles from collapsing."

"Thanks, Grandpa!"

At 3:30 that afternoon Mr. Mindel got home and all three family adults stepped into the backyard to inspect the sukkah.

There were still no right angles anywhere to be found. One end was too high, and the other sagged toward one corner. One side slanted out at a precarious angle. The whole structure waved like ripe wheat in the light breeze.

Grandpa Isaac exclaimed, "Good! It bends with the wind, just like the human spirit. Flimsy, but not so flimsy we have to worry about it collapsing."

Mr. Mindel gasped. His mouth opened and closed like a fish. His face grew blotchy red. Finally he stammered, "What ... what is *this* supposed to be?"

Mrs. Mindel patted his arm, "Rejoicing is one of the Sukkot commandments. So *enjoy* yourself. It's the law."

Grandpa nodded. "It *is* a might small ..."

Erin asked, "Is it *too* small, Grandpa?"

He studied the petite interior. "Too small for a table, but we can leave the food outside. I think it's just the right size for us."

"We couldn't find any long pieces to make the sides bigger," Ethan explained.

Grandpa Isaac said, "Cozy is good. It connects us with nature and the natural world. And sukkah frailty reminds us of human poverty and suffering."

"This is no sukkah," stammered Mr. Mindel. "This is a disaster!"

Mrs. Mindel said, "No. This is our sukkah." Before her husband could protest again, she said, "There was once a town in Eastern Europe that was so poor they could only afford to build one sukkah. They gathered all their money and sent the rabbi to the city to buy supplies. On his way he saw a man, crying. 'Why do you cry?' asked the rabbi. 'My horse has died,' replied the man. 'I am a delivery man and this horse was my life.' 'How much would a new horse cost?' 'Fifty rubbles,' answered the man."

Mrs. Mindel cleared her throat and continued. "Fifty rubbles was all the rabbi had. Still he gave the money to the man to replace the dead horse. When he returned to his village, the people were outraged because they would have no sukkah for Sukkot. But the rabbi said, 'The whole world is going to make blessings in a sukkah. This year we will make our blessings over a dead horse.'"

"I like that story," said Grandpa Isaac.

Mr. Mindel left, shaking his head.

Mrs. Mindel said to her children, "As you start on the roof, children, remember that Sukkot is a joyous time. Sing while you work."

"I'm proud of your efforts, your *mitzvahs*," said Grandpa Isaac. "And your father will be, too, once he really studies it. Just remember, extra bracing never hurts."

Before sunset Erin and Ethan trooped back inside, bone weary, covered with sweat. "We finished."

Ethan looked worried. "The Torah says a sukkah must be easily put up and taken down. I don't think we did it right. This one was real hard to put up."

Mrs. Mindel peered out the back kitchen window. "But it will be *real* easy to take down."

The next evening the Mindel family gathered for their first Sukkot meal in the sukkah. The structure still drooped and slanted. But it glowed with the love and energy of its building and its decorating. Paper flowers and doves hung from the roof. Pictures were taped around the leaky walls. A green tarp and old rug were laid out on the floor.

Mrs. Mindel said, "Lovely work, children."

Grandpa Isaac said, "We can all fit in here if we squeeze a bit. No spreading out. This is definitely togetherness time."

Mrs. Mindel added, "I put up a card table next to the sukkah. We'll leave the food outside."

As plates were filled and passed, Mr. Mindel said, "If someone would get their elbow out of my nose, I'd like a bite of stuffed artichoke. ... That is, if someone would feed me. I can't move either of my hands."

As he munched on the bite Erin fed to him, Mr. Mindel finally smiled. "This was a great effort children, a true *mitzvah*." Then he laughed at the cramped quarters. "This is a Sukkot we'll always remember!"

Erin and Ethan both glowed. "We sure will. This is the best Sukkot ever!"

Follow-up Questions to Explore

1. In this story two children build a very inadequate version of a structure that is essential to a celebration. Have you ever tried to build or make something for one of your celebrations and, even though you tried as hard as you could, done a lousy job of it? Did that ruin the celebration? Do you think it's all right for children to get to participate in this way in celebrations, or should the work be left for adults who can do it better?

Answer

Discuss these questions in class and compare your answers to those of your classmates.

2. Sukkot revolves around something the family builds, a sukkah. Do any of your celebrations revolve around things you build or make?

Answer

Discuss this question in class and compare your answer to those of your classmates. If you're struggling to think of any, what about Valentine's Day cards, a Maypole, Thanksgiving dinner, or a Christmas tree?

Suggested Activities

1. How many of the students in your class have ever built a clubhouse or tree house? In groups, or as a class, design the "perfect" tree house. What kind of tree would you use? What would the tree house look like? What would it have in it? What kind of wood would you use? Draw a picture and building plans for this tree house. Now design a tree house you think you could really afford and build. What is the difference between these two designs?

OCTOBER

Ch'ung Yeung Chieh

A Chinese
Historical Celebration

At a Glance

SOME CELEBRATIONS ARE CONDUCTED IN GREATEST SERIOUSNESS. Some seem a mere excuse for fun and play. Ch'ung Yeung Chieh (the Chinese kite-flying ceremony) looks like one of the latter. However, Ch'ung Yeung Chieh commemorates, and reenacts, a most serious and sad event in Chinese history.

To watch Ch'ung Yeung Chieh is to watch families swarm to the tops of high hills and spend the day flying kites. These are not ordinary kites. These are elaborate, giant kites painted in a rainbow of the brightest colors and fashioned into every imaginable shape. Many are built with wires, tubes, and even flutes and gourds to hum, whistle, wail, blow, and chime while they fly.

Beyond displaying their kites, each flyer is engaged in aerial combat. Ch'ung Yeung Chieh is a day of kite dog fighting in which each kite flyer tries to either knock down all other kites or cut opponents' kite strings with his own.

The last kite flying is the winner. All who watch or participate spend a delightful day. And maybe, during the excitement and fun, some remember the two-thousand-year-old tragedy that started the celebration.

Ch'ung Yeung Chieh

Tsuan Chou Chi eagerly greeted his eight-year-old son, Kam Hong, at first light in the family's small cinder-block house on the outskirts of Foochow (Fuzhou), China. Outside, a crisp, clear morning was emerging this October 3, 1987.

"And how are you, my son, on this day of the chrysanthemum moon, the day of the double ninth?" Chou Chi's eyes sparkled with excitement. He repeatedly rubbed his hands together in anticipation.

"What's the double ninth?" asked Kam.

"The ninth day of the ninth moon. The day of Ch'ung Yeung Chieh."

"Kite-flying day!" repeated Kam. The words washed the sleep from his round face leaving an eager glow to match his father's.

"First breakfast, Kam Hong. Then we must dress and hurry to Fei-fang Hill."

Father and son both gulped their breakfast of soup, vegetables, and rice. Then Chou Chi carried a wooden chest from a tall cabinet. With both hands he carefully raised the intricately carved lid with its picture of the emperor flying eight kites while he sipped warm plum wine.

From inside Chou Chi lifted two curved claws, each fastened to a leather thong. Placing one around his neck, he handed the other to Kam.

"The claw of a tiger to make us strong."

Next he lifted two polished peach stones, also on long leather thongs. "An amulet of peach stone to ward off misfortune."

Next came two bent nails. "Tie the nail of a coffin around your ankle to protect you from accidents."

Chou Chi paused and rubbed his hands before reaching into the box a last time. "Something new I have just been able to purchase. Jade amulets, to bring us the most powerful good luck."

Kam held up the polished green gemstone to the morning light before slipping his around his neck. "Father! These are beautiful!"

"Jade is the stone of the seven virtues. Wearing jade, we'll be sure to triumph!"

By this time Kam's six-year-old sister was also up, rubbing her eyes. Their mother had been up since well before dawn working on the picnic lunch the family would eat during the kite-flying ceremony.

"And now for our new kite," announced Chou Chi. "I finished repainting it last night."

Chou Chi carried a monstrous paper winged tiger from the back room. Sharp claws and fangs of glittering red streamers trailed off one side. The eyes were the color of glowing jade. The body was painted with curving stripes of yellow, orange, and black. The wings were iridescent red.

"Oh, my!" breathed Kam. "It's a magnificent tiger, Father." Kam feared if he reached forward to touch the beast it would snap his hand off, so fierce and real did it look.

"Look here," directed Chou Chi, holding the kite over his head and pointing to five bamboo tubes he had tied into the string rigging underneath. "These will howl like a tiger on the prowl once they catch the wind! This tiger might just *frighten* the other kites out of the sky."

Kam still stared, unable to move. "Oh, my!" he muttered, unable to absorb the enormous grandeur of their kite-beast.

"Now feel our new kite string," commanded Chou Chi.

Kam reached out and rubbed his hand along the thick string. "Ow! It's too rough. It almost cut my hand."

"It's a new Japanese high-strength string," chortled Chou Chi. "You'll tear other kite strings to shreds with this line. You'll down hundreds of other kites *this* year!"

"Oh, my!" repeated Kam, visualizing how wonderful he would look in another hour controlling this monster kite with his own hands as it soared through the sky devouring other hapless kites.

Soon father and son, mother and daughter, carrying the tiger and family picnic between them, joined a long line of families marching to the top of Fei-fang Hill, one of the highest of the grassy hills surrounding Foochow. The top offers a breathtaking view of Foochow, the winding Minjiang River valley, and even the East China Sea far off to the east.

Each family carried a huge kite—some shaped like owls, some like turtles or dragons, some like giant boxes, some like giant fish, some like birds or butterflies. From above, the procession must have looked like a parade of brightly colored monstrous animals crawling slowly to the hilltop.

"Why can't we fly kites from a city park?" panted Kam.

"This is Ch'ung Yeung Chieh, the festival of kite flying and of high places. We march to the hilltops because two thousand years ago a simple man in Foochow named Huan Ching was pupil to the famous magician Fei-Ch'ang-Fang. On this day the magician told Huan to run with his family and prized possessions to the hilltop without delay.

"Huan tried to convince his neighbors to flee also. But it was a clear, calm day and they laughed at him. By the time he gathered his family, there was no time to collect possessions. The family barely made it to high safety before a flash flood roared down the valley, killing every person and animal, destroying every house and tree.

"We go to hilltops to commemorate Huan Ching's escape from death. ... That and because hilltops are a great place to fly kites."

Kam asked, "And why do we fly kites this day?"

"Huan Ching survived, but he lost everything in the disaster. Exactly one year later, he returned to the hilltop with a kite. It was said that kites can fly misfortune away into the sky. Huan gave all his sorrow and misfortune to a kite and flew it from a hilltop all day long.

"We fly kites to honor Huan. ... That and because kite flying is fun."

As the family neared the top, Kam asked, "And why do we have kite wars?"

"Kite wars," laughed Chou Chi, "have no historical meaning. They evolved over the years just because they are fun!"

The sky above Fei-fang Hill was already full of frogs, centipedes, dragons, owls, and birds. An eerie wail from noisemakers attached to the kites floated across the crowd, eagerly watching as kites dipped and climbed in the stiff breeze.

Wearing gloves to protect his hands, Kam held the string while Chou Chi raised the mighty tiger over his head and angled it into the wind. The bamboo tubes began to moan, the wings to flutter, and Kam's tiger leapt into the air. Streamer claws and fangs snapped in the wind as the tiger climbed hungrily into the crowded sky.

The crowd pointed and cheered the new tiger. Then they gasped as an enormous box kite took to the air, so big it took three men to control the strings and keep it from flying away. As big as a small house, the red-and-yellow monster box seemed to crash straight through smaller kites as it muscled its way into the sky.

"Stay away from that one, Kam Hong," warned Chou Chi. "It could tear our tiger to pieces."

And so the kite wars began.

Flyers tried to maneuver their kites to cross strings with another kite. Then the flyer would pull and vibrate his string to cut the string of the opponent's kite. It takes great skill to cut through a kite string in this way. Some flyers worked their kites high into the sky and then pulled them into a steep nose dive, crashing straight down onto another unsuspecting kite and knocking it from the sky.

Each time a kite fluttered to the ground, cut or knocked out of the competition, the crowd appreciatively cheered the skill and effort of the fallen kite flyer.

Kam banked his tiger to the left and crossed strings with a rainbow-bright owl. With quick, jerking tugs, Kam sawed his kite string against the owl's.

The owl's flyer tried to bank left and escape. Kam banked with him, still sawing, until with a sharp snap the owl broke loose from its flyer's string and fluttered to the ground.

Kam's tiger roared and swooped right, searching for another victim.

"There's a dragon below and to your right," cried Chou Chi. "Get him!"

Kam pulled on his kite string. The tiger roared across the sky and crossed strings with a fearsome-looking dragon. Both flyers jerked on their strings, trying to cut the other's line.

"Watch out for the box kite!" cried Chou Chi.

The monstrous box kite lumbered through the air and crossed strings with Kam. The box's four thick control strings seemed to surround Kam's one.

Kam's tiger was trapped between the dragon's string on one side and the giant box's lines on the other.

"Pull! Dip lower! Slide out!" yelled Chou Chi.

Kam curved his tiger kite hard against the dragon's string and pulled with all his might. Snap! The dragon's string broke. Kam yanked hard the other way. His tiger dove left and curved away from the giant box.

The four-person box kite team also pulled hard to the left, following Kam's fleeing tiger. Kam pulled right and dipped his tiger into a dive. The box tried to follow but lost its hold on the wind and fluttered for an instant helplessly in the sky.

Kam had escaped.

The crowd cheered its approval of his maneuver.

The day wore on. Fewer and fewer kites soared through the gusty winds. The sun circled around the hill to cast the kites' long shadows across Foochow below. Kam's father fed him the special *teng-kao* cakes his mother had made for their picnic. These cakes were made of sticky rice pastry filled with spiced meats and fruits and then steamed.

The cakes warmed Kam's stomach and eased the ache in his arms from struggling against tiger and wind all day.

Then Kam saw an opportunity. The great box was attacking a fish kite. Kam swooped his line across two of the box's control strings and began to jerk his line to cut through those strings. Just as the fish's line snapped, so did two of the box's four lines.

The mammoth box lurched to the right and shuddered in the sky as its team of flyers struggled to compensate for the loss of two strings. Kam's tiger dipped right and attacked the third of the box's strings.

Snap! Before the box flyers could regain control, that third string broke under the attack of Kam's mighty tiger. The box fluttered out of control and, like a wounded duck, sank to the ground.

The crowd roared. Kam's tiger soared into the sky, roaring with the crowd through its bamboo voice.

"Well done, Kam!" cheered his father. "With the great box gone you will triumph for sure."

A fight high in the sky between a caterpillar and a butterfly sent the losing butterfly spiraling toward the ground far below. *Crash!* The butterfly smashed straight down onto Kam's tiger, snapping the wood supports for one wing. The wounded tiger hung in the air for a moment as if clawing for a hold on the sky. Then, its back and wing broken, it sank with a final eerie moan to the grass.

Kam stood, stunned, unable even to blink as he stared at his fallen champion.

His father chuckled, "That is the way of things. The tiger rules the heavens one minute and is brought down by the flutter of a butterfly the next." Then he added, "At least, that is certainly the way of Ch'ung Yeung Chieh."

Chou Chi lifted his son's chin to ward off any tears. "You were a magnificent kite flyer today, Kam Hong, the best on this hill. I couldn't be prouder of you. This has been a glorious day. Come, let's salute the kites that remain in the air and head for home. And remember, we are far luckier than poor Huan Ching. We have a home, a town, and our possessions to walk home to."

As the family carried their broken tiger and empty picnic basket down Fei-fang Hill, Kam added, "And we have a whole year to make our tiger even better than before!"

Follow-up Questions to Explore

1. While other elements of Ch'ung Yeung Chieh are symbolic of historic events, the kite wars have no historic significance. They are just for fun. Do you think it's all right for elements of a celebration, or a whole celebration, to have no purpose other than fun?

Answer

Discuss this question in class and compare your answers to those of your classmates. Isn't April Fool's Day just for fun? Much of the traditional May Day celebration is also. So is Holi in India. What other "just-for-fun" celebrations can you think of?

2. Ch'ung Yeung Chieh recalls a natural disaster in Chinese history, a time when a massive flash flood killed thousands of people and destroyed whole villages. Do you think people should be more serious and somber during a celebration remembering such a tragedy? Why or why not?

Answer

Discuss these questions in class and compare your answers to those of your classmates.

Suggested Activities

1. Research kites. What makes a kite fly? Why are they designed and shaped the way they are? How many possible designs are there? Why do kites usually have a tail? Build or purchase kites and hold kite-flying contests.

2. Research past natural disasters in your state or county. What happened? Why? Has anything been done to prevent the same type of disaster from happening again? How is this disaster and its victims remembered?

Pirate Week

A Cayman Islands
History and Culture Celebration

At a Glance

MANY CELEBRATIONS HONOR THE HISTORY AND HERITAGE of a country's culture. Pirate Week in the Cayman Islands is such a celebration. It is a relatively new festival, started in 1977. When first created, one of its main purposes was to increase tourism.

But celebrations take on a life of their own. Pirate Week, held near the end of October each year, has quickly grown to be more a celebration of the unique culture of these Caribbean islands than a re-creation of the long-gone pirate days. Certainly pirates were a part of the Cayman Islands' cultural history. But honoring a proud cultural past has steadily pushed its way to the fore of Pirate Week planning and events. As it has, the celebration has strengthened, and the role and contributions of buccaneers and pirates to the culture are being better understood and honored.

Celebrations evolve to meet the needs of the people. Reconnecting with our cultural heritage is one strong need we fulfill through celebrations. Pirate Week has evolved into such a festival.

Pirate Week

A light onshore breeze blew in from the white puffs of cotton that dotted the mid-morning sky on October 28, 1994. A warm sea lazily lapped against the sparkling ribbon of beach as if the ocean, too, were on vacation here and wanted some time to relax. Two women walked side by side, their feet squeaking in the powdery sand.

One was tall, white-haired, and deeply tanned from years of living on these tropical islands, and walked with long, easy strides as if soft sand was the easiest thing in the world to walk on. The other was short, eleven years old, had straight brown hair she wished would curl, overly long and gangly arms and legs, and had recently been fitted with braces that still caused her cheeks to flush with embarrassment every time she smiled or laughed.

"I'm glad you have finally made it to Grand Cayman Island for a visit, Katherine," said the older woman.

"My dad's been looking forward to Pirate Week for months, walking around the house saying, 'Avast ye lubbers!', 'Arrrr, maties!', and 'Yo-ho-ho and a bottle of rum.'"

The older woman laughed, "Even as a boy, your father loved pirates far more than cowboys or space."

"Grandma Samantha ..." began eleven-year-old Katherine Waller.

"My friends call me Sam," interrupted her grandmother. "Now that you're eleven, you should, too."

Katherine smiled and repeated, "Sam." Then she remembered her braces and shut down her smile. "*My* friends call me Kathy instead of Katherine."

The older woman tilted her head, thinking. "If you don't mind, I'll call you Kate. It's a stronger name. A visit to these islands during Pirate Week calls for powerful names."

"Sam," Kate started again, "why do you live way down here?"

"I like the warm climate. I love the ocean. The water's more beautiful here than anywhere else on earth. And we have a family link to the Cayman Islands."

"We do?"

As they rounded a curve in the beach sand gave way to ragged clumps of rock. "We've reached Pull-And-Be-Damned Point, named by desperate sailors who had to row with all their might past these rocks before the current smashed their boat against jagged coral reefs. There are strong currents and dangerous reefs in these waters. Now it's time to turn back."

Katherine started to ask more about the point's name, then screamed. "A monster!"

"It's just a turtle, Kate," laughed Sam.

"I *know* turtles," said Kate. "They're small and cute. You hold them in your hand and put them in glass bowls."

"We have *big* turtles—sea turtles. That one's probably six hundred pounds and perhaps eighty years old."

Kate stared, flabbergasted. "It's almost as big as my mom's car."

Sam said, "Columbus named these islands the Tortoise Islands. Twenty years later someone changed the name to 'Cayman' when they saw a couple of crocodiles, or caymans. Our turtles were a big part of why the pirates came here."

Curving palm trees leaned out over the beach like carefully planted shade umbrellas as Kate and her grandmother headed back up the beach toward Georgetown. Kate asked, "Did pirates *really* live here, or is this just a hokey festival dreamed up to make tourists come?"

"Look around you, Kate," answered Sam. "See any hills or mountains? No. These low-lying islands were the perfect anchorage for pirates. They were hard to spot and they offered water, shelter, meat and eggs, and …"

"There were cattle here?" interrupted Kate.

"No. *Turtles*. Lots of turtles. And finally, they offered privacy and open land for hiding treasure."

Kate gasped, "There's buried treasure here?"

"Tons of stolen gold, silver, and jewels were buried here. Who knows how much remains? Most of the pirates who buried it were captured and killed before they spent a single doubloon."

As they walked, Kate dreamed of coconut-hard, yellow-toothed pirates dragging heavy chests of doubloons and pieces of eight across this very beach.

"Not this beach," corrected Sam. "Most of the pirates hid their booty either on the East End or on Little Cayman Island. There was a regular British colony and town here at Georgetown. Pirates, buccaneers, and privateers only stopped here to buy—or steal—supplies."

"With cannon blazing?" asked Kate.

"Sometimes."

Kate said, "You said we had a family connection with the islands. Was there a pirate in our family?"

"Close," answered Sam who chuckled at the excited gleam in Kate's eye. "Exciting to think there's pirate blood in your veins, isn't it?"

Kate nodded. "My dad would be thrilled."

"It was my great-great-great-great-great-great-grandmother who moved here from England in the early 1700s. Now, at that time most of the pirates were really privateers—men with their own ships who raided the ships and outposts only of their declared enemies. Most privateers and buccaneers in these waters were the sworn enemies of Spain. That made them more or less allies of the English. One pirate, Henry Morgan, was knighted by King Charles II for all the Spanish ships he sunk and Spanish towns he sacked.

"But life and times were hard in the late 1600s and early 1700s. One privateer after another realized there was no need to *buy* supplies, even with stolen money, when they had the power to *take* them. Privateers became pirates and plundered whomever and wherever they wanted. But few attacked Georgetown and Bodden Town here on the Cayman Islands because this is where most called home.

"The fiercest of all the pirates was Edward Teach, called Blackbeard. He specialized in being cruel, in terrorizing. And he was very successful at it. Blackbeard was the first to use a black pirate flag."

"I thought they were all black," said Kate.

"Until Teach, they were red—blood red. He thought black looked more evil. His clothes, beard, and flag were all black. Blackbeard had two hideouts, one on the East End and one on Little Cayman.

"Now we come to my great-great-great-great-great-great-grandmother. She became a minder for Edward Teach."

"What's a minder?" interrupted Kate.

"A treasure minder, a local who was trusted by the pirates and was paid to watch over treasure stores while the pirate was away. It's said her house was torn apart board by board and her yard was dug up twenty feet deep when she died. They never found a penny."

"It's still buried somewhere?"

Sam shrugged and sighed. "All those who know died long centuries ago … Ah. We're back to home."

Nestled in a grove of acacia and palm trees, Sam lived in a one-story white wood house with a wide, wraparound porch and green shutters framing each window. Kate's father called to them from the porch, "Arrrrr, ye swabs. I'll runs ye up the yardarm!"

Kate rolled her eyes. Sam patted her hand. "Humor him. Remember, it's in his blood."

Sitting at the porch table, Mr. and Mrs. Waller were pouring over Pirate Week schedules as if they were treasure maps.

"Look at all these activities, Kathy. We'll never be able to do it all," said Mrs. Waller.

"It's Kate," said Kate, feet planted, eyes glinting in a strong and powerful way.

"What is?"

"My name. Kate's a more powerful name and fits with the image of a pirate queen."

"I see …" said Mrs. Waller, though the look on her face said she didn't really see at all. She turned to her mother-in-law. "What's a 'caboose cooking' demonstration?"

"A unique local style of outdoor cooking," answered Sam. "Sort of our version of a barbecue. You really must try some of the traditional local dishes: conch stew, coconut 'rundown' tarts, and fish tea."

"What about turtle?" asked Kate. "That's what the pirates ate."

"And ate most of them up, I'm afraid. There are precious few turtles left and those are protected."

"Are the thatching and rope-making classes worthwhile, ye scurvy scum?" asked Mr. Waller.

Kate groaned. Sam laughed. "And the mahogany squaring. Those were all crafts developed right here to support the sailing-ships industry."

"You mean the pirates," said Kate.

"Not just pirates. Any ships who could pay were welcome in Georgetown harbor. Some of the finest masts, ropes, and rigging in the world were made here."

Mrs. Waller said, "I never knew there was such a unique culture on these islands."

Sam answered, "The Cayman Islands were the only place where pirate and British colonial cultures mingled. Pirates represented a big part of the local economy. It helped us grow in a unique way."

"I'm sold, ye bilge rats," said Mr. Waller, rattling a pretend sword. "Arrrr, we be settin' sail fer the East End Heritage Center, says I."

Kate sadly shook her head. "Dad, open your eye. You don't wear a patch." Then she added, "I want to poke around downtown. Besides, I don't think I can take much more of Captain Dad."

Downtown alone, Kate sat on a stone wall called Drummond's Wall, built as a last line of defense against marauding pirates. She gazed across the clear and dazzlingly blue waters of the harbor.

Kate closed her eyes and saw the billowing sails of a three-masted ship with a fluttering red flag with skull and crossed sabers flying from the main mast.

A pirate ship was attacking the harbor!

On board, the crew of grizzled buccaneers opened the gun ports and wheeled fifteen loaded cannon into the breeches.

"Look lively, ye swabs!" cried the captain, pacing the deck. "Muskets to the riggin'! Move ye fo'c'ale scum afore I shoots ye meself!"

Barefoot and tattered men, tough as nails, fierce as typhoons, scrambled up the rigging carrying long, smooth-barrel muskets.

"Helm, swing her around fer a broadsides," cried the captain.

"Aye, Captain Kate. Swingin' hard to port."

The guns be primed and ready, Cap'n Kate," reported the head gunner, Grizzly Slasher.

"Fire!" bellowed Captain Kate, her straight brown hair billowing out behind her like a banner in the stiff wind.

Fire belched from fifteen cannon on the starboard side. Thick gray smoke obscured the ship. The thunderous explosion roared like a shock wave across the harbor. Fortress walls, moored ships, and harbor buildings dissolved in the mighty blast of pirate guns.

"Give 'em another broadside!" cried Captain Kate. "Fire!"

Again the cannon roared. Cannonballs screeched across the harbor to demolish the town defenses. The Georgetown fortress was reduced to a blazing ruin.

"Helm, bring us in to the docks!" yelled Captain Kate, shaking her blood red saber at the terrified town. "We'll burn every building!"

"Arrrrr!" cried the crew, unsheathing saber and long knife. "She's the fiercest pirate of them all," said one to his mate.

"Aye, and the only pirate who wears silver teeth!"

"Cap'n," called the mate. "It's a message from the town."

"Do they surrender?" growled Captain Kate. "We'll sack the town anyway."

"No, cap'n. It be yer parents a-callin'."

"Kathy? … Kath … er Kate. Are you daydreaming?" Kate's mother shook her shoulder to get her attention.

"What? Oh, just thinking, Mom."

"We hurried back because there's a mock pirate attack scheduled for 4:30. Doesn't that sound like fun?"

Kate smiled and shook her head. "I feel like I've already seen that part. I want to explore the East End with Sam and do some *digging*."

Follow-up Questions to Explore

1. Do you think it's all right to celebrate something that was more bad than good, like the pirates? Were there aspects or elements of the pirates and buccaneers that you would call more good than bad?

Answer

Discuss these questions in class and compare your answers to those of your classmates.

2. Why were many of the pirates called buccaneers?

Answer

The little dome-shaped smokehouses where natives on Hispaniola Island smoked the meat of wild cattle and boar were called *bouccanes*. Those who smoked the meat were called *boucaniers*. The smoked meat was called *boucanee* (which is the origin of the word for our breakfast favorite, bacon). Pirates bought vast stores of this dried, smoked meat since it would keep during long voyages at sea without refrigeration. Over time, the pirates began to be called by the name of the meat they so frequently bought and ate.

Suggested Activities

1. Research fictional and real pirates and plan a pirate day in class. Create treasure maps for treasure you hide. Research pirate clothes and make simple costumes. Research pirate foods, the hearty fare that wouldn't spoil during long voyages through the tropics with no refrigeration, and eat pirate meals. Collect and read aloud pirate stories and books.

November

Day of the Dead

A Mexican Celebration
of Family Rememberance

At a Glance

CALLED DIA DE LOS MUERTOS, THE DAY OF THE DEAD falls on the date of the modern Christian celebration of All Souls Day, November 2, one day after the celebration of All Saints Day on November 1, which follows All Souls Eve (known as Halloween) on the night of October 31.

It would be more correct, however, to say that All Souls Day falls on the Day of the Dead. For the Day of the Dead celebration in Mexico predates any Christian celebrations. The celebration harks back to an Aztec festival honoring the goddess Mictecacihuatl, the "Lady of the Dead." Catholic priests moved the Mictecacihuatl celebration to coincide with All Souls Day as part of an effort to convert the Native people to Christianity.

It is interesting that Day of the Dead and our Halloween, two celebrations honoring dead spirits, fall on virtually the same day. They are, however, almost exact opposites. Halloween focuses on scaring away evil spirits and on creating fear and frights through spirits, ghosts, and goblins. The Day of the Dead is a joyous celebration of life to which all family members, those now living and those now dead, are invited. There is no sense of fear in the Day of the Dead celebration. It is a happy, playful family and community celebration.

In recent years, the Day of the Dead celebration has become less important in urban centers of Mexico, but in smaller, rural towns it is still a major annual event.

Day of the Dead

Clareta Menendez nodded with satisfaction at the large blob of dark dough on the table before her. She brushed several loose hairs out of her face with the back of her hand because her fingers were still covered in flour.

"Why is the bread so dark, mama?" asked five-year-old Pepe, eagerly licking the dough from his fingers.

"It's not *bread* yet. It's just dough," corrected his six-year-old sister, Aleta. The Menendezes named their daughter "Aleta," which means "winged," in hopes it would help her soar through life with the ease of a bird. But Aleta was by far the most serious and solidly grounded of the whole family.

"It's pan de muertos ["bread of the dead"]. It's a special bread, Pepe," explained their mother. "It's dark because we used special, dark flour, and because I put in extra molasses to make it sweet."

"Sweet? Let's eat some now," begged Pepe.

"It's not bread yet," answered Aleta. "We can't eat it while it's still dough."

"*I* can," smiled Pepe.

Their mother laughed and again brushed back the few scraggling hairs that had escaped from her barrette. The first few flecks of gray tinged her coal black hair. She explained, "Pan de muertos is for the Dia de los Muertos [Day of the Dead] celebration tomorrow. We won't eat any of it until after we visit the cemetery."

The Menendezes were one of the thousand families living in the mountain town of Jalpa, which clung to the eastern side of the Sierra Madre Mountains along the Santiago River, forty miles up from Guadalajara. By early November, several of the higher peaks were dusted with snow. The Jalpa cemetery covered the top of a lovely hill just above town. From there visitors had a breathtaking view of mountain peaks, gurgling river, and long, sloping valley.

"Will dead people really eat the bread, mama?" asked Pepe, suddenly worried. "Will they eat it all up?"

"The bread will make the dead feel more comfortable and welcome on their special day. Don't worry, Pepe, you'll get to eat plenty tomorrow."

Relieved, Pepe smiled and turned back to licking dough off his fingers. Pepe's and Aleta's teenage brother, Carlos, rushed in. If anyone in the family should have been named "Aleta," or winged, it should have been Carlos. He flew through life like a racing eagle. "Is my costume ready, mama?"

"Not yet," she answered. "If you're in such a rush, mend it yourself."

"I can't fix that big a tear! *You* have to."

Mrs. Menendez sighed. "All right. But be more careful this year."

"Careful?" laughed Carlos. "On the Day of the Dead? It's supposed to be wild!"

Six-year-old Aleta scowled, deep in thought. "If they are dead and we can't see them, how do you know they come to visit on the Dia de los Muertos?"

"We *believe* that they do," answered her mother. "Several times I have *felt* your great-grandmother sitting beside me. I could almost hear her laugh."

Aleta shook her head. "I think cemeteries and dead people are creepy."

"Oh, no," said her mother. "They are our ancestors, our family. And they aren't really dead. Death is a door between two lives. The cemetery is like a doorway. On the Day of the Dead, we go to the doorway and invite our loved ones to join us for a celebration of life. For a few hours our whole family is together again in spirit. There's nothing creepy about it."

"Of course there is," protested Carlos. "Wait till you see me in my skeleton costume. I'll be the creepiest ever!"

Mr. Menendez stood in the kitchen doorway. A short, thick man with oversized, callused hands, he had worked in the fields his whole life. "That's what I love about the Mexican people. We can make fun of anything, anytime. You'd think that honoring our departed on Dia de los Muertos would be religious and serious."

He quickly added, "And it is … partly. But, you watch, most of the town will be laughing, poking fun at death with Carlos tomorrow."

"I'll mend your costume before I go to sleep," Mrs. Menendez said to Carlos.

Aleta said, "He wants to look perfect for his girlfriend."

Pepe giggled, "Carlos has a girlfriend. Carlos has a girlfriend."

Carlos turned beet red and stomped out of the kitchen.

In the morning the whole family, along with most other families in Jalpa, climbed the short hill to the cemetery. Each family member wore their best clothes, the women wearing elaborately embroidered blouses. Each person carried a lit candle as they climbed the winding path under gray, cloudy skies. Carlos and Mr. Menendez also struggled with heavy baskets and boxes of food.

It was a happy, not a solemn time. Many families sang songs as they walked. Flutes softly played. Some told stories of dead ancestors. The morning air sliding down from the mountains felt cool and brisk.

The Menendezes stopped at the graves of Mr. Menendez's parents. There they laid cut marigolds to outline the shape of a large cross and placed candles at each corner. They sprinkled marigold petals in the middle to create a brilliant yellow carpet over the graves.

They spread out a picnic blanket nearby. On it, Mrs. Menendez spread plates of tamales, corn pies, pots of beans and rice, bowls of limes and avocados, and a basket with pan de muertos. "These are some of your grandparents' favorite dishes," explained Mrs. Menendez.

"Did you bring the chocolate?" asked Mr. Menendez.

"My *tia* and *tio* [grandmother and grandfather] liked chocolate?" asked Pepe.

"No. But your father does," said Mrs. Menendez.

"My mother liked to watch me eat it, because I enjoyed it so much," he answered.

Mr. Menendez told stories of his parents and grandparents. His impersonations of the various family members (and especially of himself as a young, mischievous child) made the family roar with laughter.

Then they ate their great feast in silence, enjoying the view, thinking of past family members, listening to the laughter and music from other families.

Carlos was the first to rise. "Can I go now?"

"Not until we clean up," said Mrs. Menendez.

"Then hurry up," Carlos insisted. "I can't be late. My friends and I are doing a parade."

"He and his girlfriend get to be the bride and groom," teased Aleta.

"Who told you?" blushed Carlos.

Pepe giggled, "Carlos has a girlfriend. Carlos has a girlfriend."

Carlos galloped back into Jalpa ahead of the family. Mrs. Menendez turned toward the church for Mass and to pray for departed ancestors. Mr. Menendez decided to take Pepe and Aleta to see the parades and Dia de los Muertos displays in the marketplace.

"Not too many sweets," warned Mrs. Menendez.

"They'll only get a few small ones," her husband answered.

"I meant *you*."

Music from roving drums, flutes, and guitars echoed across the town center of Jalpa. Festive crowds milled around the shops and lined the streets to watch impromptu parades.

Bakery shelves were stacked with sugar skulls, chocolate skulls and coffins, and bread baked into skull and skeleton shapes with fiery red or green candy eyes. So were carts in the market square. It felt more like a birthday party than a day to remember the dead.

The crowd cheered as a new parade started into the square, led by three drummers and a flute player.

"That one is Carlos's," cried Aleta. "Hurry!"

They ran for front-row seats as the small parade passed by. Six boys carried a life-sized coffin on their shoulders. As they neared the spot where Mr. Menendez and his children sat, the coffin lid began to creak open. Bony white fingers crept out. Wider and wider opened the lid on its rusty hinges as the crowd roared approval. Bone by bone the arm of a skeleton emerged from the open coffin. Finally the head and shoulders popped out and the crowd cheered.

In front of the casket marched a bride and groom.

"Look! It's Carlos!" cried Pepe.

"And his girlfriend," teased Aleta.

Dressed in a black suit and high hat, Carlos marched arm in arm with a young woman, dressed in a high-neck, flowing bride's gown and carrying a bouquet of bright marigolds. Both wore skull masks and skeleton gloves so that no human skin showed. The crowd laughed and tossed candied skulls and chocolate skeletons, much as we would rice at a wedding.

"Two skeletons getting married is funny," laughed Pepe.

The skeleton rose to a sitting position in the coffin; its hollow eye sockets seemed to stare at people as the head bobbed on its bony neck. One bony arm reached out, as if floating through the air, and pointed a waving finger toward Pepe. He squealed in delight and covered up his eyes as he laughed.

Carlos called out, "See how much life the dead have!"

Again the crowd laughed and cheered, and the skeleton slowly sank back into its coffin. At the square in front of the church the parade disbanded. The coffin was carried back to its storage shed for next year. Carlos and his girlfriend melted into the crowd, now only two of many in outrageous skeleton costumes. Other parades would march through the square. Soon bands would form and dancing would start.

Mr. Menendez led Aleta and Pepe home as the sun disappeared behind the high western mountaintops. "Next year," announced Pepe, pointing a bobbing finger off toward the low rooftops, "I want to be the skeleton in the coffin for the parade!"

Follow-up Questions to Explore

1. Dia de los Muertos pokes fun at the idea of death. Do you think that's all right to do, or do you think death is too serious a topic for fun?

Answer

Compare your answer with those of your classmates.

2. Dia de los Muertos is partly a serious religious celebration and partly a wild public display. Can you think of other celebrations that combine a serious side and a wild, playful side?

Answer

Holi in India, Tanabata Matsuri in Japan, and American Christmas are three good examples. See how many you can name.

Suggested Activities

1. Research how cultures across the globe honor and remember their dead family members and close friends. Mexicans do it through their Dia de los Muertos celebration. How do other cultures do it? Make a chart of the different cultures, their celebrations to honor the dead, and the features of those celebrations. List these celebrations on sticky notes and place them on a world map.

2. Research traditional Dia de los Muertos foods in different regions of Mexico. Print out the recipes and plan an in-class fiesta. Research Dia de los Muertos traditions and interview Mexican adults in your community to learn what they do for this celebration. To accompany your fiesta, plan a celebration in the Dia de los Muertos tradition to honor deceased family members of your students.

Homowo

A Nigerian
Harvest Celebration

At a Glance

HARVEST TIME IS A GREAT CAUSE FOR CELEBRATION. Almost every country features at least one major festival at the end of the growing season. Harvest celebrations serve several important purposes. They are joyous occasions to reaffirm the survival of the community as a new, life-sustaining crop is stocked to supply the population with another year's food.

Harvest celebrations are also a time to pause from the rigorous and constant labor of the growing and harvest seasons for a day of dance and play. They are often a time for formal and somber thanksgiving. Finally, they can serve as an opportunity to conduct community or tribal business. The late fall Homowo, or "Hunger Hooting," festival of the Ibos people of Nigeria is such a combined celebration.

Homowo

The day of November 10, 1988, had barely started. The sun had just cleared the jacaranda trees and waving grasslands that stretched east from the town of Okene, Nigeria. Already the day was hot and steamy. The rainy season was over, but still the ground was saturated with enough water to turn the land into a steam bath. The great burning disk they called the sun promised to make the afternoon sizzle.

Agila Okodi rubbed her face with her hands to sweep the sleep away. The last week had seemed like cruel, tortuous work for an eight-year-old girl. She struggled to coax her body into getting ready for yet another day of harvesting. But how could she? The yams were too big for an eight-year-old girl to manage, and they grew far too deep for her to easily dig up.

Agila cocked her head, listening. "Father, I hear drums. Why are drums playing this morning?"

Already tapping his feet, swaying his hips, her father smiled. "Ah, don't you love to hear the drums?"

"But why are they playing, Father?"

Agila's father, Tafawa Okodi, was tall and lean with long, sinewy limbs. His head and shoulders began to bob and sway with his hips. "Drumming makes me want to dance. Drumming means a celebration."

She crossed her thin arms and planted her feet before her towering father. "But *which* celebration, Father?!"

He laughed as he danced around his statuelike daughter. "*Every* celebration means dancing and music and laughing and feasting. Who cares which one?"

"*I* do," Agila insisted. "Stop dancing and tell me!"

Tafawa paused and cupped his daughter's face in his great brown hands. "Always the serious one, this daughter of mine. I think you are better suited to be

193

a scientist than a farmer." He smiled, showing great rows of pearl white teeth. "All right, my inquisitive daughter. What did you do all day yesterday?"

"Picked yams."

"And the day before?"

"Picked yams."

"And what will you do today?"

Agila sighed and tried to muster some faint trace of enthusiasm for the crops that kept her family alive. "Pick yams again."

"No!" cried her father. "Listen to the drums! It's Homowo! The day of Hunger Hooting, the Yam Harvest Festival."

"How can the drums tell you that?"

"Listen! Those are the big *atumpan* drums—covered with elephant skin and so big they have to be held up with props. Big atumpan drums aren't like puny handheld drums made from the *kyendur* tree. Atumpan drums tell us stories, they talk to us. These drums talk about the emir and the harvest."

"What do they say, *exactly?*" insisted Agila.

"Drums don't convey individual words, only general feelings, impressions. These say that this year's harvest is good, and that our chief, the emir, will hold a *durbar* today."

Agila nodded in thought. A *durbar* was a ceremonial meeting of all the local chiefs of the Ibos people. That meant parades. Homowo meant dancing to the pounding drums, eating, hunger hooting, and playing. A wide smile flashed across her black face. This day suddenly sounded much better than picking yams.

Living mostly in small towns of close-packed, tin-roofed, cement-block-walled houses, and rural villages of mud-walled, thatched-roofed huts, the Ibos people were farmers in the rich southern and southeastern regions of Nigeria. As if drawn outside by the impatient call of the drums, Agila and her father stepped out to a dirt road in front of their tin-roofed house. Others popped out of nearby houses onto this road at the edge of Okene. Standing barefoot in the road, Tafawa's feet began to tap and shuffle, kicking up a thin cloud of red-brown dust.

It felt as if the drums commanded his heart and feet to dance, as if his feet dared not disobey. But then, any celebration in rural Nigeria is a call, a command, to dance to the pounding rhythm of the drums. No Nigerian celebration is complete without dancing to the drums.

Agila kicked at the dirt and shook her head. "They should pave all the streets and roads. Then we wouldn't have to worry about dust and mud and maybe it would reduce the swarms of tsetse flies."

Tafawa laughed. "And I suppose you think we should all wear shoes, that that would be more scientifically correct?"

"No, Father, who would want to cramp their feet in hot, stuffy shoes when they can go bare and free?"

Tafawa took his daughter's hand and led her out of town in the direction of the calling drums. Yam fields spread out before them on either side of the road in the early morning yellow light. "Just for today, stop being the scientist and celebrate. It's Homowo! Now hurry. Your mother is already at the park." Then he added, "Besides, the roads have always been dirt—except for a few downtown streets. Even the main road along the Osse River to Owo is dirt."

Yams and work were forgotten as Agila and Tafawa filed into the happy trail of dancers hurrying to the grassy field at the north edge of Okene, drawn forward by the sound of the drums just as iron filings are pulled forward by the call of a magnet.

Okene is surrounded by cultivated fields, except on the northwest side where thick forest hovers like a snarling menace at the edge of town. Tall cedar and mahogany trees jam their branches into those of giant cottonwood and gnarled baobab. Creeping vines like giant squid tentacles slither over all. Swarms of tsetse flies buzz in the shade of the forest at the edge of the grassy field the people of Okene call their park.

In the center of this field rows of drums stood at attention like faithful soldiers. Some were being played by powerful drummers. As they tired, or drifted back to family groups to eat, rest, and laugh, others sprang forward to take their place. The drums played without stop at Nigerian festivals.

Periodically, one of the drummers would throw back his head and hoot to the sky. The call rippled like the wind across the crowded park, with each person rearing back, laughing, to hoot like a screeching owl. A thousand people hooted away the pangs of hunger that lurked in the shadows like an unwanted guest through the months before harvest began.

The rich food smells at the park were almost as powerful as the incessant beat of the drums. Every family brought a banquet of food for a giant potluck—palm-nut soup, river fish, *kpokpoi* (a sweet cornmeal and palm-oil bread), meats, corn bread, melons, and other sweet fruits. And everywhere were stacks of yams—raw, boiled, baked, mashed, and fried. Yams as big as a grown man's thigh were stacked like sandbags in long rows, waiting their turn in the cooking fires and pots.

Family clusters ate and laughed. Some rose and danced, only to collapse back to the grass to pant and eat some more. Children ran and played between bites. Neighbors and clan members visited, strolling around the grassy park.

The giant atumpan drums began to speak again. The durbar was about to start. Adults brushed away the crumbs for ants and birds to enjoy. Many grabbed drums from the long rows standing on the grass. All hurried back into the center of Okene to either be in the durbar parade or to admire it. Hundreds of drums would precede, surround, and follow the parade. In it, each of the local chiefs would be carried in a wooden chair, elevated onto the shoulders of men from the chief's clan.

The chairs were lined with soft furs and blankets to protect the chief and to display his wealth and power. Wide, brightly colored umbrellas were mounted to each chair to shade and cool the chief.

The emir, or head chief, would ride first, in the place of honor. According to tradition, the emir would shower the cheering crowd with coins. For among the Ibos people, the wealth of a man is not measured by how much money he has, but by how many people he can and does help. The more a man helps others, the wealthier he must be.

Agila and the other children were left with a few supervising adults to play away the afternoon. Agila joined twenty friends in a Homowo game of *Akila*. The girls divided into two teams, standing in facing lines. A drummer set a steady beat and all girls bounced or hopped to this beat. One girl from each team jumped forward, still bouncing with the drumbeat. The drummer cried a signal. On the next bounce, both girls stretched one leg forward. If they stretched out the same leg, Agila's team scored a point. If they stretched out opposite legs, the other team scored. Either way, both teams hooted with pleasure. Then these two girls hopped back into line and the next two hopped out.

But Agila couldn't concentrate on the game. The distant pounding drums of the durbar parade snaking their way through Okene made her curious. How many chiefs were being carried in the parade? What did the emir look like? Was he kind or stern? Did he smile or frown?

She dropped out of the game with her team still four points ahead and followed the calling of the drums to a large market square. A thick ring of people hid whatever was happening in the middle. She wormed her way through a forest of tall, straight, black legs. Before her she saw a wide circle of umbrellas. Underneath sat a circle of serious-looking men. Assistants held the umbrellas and fanned their chiefs with wide palm branches.

Agila heard a booming, resonant voice. "What business is next for the durbar?"

She leaned forward and craned her head around to the left to better see the man wearing a flowing coat of spun gold. Agila lost her balance and tripped over the foot of one of the assistants. She tumbled into the clearing and sprawled face-first into the dirt, raising a sizable dust cloud.

"And who is this who comes before the council of chiefs?"

Agila bounded back to her feet, dusting herself off as she rose. A flash of embarrassed panic washed over her. All in the circle stared at her. This could be *big* trouble. But the man in gold (whom she knew must be the emir) was smiling. The smile spread thick confidence through Agila's body and into her voice.

"I am Agila Okodi," she answered, her voice gaining strength with every word. "And, since you asked, I think you should make yam harvest easier for children."

"How so, easier?" chuckled the emir. Many in the circle of chiefs chuckled with him at this bold child.

"You should order the farmers to grow smaller kinds of yams that would be easier for children to pull. And they should be ones that grow closer to the surface so there would be less digging. Every child of the Ibos people would thank and admire you."

The emir leaned forward and thoughtfully cupped his chin in one hand. "*Every* child, you say?" He stroked his chin for a long moment, then laughed. "Maybe this one belongs on my science council."

All the chiefs joined their emir in laughter.

"I accept. When's the next meeting?" answered Agila, not sure whether the laughter meant they thought her idea was a good one or not, as an assistant whisked her out of the circle.

"Everyone likes stories. But not when they sound like lies," scolded her father when Agila told him that night of her being appointed to the emir's science council.

"But it's the truth," Agila demanded.

And then the big atumpan drums began to speak. Tafawa held up one hand to silence his daughter as he listened.

"What do they say, Father?"

A confused look crossed Tafawa's face as he listened. "The drums speak of thanks to the little girl with the big ideas. Now what could that mean?"

Agila glowed. "I better go study before they call a meeting."

Follow-up Questions to Explore

1. Why do you think people actually "hoot" during Homowo?

Answer

> Much of Nigeria is a poor, rural area. People scrape by, living from harvest to harvest. Often little food is available as last year's crop is consumed and this year's crop is not yet ready for harvest. The time of harvest is a time of plenty, and thus a time of great joy, a time to throw back your head and laugh, a time to forget last year's hunger and ignore the possible hunger of next year. It is a time to hoot away the lurking menace of hunger and celebrate the bounty of the earth.

2. At Homowo and at other Nigerian festivals, women cook and men drum. Do you think it is right to have separate roles for different sexes? Are there similar divisions for some of your festivals?

Answer

> Discuss these questions in class and compare your answers to those of your classmates. In most cultures, and at most celebrations, women cook and clean, the hardest chores of all. One possible exception is the American Fourth of July. Here the food, while usually prepared by women, is often cooked by men since American men typically do the barbecuing.

> Boy's and Girl's Days in Japan have entirely separate celebrations for the two sexes. During Native American festivals certain dances are for men, others are for women. During the Passover Seder, certain roles or actions are to be performed by males, others by women. Many of our celebrations show these kinds of built-in gender differences.

Suggested Activities

1. In this story the children play a Homowo game called *Akila*. Reread the story to be sure you understand the rules, and play *Akila* yourselves. Remember to throw back your head and hoot at the sky. This is Homowo! Does *Akila* remind you of any other games you play?

2. Homowo is a harvest festival. Research harvest festivals around the world. List each on a sticky note and place them on a world map. Make a chart of world harvest festivals, the time of the festival, the major crop harvest they celebrate, and the major activities of the celebration.

Thanksgiving

A Celebration of Harvest and Thanks in the United States

At a Glance

VIRTUALLY EVERY CULTURE IN THE WORLD HAS, or has had, a harvest celebration. Most happen just after the last of the crops are harvested. But not all. Virtually every culture also has, or has had, celebrations to give thanks for past blessings, or to ask for future blessings. Many of these have been onetime events. Others are regular, annual celebrations.

Few major celebrations in the world have combined these two purposes. One of these is our annual Thanksgiving. To make the celebration even more intriguing, we also use it for a third purpose: to honor a historical event of our early ancestors—the Pilgrims' struggle to survive their first years in Plymouth Colony and their first harvest Thanksgiving celebration in 1621.

One celebration. Three purposes. But it was neither a natural nor an easy evolution to create our modern Thanksgiving. Its history is unique in the world and one we each would do well to know.

⟲ Thanksgiving ⟳

A slate gray sky hung low over the fields, barns, and silos of southern Illinois. The corn was in. The leaves had fallen, withered, and been raked. The land had faded from the lush greens and golds of summer to dull shades of brown—the tan of cornstalk stubble, the gray-brown of bare tree trunks, the deep brown of the dirt itself.

In early November, the students in Mrs. Washanger's fourth-grade class didn't gaze out the window much. There was nothing to see but shade upon shade of dismal brown. This was certainly true in 1993 when, on November 10, Mrs. Washanger stood tall, straight, and a trifle chubby, before her class. Her smile was always warm and inviting. But her piercing blue eyes told the students this was a serious discussion.

"On November 1, I asked a series of questions about Thanksgiving and told several of you to remember the answers you gave. My first question was what is the purpose of Thanksgiving. Do you remember those answers now?"

Next to the windows, freckle-faced, green-eyed Jacob Morton paused before he spoke to plaster down his cowlick that always stood up like peacock feathers. "I said Thanksgiving is a harvest festival. It's when we give thanks for a successful harvest." Most in the class nodded agreement. Behind him his best friend whispered, "Way to go, Jac-o."

Karen Kester, a big-boned girl who was the best baseball slugger in the class and whose straight auburn hair was the same shade as Mrs. Washanger's, nodded. "I said the purpose of Thanksgiving was eating, 'cause that's mostly all we do." Several in the class snickered.

Behind her Daniel Pinkerson, a small boy with thick black hair and sad puppy-dog eyes said, "I said the purpose of Thanksgiving must be sports, 'cause what we do is watch football games all day." Most in the class giggled. Two boys in the back booed.

Elizabeth Ellison raised her hand from her front-row desk. She rated the front row because she was the class math whiz. Her blond hair was pulled back and tied in a pink bow. "I said the purpose of Thanksgiving is to give thanks for our blessings." The class shifted uncomfortably. That sounded right. But everyone knew Thanksgiving was all about turkeys, harvest, and Pilgrims.

Mrs. Washanger smiled. "Very good. Second, I asked, 'If Thanksgiving is about being thankful, what are we supposed to be thankful for?' Do you remember how you answered?"

"Eating!" answered Karen Kester with her knees stuck into the aisle since she was almost too big for her desk.

"Sports and football," answered Daniel Pinkerson.

"That we aren't turkeys," said another boy in the back and everyone laughed.

"The harvest," insisted Jacob Morton, holding down his cowlick.

"Peace," said someone else.

"Our blessings," repeated Elizabeth Ellison.

"Families," whispered a girl near the door.

Mrs. Washanger gently clapped her hands for quiet. "Finally, I asked the four of you ..." Here she pointed in turn at Karen, Elizabeth, Daniel, and Jacob, "... who started our Thanksgiving tradition. How did you answer *that* question?"

"The Pilgrims," answered Elizabeth, hands clasped confidently on her desk.

Daniel said, "I said it was probably a trick question and the Indians must have started it." The class laughed.

Karen blushed. "I said I didn't know."

"Definitely the Pilgrims," answered Daniel with a firm nod.

"That's how you answered ten days ago before you did any research," smiled Mrs. Washanger. "Then I asked each of you four to research Thanksgiving and find out who is right and who is wrong. Do you have your reports?"

The four students nodded and shuffled through backpacks and notebooks for the papers.

"Please stand in front of the class and tell us what you have found."

The four students shuffled to the front and glanced nervously at each other to see who would have to go first. Elizabeth Ellison stepped forward, smoothed out her plaid jumper, and raised her paper to read.

"I first said that the purpose of Thanksgiving is to give thanks for our blessings. But everything I read about Thanksgiving talked about the Pilgrims. Nothing talked about our blessings, or about what crops we harvest, or even why Thanksgiving is in late November, over a month after all the crops are harvested. (I heard that most harvest festivals are held on the last day of harvest or just after the crops are in.)

"So now I guess the real purpose of Thanksgiving must be to remember the Pilgrims. This is what I found." Elizabeth lifted her paper closer to her face to read more easily.

"A hundred and two Pilgrims landed at Plymouth on December 11, 1620. A harsh winter and disease killed forty-six of them by the next fall. There were only fifty-six Pilgrims in the whole colony! That's fewer people than just the fourth-graders at this school, and we're just one small school! Then William Bradford was elected governor and declared a day of thanksgiving because they had had a good harvest and the second winter wouldn't be as bad as the first. He decided to invite a few local Indians—I guess because they had helped the Pilgrims with planting and hunting. Over ninety showed up for Thanksgiving and they had a party that lasted for three days."

Elizabeth folded her papers and slipped them back into a notebook as she concluded. "I guess Thanksgiving is all about honoring the Pilgrims and the hardships they endured to start a new country."

A few children clapped. Elizabeth smiled and blushed.

"Wrong! Wrong!" shouted Daniel, wiping his hair back out of his eyes. "I read all that stuff about the Pilgrims. And you left out the main point. What they did during that three-day Thanksgiving was hold sports events. They had foot races, and long-jump and high-jump contests. They had archery contests and musket-shooting contests."

Daniel sucked in a great breath and continued, now speaking so fast his words all ran together. "Sure they ate. They had to. They were hungry from all the sports. But the point is, the Thanksgiving in 1621 was like the first Olympics. Sports have been part of Thanksgiving ever since. That's why we always have football games on Thanksgiving now. On Thanksgiving we give thanks by playing sports. Then we're real hungry and so we eat a lot."

Boys cheered. Girls groaned. Daniel bowed.

"No! No! NO!" cried Karen Kester. "I like sports as much as anyone. And you know I'm better than anyone in this class. But sports has nothing to do with why we celebrate Thanksgiving. Sports is just what you do that day if you're bored. Families come together for Thanksgiving dinner. Every picture you ever see of Thanksgiving is of a table and a big meal and people eating.

"It's turkey, dressing, cranberry sauce, and pumpkin pie that we think of when we think of Thanksgiving. None of those menu items, by the way, were on the Pilgrims' first Thanksgiving menu except maybe whole cranberries."

"They did too eat turkey!" shouted a girl in the back of the class.

"When they said 'turkey'," explained Karen, "they meant any of several bald-headed game birds. What they probably ate were small game birds, like quail, maybe."

Karen shuffled her papers and continued. "Thanksgiving is a time to celebrate eating—my mom said 'overeating.' But maybe what we're really celebrating is that we have plenty to eat, so much that we can afford to overeat one day and not worry about running out. So I guess maybe we *are* celebrating the harvest."

Then she added, "But we don't talk about harvests. We only talk about food and eating!" And she folded her arms to show she was through.

"Wrong, wrong, wrong!" said freckle-faced Jacob Morton, waving his hands as if trying to erase her words from the air. "I'm the one who first said Thanksgiving is a harvest celebration. But it isn't. I read up on the history of Thanksgiving and Elizabeth is the one who was right when she said the purpose of Thanksgiving is to give thanks for our blessings—mostly, I think, victories in battle—those kinds of blessings."

He shuffled through his papers to find the first page. "Everyone so far was right. The Pilgrims held the first Thanksgiving in November of 1621. But they didn't hold another one the next year. Then they did it again in 1623. But that Thanksgiving wasn't a harvest festival. No! A big drought in May of 1623 almost wiped out all the Pilgrims' crops. Governor Bradford called for a day of prayer for rain. Next day it *did* rain, and he proclaimed that the fourth Thursday in November would be a day of thanksgiving for that rain. See? They gave thanks for their blessings."

Jacob shifted to his second page and continued. "There weren't any regular Thanksgivings for over two hundred years. In 1777 the Continental Congress declared a November Thanksgiving day to celebrate the army's victory over the British at Saratoga. All the colonies had it, but it didn't stick.

"Then in 1789 President Washington tried to make the fourth Thursday of November a national Thanksgiving Day in honor of the Pilgrims and America's victory in the Revolutionary War. But most Americans thought that …" Here Jacob followed the words with his finger to ensure he read the quote correctly. "'The hardships of a handful of early settlers wasn't worthy of national recognition.' Besides many southerners thought Thanksgiving was a Yankee holiday and didn't want to do it. Thomas Jefferson argued against Thanksgiving for all eight years he was president."

"Is that all, Jacob?" asked Mrs. Washanger.

"Almost, Ma'am. Beginning in the 1820s, a lady named Sarah Hale wrote lots of articles calling for a national Thanksgiving Day. Did you know that the first Thanksgiving here in Illinois didn't happen until 1838?! And that one was celebrated here in Springfield.

"But it was 1863 when Thanksgiving first became an annual, national celebration. President Lincoln declared the last Thursday of November to be a day of Thanksgiving to celebrate the victory at Gettysburg, to honor the fallen soldiers at Gettysburg, and to pray for peace. We've had a Thanksgiving ever since."

Jacob put down his papers. "So, you see, we celebrate Thanksgiving to give thanks for our victories and successes. And Abraham Lincoln started it."

Most children nodded. The back two rows tried to restage the Battle of Gettysburg except with machine guns instead of muskets.

"Thank you all," said Mrs. Washanger.

"Wait!" cried Karen. "That wasn't true. The Indians started Thanksgiving, not Lincoln. Squanto, an Indian who spoke English, saved the Pilgrims. And Chief Massasoit helped supply them. He brought most of the people who attended that first Thanksgiving, and almost all the meat. Indians should get the credit."

"That's not right!" yelled Jacob and Daniel. In a flash the whole class was arguing and yelling, taking sides with one of the four reports.

Mrs. Washanger clapped her hands. All grew quiet and waited for her to decree whose version was correct. Mrs. Washanger smiled and thanked the four students for their reports. Once they were seated she said, "You were all correct. And what a wonderful day Thanksgiving is to let us give thanks in so many ways for so much. We are truly blessed and have much to be thankful for. Having a celebration like Thanksgiving every year is one of those things."

Follow-up Questions to Explore

1. What do you think about when you celebrate Thanksgiving? What does your family talk about? What do they say is the purpose for your Thanksgiving feast?

Answer

Discuss these questions in class and compare your answers to those of your classmates. How do your answers compare to the historic purposes for the celebration?

2. The first Thanksgiving was held in 1621. After two tries, it was abandoned. During the 1700s and early 1800s, Thanksgiving was tried and forgotten, honored and abandoned, celebrated and banned in communities and regions across the country. Can you think of other celebrations that have started and stopped?

Answer

May Day is one good example. Since its first celebration in Roman times, it has started and stopped dozens of times in countries around the world. But somehow May Day, like spring itself, always comes back, and even in the darkest times, seems to forever keep a toehold somewhere among the peoples of earth. Can you find other examples?

Suggested Activities

1. Research the complete history of Thanksgiving, the years it was held, the years it was banned, the attempts to start it, the attempts to stop it, the people who promoted it, and the people who were opposed to it. List what you find on a timeline from 1621 to the present. Include beliefs, attitudes, and popular images of the Thanksgiving celebration along the way.

2. Describe both Thanksgiving in general, and the first Thanksgiving feast in particular, from the two different points of view of a white Pilgrim child (or modern white child) of your own age and a Native American of the same age. Research the "real" foods. Prepare them and have a traditional Thanksgiving feast.

DECEMBER

Saint Nicholas Day

A European Christian Celebration
of a Famous Saint

At a Glance

Did YOU EVER WONDER WHERE SANTA CLAUS CAME FROM? Santa was never part of the first Christmas. He didn't exist for Christmases in A.D. 500, A.D. 1000, or even A.D. 1500. Yet so much of our modern Christmas lore and ceremony center around this overweight, overgrown, elflike, benevolent magician who employs countless miniature elves; rides a sleigh to every house, apartment, hut, and trailer in one single night; slides down chimneys—even in houses that don't have chimneys—without ever getting the least bit dirty; who simultaneously lives in every department store, mall, and parade for the entire month before Christmas; and who drives the whole gift-giving machinery of the "holiday shopping season."

Who is this fellow and where did he come from?

The story begins with a fourth-century Christian bishop, Nicholas, born in Asia Minor and archbishop of Myra in Lycia (part of modern-day Turkey). Stories abound about his acts of giving and heroic deeds, the miracles he performed, of his support of children, of his selfless generosity. He was sainted by the Catholic Church in the sixth century. By the twelfth century he had become the patron saint of Russia, of thieves, of boys, of girls, of mariners, of the weak and poor, of scholars, of merchants, of Amsterdam, and of much of Germany. We will never know how many of the myriad stories about Saint Nicholas are true. True or not, these stories quickly made Saint Nicholas the most famous of all Christian saints.

Saint Nicholas is a revered figure in Europe. His celebration day was set almost fifteen hundred years ago to be the date of his death, December 6. For the last thousand years on December 6 Saint Nicholas has given gifts—small token gifts—to the children of Western Europe.

Saint Nicholas first came to America in the early eighteenth century with Dutch immigrants to the Dutch colony at New Amsterdam (later renamed New York). The Dutch spelling of Saint Nicholas's name was *Sinter Klaas*.

It took several hundred years for *Sinter Klaas* to become "Santa Claus," for his celebration to shift dates from December 6 to merge with the emerging American celebration of Christmas (Christmas was not acknowledged in England or America as a holiday until well into the nineteenth century), and for the merchants of America to convert St. Nick into the icon of Christmas buying and material giving.

But in Europe the celebration of Saint Nicholas still flourishes as it has for a thousand years, especially in the Low Countries of northern Europe.

Saint Nicholas Day

"Lift me higher, Papa! I can't see!" commanded five-year-old Gusta, her hair, the color of ripened wheat, billowing in flowing waves in the chill December wind.

"I can't see *either* with you sitting on my head," Dewitt Dekker, her father, shouted in order to be heard above the cheering crowd. "Wave."

Wearing flowing scarlet robes and a tall bishop's miter, with snow-white beard and tall black boots, and carrying a crooked staff of gold, Saint Nicholas himself strode down the gangplank of the small freighter on which he had arrived at Amsterdam's inner harbor this morning of December 6, 1992. Fireworks exploded overhead. Cannon roared in salute to the visiting saint. Church bells across the city rang joyous melodies of welcome. The overflow crowd lining the docks and parade route to City Hall erupted into wild cheering.

Gusta screamed loudest of all as she frantically waved both tiny hands. "It's Saint Nicholas! It's him!"

At the head of the short pier where his boat docked, the saint mounted his waiting white horse, its breath steaming into the biting early morning air. The mayor and other dignitaries bowed low and then scurried to reach their cars and follow Amsterdam's patron saint on his ride through the city.

"He's here!" Gusta squealed as Saint Nicholas rode past, waving to the cheering boys and girls. Gusta slid into her father's arms. "Papa! Saint Nicholas *looked* at me." Her stunned face glowed. "We have to go home!"

"Don't you want to watch the rest of the parade?" he asked.

"I have to get ready!" she answered.

The Dekker family lived in a three-story row house jammed, city-style, right against the sidewalk in a working-class neighborhood on Amsterdam's southeast side. It was a good half-mile from their house to the nearest of Amsterdam's downtown canals and waterways, which was a great disappointment to the Dekkers' seven-year-old son, Karel. In his prayers each night Karel wished for either the family to move onto a canal or for a canal to worm its way through Amsterdam to them.

The house smelled of baking and cleaning as Dewitt and Gusta rushed in. Mrs. Alida Dekker and Karel were icing fresh *speculatius* cookies (a thin-dough cookie made with lots of brown sugar, butter, and sour cream, and cut into likenesses of St. Nick). It looked like Karel's face, hair, and arms were covered with more icing and dough than he had managed to get into the cookies. Rows of Gusta's favorite Saint Nicholas Day cookie, *taai-taai* (a crisp ginger cookie), cooled on a rack, filling the house with their wonderful smell.

Mrs. Dekker's mother, Grandma Lina, had been in charge of cleaning, with special attention paid to the front room where Saint Nicholas himself would visit the family.

"Saint Nicholas *looked* at me!" shouted Gusta.

Karel brushed a few hairs out of his face with the back of his hand, smearing icing across his forehead. "I'm being very helpful. Aren't I, Mommy?"

"Yes, you are."

"So, you'll tell Saint Nicholas how good we are?"

Alida pretended to be lost in serious thought. But her eyes sparkled with delight and laughter. "I haven't decided whether or not to speak on your behalf this year."

"Mother! You have to! I've been helping *all day!*"

"*Today*, sure. But there was that day last week …"

"You *can't* tell Saint Nicholas about *that!*" Karel interrupted. "It was an accident. It wasn't my fault!"

Mrs. Dekker had to struggle to hold her serious frown. "Still, he does want a full report …"

"Pleeeease, Mommy," Karel begged. "Pleeeease don't tell him. I'll be good next year. I promise."

"I'll think about it," Alida managed to say without laughing.

Gusta raced for the stairs. "I have to get my basket for Saint Nicholas ready."

"And I have to write a poem for him," added Karel, following his sister. "Saint Nicholas loves poems. Maybe, 'I'll always be your *pal* … if you give us a *canal!*'"

Gusta rolled her eyes and the children disappeared upstairs.

From the kitchen doorway, Dewitt said, "You *enjoyed* tormenting the poor boy."

Now Alida let her laughter escape. "It's so much fun to watch his face when he's worried about what Saint Nicholas will think."

The rest of the afternoon, Gusta and Karel labored to decorate and fill their straw baskets for Saint Nicholas: decorations to let Saint Nicholas know they had been good; sweets and poems for the saint himself; and lumps of sugar, carrots, and hay for his white horse. When finished, the baskets were placed by the front window.

Gusta's lower lip trembled as she compared her basket to her brother's. "I don't have a poem for Saint Nicholas 'cause I can't write yet."

"He knows, sweetie," said Alida. "You made a *lovely* basket."

"Elves and fairies watch us and write in his book," whispered Karel. "So Saint Nicholas knows *everything!*" Then he added, "Except about last week. He *can't* know about that!"

At dusk came dinner. As the dishes were cleared, Dewitt and Grandma Lina bundled in coats at the door.

"We're off to the bakery. Be back in a couple of hours."

"But you'll miss Saint Nicholas," exclaimed Gusta.

"We'll probably be back in time," Mr. Dekker answered. "But if we're not, you be extra good while he's here."

"We will, Papa," the children shouted.

"Good luck," called Mrs. Dekker. "If you win, Mother, pick something we *all* will enjoy."

A Saint Nicholas evening tradition started at Amsterdam bakeries several centuries ago. It started as simple raffle drawings for the remaining holiday cookies and cakes. Over time, it grew into a night of high-stakes dice gambling on the bakery floors, with large sums of money changing hands between bettors. The winners get first choice of the special Saint Nicholas marzipan cakes and current-raison breads each store bakes for the evening's festivities.

At home Gusta and Karel pretended to be busy coloring. Always the corner of one eye was glued to the door.

A stout rapping boomed through the house. Both children shrank against the far wall, hearts pounding like helpless deer trapped in the mesmerizing headlights of an oncoming car.

Mrs. Dekker opened the door.

A cold wind swirled in. With it, Saint Nicholas stepped inside—tall, commanding, regal, saintlike. His piercing blue eyes shone out over a thick white beard.

Behind him came a young man dressed as an angel carrying a thick leather-bound book. Behind the angel lurked three ruffians dressed as devils with blackened faces and beet red eyes. They slunk in rattling chains, making fierce cries and yelps. The devils leered at the children from behind the bishop's robes.

A great silence fell over the room.

Saint Nicholas pounded his crook on the floor and demanded, "Bring the children of this house forward to be examined."

Stomachs churning, breath coming in ragged gasps, Gusta and Karel hesitated, backs pressed into the wall, hoping the other would advance first. Saint Nicholas held out one hand. "Give me the book."

The angel seemed to float forward, opening the great book to a page marked with a red ribbon, and handed the volume to the saint.

Nicholas's eyebrows furrowed as he studied the page. "Hmmmmmm." He glared at the children, seeming to pierce the darkest corners of their very souls.

He knows, thought Karel.

"Have these children been good?" asked the saint, turning to Mrs. Dekker.

Terror spread across Karel's face. *Don't tell, Mother! Please don't tell!* The devils crept forward cackling, rubbing their bony fingers. One reached into a long bag slung over his back for the grinding mill—like a giant pepper grinder. Every child knew that the devils were there to drag bad children to the attic and grind them into pepper nuts to sprinkle on the ginger cookies of good children.

He knows! The devils will get me!

"These children have both been very good all year, Your Grace," smiled their mother.

The devils howled in disappointment and retreated.

Saint Nicholas nodded. "I thought so. I shall return later."

The angel flipped a small candy to each child and the procession swept out the door and down to the next house.

Gusta and Karel collapsed to the floor, overcome with relief and joy.

Minutes later, Mr. Dekker returned. "The bakery's mobbed. I didn't even *try* to get inside. But Granny Lina dove right into the thick of it. She's doing so well she's going to stay a while longer."

"Papa, *he* came!" burst Gusta.

"Who came?" Mr. Dekker asked.

"Saint Nicholas! And you missed him again."

"What a shame I missed it," he smiled.

"And he said we were good children!" stammered Karel, glowing with relief.

"That's wonderful news!" said Mr. Dekker. "I can't believe I missed him again this year. Up to bed now. You don't want to be awake when Saint Nicholas returns."

Deep in the night, Saint Nicholas returned to the homes of good children to leave sweets and small token gifts. But every child also knows that he sometimes stopped at the homes of bad children to leave charred willow whips and lumps of coal.

Early the next morning, Gusta and Karel bounded down the stairs from their third-floor rooms to the big front parlor. The wood floor felt icicle cold because no one else was up yet to start a fire or switch on the wall heater. Neither child cared. Had Saint Nicholas returned? Had he left symbols of good or evil?

Their hearts skipped a beat as they realized their baskets were not sitting under the window. Saint Nicholas Day magic had worked again! Karel dropped to his hands and knees to search the corners of the room. Gusta climbed onto each chair to peer behind it. Where had Saint Nicholas hidden the baskets both children knew were now stuffed with scrumptious treats to eat?

"Here!" cried Gusta pointing to a high shelf.

"Here!" cried Karel reaching under the heavy couch.

The children sat on the floor munching the first of their marzipan delights. "Did you notice that Saint Nicholas looked a little like our father?" asked Gusta.

"Shhhh," hissed Karel. "Elves might be listening!" He paused for a mouthful of sugar cookie. "Besides, I don't want anything to ruin the magic of these Saint Nicholas Day treats!"

Follow-up Questions to Explore

1. Compare Saint Nicholas and Santa Claus. What are their similarities and differences? Did one evolve from the other? Which from which?

Answer

Discuss these questions in class and compare your answers to those of your classmates.

2. The American image of Santa Claus evolved over several hundred years from the European celebration for a real person, Saint Nicholas. Do you think it is all right that Americans changed a celebration for a real person into our own reinvented image and don't give any credit or acknowledgment to the original person, Saint Nicholas? Why do you think Americans changed Saint Nicholas into Santa Claus?

Answer

Discuss these questions in class and compare your answers to those of your classmates.

Suggested Activities

1. Saint Nicholas is celebrated all across Europe. Research the history of this man. Research the history and traditions of Saint Nicholas Day in the different European countries. What does Saint Nicholas represent? What does he do for the children? What do they do for him? What are the beliefs surrounding Saint Nicholas? What treats are made for Saint Nicholas? What treats are given to children by Saint Nicholas? What traditional treats are made for the family to enjoy during this celebration? Download or research recipes for traditional Saint Nicholas Day treats from different countries. Prepare and share these recipes.

Our Lady of Guadalupe

A Mexican and Catholic Celebration of a Historic Religious Miracle

At a Glance

MANY OF OUR CELEBRATIONS HONOR RELIGIOUS, OR SACRED, PURPOSES. Some of these started as religious recognition of seasonal events, some to mark events in church history, some to mark events in the annual church calendar, and a few to mark the occurrence of miracles. One such miracle happened in Mexico in 1531, shortly after the Spanish conquest converted the country to Catholicism. It was a cruel and difficult time for the native Mexicans.

The miracle that occurred in the small village of Guadalupe in 1531 was adopted two hundred years later as a symbol for the struggling Mexican revolutionary army. With the success of the revolution and the creation of an independent Mexican state, Our Lady of Guadalupe became the patron saint of all Mexico.

There are other Catholic feasts and celebrations to honor other saints and other miracles. But in Mexico the celebration of the *Dia de Nuestra Senora de Guadalupe* (The Day of Our Lady of Guadalupe) is the most important of all. Only the shrines at Lourdes in France and Fatima in Portugal receive more visitors each year than does the Shrine of Our Lady of Guadalupe.

Our Lady of Guadalupe

Diego, his wife, Lucia, and their daughter, Anita, crossed the wide, cement plaza and pushed open a side door to the towering basilica of Our Lady of Guadalupe. Though it was December 10, the air was still tropical and warm in this small village now swallowed into the ever-expanding sprawl of Mexico City. The sky hung gray with smog instead of the clear blue they had hoped for.

"Are you sure this is the right place?" Diego asked in hushed tones as they blinked into the darkness of the basilica.

"It's right here on the map," answered Lucia, her voice echoing across the vast cathedral. Her finger jabbed at the folded tour map they had purchased for the trip. "See for yourself."

Twelve-year-old Anita added, "The name was carved in the stone front of the church, 'Nuestra Senora de Guadalupe.' This *has* to be the place, Papa."

"Then it must be the wrong time," concluded Diego.

"The Festival of Our Lady of Guadalupe is on December 12," answered his wife. "It's December 12 at home in Larado. It's December 12 in all the rest of the world. It's December 12 *here*, too."

"But there are no preparations, no crowds."

"Not so loud, Papa. Your voice carries."

"May I help you?"

The voice came from beneath the hood of a brown, floor-length robe with wrist-length sleeves. The hands were clasped. The feet wore plain sandals. The brown face smiled. "I am Brother Lupe."

Diego extended his hand. "We have come for the Celebration of Our Lady of Guadalupe. But I see no crowds or preparations."

Brother Lupe smiled. "The crowds will arrive tomorrow, as will the bustling preparations. You were wise to come a day early."

"We're from Laredo ... in Texas," said Lucia. "This is our first time here."

"But my family ancestry tracks directly back to Juan Diego. I am named for him," added Diego.

Brother Lupe's eyebrows rose in surprise. He nodded in respect. "Then you are an honored guest. If you'd like I will show you the very spot where Juan Diego's miracle took place."

Anita pointed to a piece of cloth encased in glass and hung behind the altar. "Is that it?"

"That is what the tourists and pilgrims come to see," said Brother Lupe.

"Pilgrims?" interrupted Lucia.

"Yes. Many Mexican Catholics feel it is a sacred duty to make a pilgrimage to this site. They stare at the cloth, pray, and then they leave. But the cloth is a *symbol* of the miracle, *evidence* of the miracle, but not the whole story. We must climb Tepeyac Hill to see the whole story."

Tepeyac Hill rose steeply behind the basilica. As the family climbed, Brother Lupe explained, "Tonantzin, the Aztec goddess of earth and of growing corn, was an important goddess to the common Aztec people. Her temple stood on top of this hill. When the Spanish conquered Mexico they destroyed most Aztec shrines and symbols. By 1528 Tonantzin's temple had been torn down.

"It was a terrible time for the people of this land. The Spanish were cruel and hard. Many Aztecs were slaughtered. The rest lived as slaves. The riches of the land and people were plundered. Many peasants converted to Catholicism to receive better treatment from their conquerors. One such farmer in this village of Guadalupe was Juan Diego, your ancestor. On the ninth of December in 1531 ..."

"On the ninth?" asked Anita. "I thought the miracle happened on the twelfth."

"It did," answered Lupe. "But the story starts on the ninth. That afternoon was cool and clear." Lupe waved his hand toward the sky. "There was no city to create smog back then. Juan Diego walked among the ruins of Tonantzin's temple feeling a deep sadness for the fate of himself and his people. Both the place and the goddess had been important to him throughout his life.

"Then, miraculously, the Virgin Mary appeared to Juan, standing on the ruins of Tonantzin's shrine on top of this very hill we are climbing. She beckoned him to her. The timid man was afraid and shook his head 'no.' She smiled and beckoned again. Now he fearfully inched forward. She told him to build a church on this hilltop in her honor.

"Juan felt that the Virgin's message was a sign that all would be well if the people let Christianity replace their old Aztec beliefs. He raced down the hill to tell the bishop of his meeting. But the bishop would not even see him. The next day Juan sadly returned to Tepeyac Hill. Again the Virgin Mary appeared to him. Again she asked for a church to be built. Again the bishop would not listen."

The four climbers reached the level hilltop and paused to catch their breath. Diego wiped the sweat from his face with a wide bandanna. "A third time it happened on the next day," began Brother Lupe, still panting.

"That would be on the eleventh?" asked Anita.

"Yes, exactly right. But on the twelfth, when Juan returned to this hilltop, the Virgin Mary said she would give him a sign to show to the bishop. When Juan turned around, the hilltop—which had never grown anything other than weeds and cactus—was covered in blooming Castilian rosebushes, a kind of rose foreign to Mexico.

"Juan picked the roses and wrapped them in his simple, homespun cloak to carry down the hill. When he later opened that blanket in front of the bishop, the roses vanished. Where they had lain, a portrait of the Virgin appeared on the rough cloth. That was the final miracle.

"The bishop was convinced and the church was built," concluded Lupe with a self-satisfied grin.

"Are these rocks the ruins of Tonantzin's shrine?" asked Lucia.

"These are the ruins of the original church to the Virgin Mary. The cloth with that portrait hung here for many years. When the new basilica was built and this church crumbled, the portrait was moved down the hill."

"And that's the cloth behind the altar?" asked Anita.

"Yes, and look closely at it when we go back down," said Lupe. "After 450 years the cloth has not deteriorated and the portrait's color has not faded. Not at all."

As they reached the quiet square in front of the basilica, Diego thanked Brother Lupe for his tour.

"It was a pleasure to meet and guide Juan Diego's namesake. Now rest. For on the twelfth this square will be so packed with booths, music, and dancing you won't be able to get across."

As promised, by 7 A.M. on December 12, the square and surrounding streets had become a raucous sea of people. Wooden booths lined each street and two sides of the square. Some sold balloons, with bright bunches of every possible color swaying in the light breeze. The sky had cleared, leaving a rich blue above the radiant balloons.

Some booths sold birds. Red, yellow, green, and blue songbirds seemed to chirp, "Buy me! Buy me!"

Fruit sellers and food booths were already crowded and busy. But most booths sold candles. Everywhere flickering candles lined windows, doors, and roofs. Most pilgrims carried lighted candles, so that the square was alive in a flowing river of candle flames.

The air quivered with the rhythms of fifty clusters of musicians playing on guitar and drum. Puppet stages reenacted the miracle of Juan Diego to overflow crowds.

Diego, Lucia, and Anita had to shout to hear each other as, holding hands to keep from being separated, they forced their way toward the basilica.

Everywhere costumed groups of dancers performed. Many wore elaborate feathered headdresses with feathered sleeves and leggings. Many women danced in flowing feather capes. Most danced pre-Christian, Aztec dances, the Bird Dance being the most popular.

But weaving through the wild merriment marched a thick, solemn line of worshipers. Some wore fancy dresses or suits. Most wore full flowered skirts and shawls or serapes. Many walked barefoot. Most carried lighted candles. Some walked with arms folded across their chests. All inched their way toward the wide double doors at the front of the basilica.

Inside, every seat was filled, every aisle was jammed. The basilica blazed with light from countless candles spread across every level space, each deposited by some pilgrim. The smell of burning candles and incense permeated everywhere. Mass was said throughout the day as the flood of pilgrims entered, prayed, stared at the cloth, and slowly filed out into the bright sunshine and lively festival.

For Diego and his family it was a day to overload the senses and the emotions with the sights, sounds, smells, and images of the square and the basilica. It was a day of remembrance, a day of joy, a day of loud celebration, a day of quiet prayer, a day of wonder, a day of hope. But above all, it was a day to cherish forever.

Follow-up Questions to Explore

1. Why do you think Aztec costumes and dances appear at a Christian celebration?

Answer

As the Christian church expanded across Europe and the Americas, Christian celebrations were placed on top of (on the same date as) existing local celebrations. In the early days when Christians were being persecuted, this let Christians celebrate their holidays without being caught, because everyone was celebrating. Later, it was done to encourage non-Christians to convert to Christianity.

When Spanish invaders conquered Mexico, their Catholic priests tried to incorporate Catholic rituals onto the days of, and as part of, the Aztec celebrations, in order to make Catholicism seem more familiar and attractive to the native population. Elements of ancient Aztec culture thus survived over the centuries as parts of Catholic ceremonies and celebrations.

2. This story is about a miraculous appearance by the Virgin Mary to a peasant farmer in Mexico. Do you believe in miracles? Do you know of other miracles celebrated in other religions?

Answer

Discuss these questions in class and compare your answers to those of your classmates.

Suggested Activities

1. This story takes place in the small town of Guadelupe, Mexico. Locate Guadelupe on a map. Study the community and economy of the area. What is the climate like? What do the people of Guadelupe do? What is their history?

2. This story is about the shrine for a past miracle. Research miracles and shrines. Are there other sites around the world that are thought of as sacred places because miracles happened there? What happened at each site you find? What is at the site now to commemorate the miracle? Who visits the place? What do they do there? List each miracle shrine on a sticky note and place them on a world map.

Kwanzaa

An African-American Cultural Celebration

At a Glance

MANY OF THE FESTIVALS AND CELEBRATIONS WE HONOR each year date back for hundreds of years, some for thousands. Yet at some time each was a brand-new celebration. Each began, grew, adapted, and changed over the years to meet the changing needs and customs of the people.

The newest major celebration in the world is Kwanzaa (or Kwanza), which literally means "first fruit." The first Kwanzaa was held in Los Angeles, California, in 1966. Kwanzaa was founded by Dr. Maulana Karenga, a Black Studies professor, as a culturally based celebration that could link African Americans with their African heritage. Kwanzaa is the only African culturally based celebration practiced outside of Africa.

Kwanzaa

"*Again?* Why do we have to do Kwanzaa again?" Thirteen-year-old Kalela Douglas slouched across an overstuffed chair in the living room of the family's second-floor apartment in Burbank, California. "I don't want to go *again*."

The date was December 31, 1993. Outside it was shorts weather as a warm breeze blew the smog out of the Los Angeles basin. The TV was on in the Douglases' den. Mr. Douglas and several friends watched a college football game.

Kalela peered around her chair and huffed when she realized her father hadn't heard her carefully staged protest.

She raised her voice to a near shout. "I said, 'Why do I have to go to Kwanzaa *again?*'"

Mr. Douglas leaned around into the doorway. "We don't *have* to go to Kwanzaa. We *get* to go. And we're going again because Kwanzaa lasts for seven days. This is the sixth."

Kalela kicked her feet up over the back of her chair, "But it's *New Year's*. Everyone I know is either going to a party at the beach or they're going to Pasadena to spend the night on the street for the Rose Parade."

Mr. Douglas set down his beer and stepped into the living room. "Tonight is the Karamu feast, the most important night of Kwanzaa. And not 'everyone' is going to the beach. Several of your friends will be at the community center with us."

"Why can't we just have Christmas and New Year's like normal people?"

"Are you Christian?" asked Mr. Douglas, settling onto the armrest of Kalela's chair.

"Well, no."

"Christmas is a religious celebration for Christians."

"But I like the presents and the parties!"

"That's the trouble with modern American Christmas," said Mr. Douglas. "It's too commercial. We need a celebration that speaks to our values, our culture, our heritage."

"What's wrong with presents?" demanded Kalela.

"It's fine to give Kwanzaa presents. But they should come from the heart and the hand, not from the wallet."

"What does that mean?"

Mr. Douglas chuckled, "That you should *make* the gifts you give, not *buy* them."

"Oh."

Kalela shifted uneasily in her chair, groping for a convincing argument. "Why does Kwanzaa have to take so long? Why not get it over with in one day?"

"Seven days to honor the seven African-based principles I've been teaching you. Kwanzaa is the only African cultural celebration in America."

Kalela scowled and crossed her arms. "I'm *not* African. I was born in Chicago."

"But if you trace back about twelve generations, you'll find your ancestors came from Africa, mostly West Africa."

Kalela swung her legs, kicking into the coffee table, frustrated that her arguments didn't seem to have any effect. "So, what's so great about Africa? All I see in the news is either people starving or at war."

"Get past the headlines to the people and culture," said her father, "and you'll find a rich, wise, and compassionate heritage. The first calculator—the first abacus—was invented in Africa. So was the first glue and adhesive. Cement, ink, dams, weaving looms, and security locks were all invented in Africa."

Kalela started for her room, planning to slam the door in defeat. She stopped for one last try. "Why don't we wait and say 'yippee to Africa' on Martin Luther King, Jr., Day?"

Mr. Douglas searched the shining black eyes of his daughter. "What's *really* going on here? I know you feel proud of your black culture and ancestors."

Kalela's shoulders sagged. She let out a long, slow sigh. "Do I *have* to say all those African words again tonight?"

Mr. Douglas threw back his head and laughed, then crossed the room to encircle his daughter in his arms. "You mean words like 'placemat' and 'corn'?"

"But I have to say them in … in … swili."

"Swahili," corrected her father. "Actually it's 'Kiswahili,' the only nontribal African language that is spoken over a large portion of the continent."

"But I'm supposed to be on *vacation*. Having to learn a new language feels like school. And every night there's a test."

"You did wonderfully well last night," laughed her father. "Kwanzaa is a very special time for us. Relax and enjoy it. You'll see."

The sky was dark when the Douglases left for the Burbank Community Center. Snaking lines of solid white headlights marked the crisscrossing freeways through Burbank. The Douglases gathered in a spacious side room of the center with a dozen other families—almost forty people, all local, all black.

The room had been decorated in rich African patterns in green, red, and black. A great banner hung on one wall with seven lines of writing in Swahili. Kalela knew it was the seven principles of Kwanzaa. In the center of the room a large table was set with a single placemat and six other items, the Kwanzaa symbols Kalela would have to remember and name.

The people wore flowing African robes with geometric patterns woven into wide vertical stripes. They talked and laughed. Children dashed about playing tag.

Mr. Douglas clapped his hands and welcomed everyone to Karamu, the grand feast of the Kwanzaa week. He especially welcomed the elders. Hiram Elliot, the oldest present at eighty-eight, said how important it was to remember African ways and to blend African culture with American life.

A barefoot woman with over twenty jangling bracelets of gold and silver danced her way through the telling of an African story about why the sky is so high. Kalela laughed in spite of herself.

Mr. Douglas motioned for quiet. "My daughter, Kalela, would like to introduce us all to the seven symbols of Kwanzaa."

"No she wouldn't," hissed Kalela through a forced smile.

Her father's emphatic nod motioned her toward the table.

Kalela sucked in a deep breath, tried to calm her pounding heart, and stepped to the center table, pointing to each item in turn.

"First is *mazao*, the fruits and vegetables, the result of collective labor and a symbol of harvest joy. Second is … is … *mkeka,* the placemat."

Mr. Douglas sighed in relief. His daughter continued. "*Mkeka* symbolizes tradition and welcome. Third is *kinara*, the candleholder, symbolic of continental

Africans, our parent people. Fourth is *vibuzil* … no, *vibunzi*, the ears of corn, which represent the children and our future.

"Fifth—and I would never forget this one—is *zawadi*, the gifts!" Many adults chuckled. Children cheered and repeated the word, *"Zawadi."*

"Zawadi symbolize love and commitment. Sixth is … is … Shoot! This is the hardest one."

Mr. Douglas held his breath and closed his eyes, trying to transmit the wording to his daughter.

"The sixth one is … Oh, I remember, *kikombe cha umoja*, the communal unity cup, the symbol of unity."

With a wave of relief Kalela reached the final item. "The seventh is the seven candles, *mishumaa saba*, which symbolize the seven principles of Kwanzaa, the *Nguzo Saba*."

Everyone applauded. Kalela blushed and stepped aside. A few gifts were exchanged, mostly between family members. Kalela received a beautiful beaded bracelet and shoulder bag from her parents. Knowing that her always-busy parents had taken the time to sew the seams, stitches, and beadwork themselves somehow made each item more precious to Kalela.

Two women lit the seven candles one at a time, explaining one of the seven principles with each candle, and pointing to the written version in Swahili on the wall. They also talked about African culture and their intentions for the new year. Kalela found her mind beginning to wander. Then three men beat drums and two women sang a rhythmic song in Swahili.

Carried away on the music, Kalela saw a crisp, full moon just rising over jacaranda trees at the edge of a great grassy plain. In the distance, jackals yapped and a lion roared. Kalela watched field workers return to the village, singing the same rhythmic song.

Kalela was in an African village, a West African village of thatched huts with clean-swept dirt floors where cooking fires were lit for the evening meal, where children played, where neighbors shared and helped, where there was much laughter.

Sentry guards jogged out to protect the herds and gardens through the night. Older children set aside their afternoon studies to help their parents. Kalela realized she was in a village where learning, joy, support, family, and hard work were important. These were intelligent, creative, caring people. Some painted, some wove, some carved. These were people Kalela wanted to know. These were people she felt proud of.

Mr. Douglas's elbow nudged her out of her vision. "It is time for the traditional communal drink. Would you fill the communal cup with water, the essence of life?"

All forty people gathered in a circle around the center table as Kalela filled the communal cup and brought it to her father. As he lifted the cup to his lips the circle began a chanted verse. The verse continued as the cup was passed from person to person, from lip to lip.

> For the Motherland, cradle of civilization.
> For the ancestors and their indomitable spirit.
> For the elders from whom we can learn much.
> For our youth who represent the promise for tomorrow.
> For our people, the original people.
> For our struggle and in remembrance of those who have struggled on our behalf.
> For Umoja, the principle of unity, which should guide us in all that we do.
> For the Creator who provides all things great and small.

In her mind Kalela saw the pattern of a spider web, a great web that spanned America and connected ten thousand homes across the country where Kwanzaa was being celebrated in exactly the same way this very night. The center of Kalela's web was Mother Africa herself.

Kalela hardly noticed the great Karamu feast. She hardly heard the singing, or remembered the hours of dancing. Her mind was stuffed with images of Africa and with an eager longing for Kwanzaa to start all over again next year.

Follow-up Questions to Explore

1.   What are the seven principles of Kwanzaa?

Answer

Umoja (Unity) in family, community, nation, and race. (2) *Kujichagulia* (Self-Determination) to define ourselves, name ourselves, create for ourselves, and speak for ourselves, instead of allowing others to do these things for us. (3) *Ujima* (Collective Work and Responsibility) to build our community together and make our sisters' and brothers' problems our problems and solve them together. (4) *Ujamma* (Cooperative Economics) to build our own stores and other businesses and profit from them together. (5) *Nia* (Purpose) to make our collective vocation the building of our community to restore our people to their traditional greatness. (6) *Kuumba* (Creativity) to leave our community more beautiful and beneficial than we inherited it. And (7) *Imani* (Faith) to believe in our parents, our people, our teachers, our leaders, and the righteousness of our struggle.

2. The tenants of Kwanzaa say that you should make gifts rather than buy them. Do you agree? For your celebrations that involve gift giving, do you make gifts or buy gifts? Why? Do you prefer to get handmade or purchased gifts? Why?

Answer

Discuss these questions in class and compare your answers to those of your classmates.

Suggested Activities

1. Kwanzaa uses words that come from the Swahili (or Kiswahili) language. Research this language. Where did it originate? Where is it spoken today? Search for a recording of someone speaking Swahili to hear what it sounds like. Learn some simple, basic words in Swahili *(pencil, paper, boy, girl, day, food, etc.).*

2. Kwanzaa is an African-American celebration. Most African Americans are descended from slaves. What part of Africa did the slaves come from? Research the slave trade. Who ran it? What trade routes was slave trade a part of? How were the slaves captured, and by whom? Why didn't African governments fight against the slave traders?

3. Have you ever made a birthday or Christmas gift instead of buying one? What gifts could you make? Plan and design a gift you can make for someone. Keep a diary of the making of this gift, of how you felt when you gave it, and of how the person you give it to reacts.